Controversies in Drugs Policy and Practice

Controversies in Drugs Policy and Practice

Neil McKeganey

palgrave
macmillan

First published 2011 by
PALGRAVE MACMILLAN

Palgrave Macmillan in the UK is an imprint of Macmillan Publishers Limited, registered in England, company number 785998, of Houndmills, Basingstoke, Hampshire RG21 6XS.

Palgrave Macmillan in the US is a division of St Martin's Press LLC, 175 Fifth Avenue, New York, NY 10010.

Palgrave Macmillan is the global academic imprint of the above companies and has companies and representatives throughout the world.

Palgrave® and Macmillan® are registered trademarks in the United States, the United Kingdom, Europe and other countries.

ISBN 978–0–230–23594–6 hardback
ISBN 978–0–230–23595–3 paperback

This book is printed on paper suitable for recycling and made from fully managed and sustained forest sources. Logging, pulping and manufacturing processes are expected to conform to the environmental regulations of the country of origin.

A catalogue record for this book is available from the British Library.

A catalog record for this book is available from the Library of Congress.

10   9   8   7   6   5   4   3   2   1
20   19   18   17   16   15   14   13   12   11

Printed in China

For Elsie and For Elise

Contents

Acknowledgements

It is one of the great privileges of being an academic that you have the opportunity of talking at length with so many individuals whose differing views and experiences help shape your own thinking and make the process of learning so enjoyable. In my case I have benefited from conversations with colleagues over many years. In particular, I would like to acknowledge my debt to Charlie Lloyd, Jim McIntosh, Michael Bloor, Robert Du-Pont, Joy Barlow, Griffith Edwards, Kathy Gyngell, Deirdre Boyd, Joanne Neale, Danny Kushlick, David Hunter, David Raynes, Mary Brett, Steve Rolles, Gerald Barlow, Lochy McLean, Rev John Mathews, Alisdair Young, Norman Stone, Theodore Dalyrmple, Joe Winston, Uday Mukerji, Gordon Hay, Joe McGallagly, Phil Hanlon, David Clark, John Mullen, Joan McFadden, Roger Howard, John Strang, Archie Fulton and many others. That list contains people who would agree with much of what I have written, some who would agree with little of what I have written and a few who would agree with nothing I have written. But debate does not need to find agreement to be helpful in furthering one's own thinking.

Professor Marina Barnard (iwaly) has somehow always found the time to read what I have written and to provide a response that balances criticism and encouragement. So much of what I have written started out as a discussion with Marina that I no longer know where her ideas end and mine begin. I am grateful to the University of Glasgow for the support it has provided to the Centre for Drug Misuse Research over many years and to Vice Principal Peter Holmes for the support he provided to me when I needed it most. I would like to acknowledge my debt to Evelyn Crombie with whom I have worked for 20 years and who has managed to create an office of normality and structure around me despite my inclination towards chaos. Finally, I would like to acknowledge my debt to my three children Rebecca, Gabriel and Daniella for reminding me that there are more important things in life than work.

Introduction

There are few topics that generate more controversy, more dissent and more heated views on one side or another than that to do with the use of illegal drugs – should drugs be legalized? Is drug use primarily a health issue or a criminal justice matter? Should drug users be provided with heroin? Should drug treatment services be aiming to get drug users off drugs or enabling them to use their drugs with lower levels of harm? Is the use of drugs a human rights issue and should people be allowed to use whatever drugs they choose without the state feeling that it has a right to intervene in their lives? Should drug-dependent parents be left to look after their children or should those children be taken into care? What should be the approach of the police in tackling the drugs problem? Are enforcement efforts an expensive waste of resources or an invaluable protection against a problem that could grow so large as to threaten the very sustainability of our society? Should drug use and drug users be stigmatized in an attempt to limit the further spread of illegal drug use or is this to victimize an already vulnerable and marginalized group?

This book sits at the intersection of many of these arguments that have characterized our attempts to deal with the problem of illegal drugs over at least the last 20 years. Each of the chapters explores a different facet of the drugs controversy looking in detail at the nature of the concerns, the beliefs, the evidence, the arguments, the possible solutions and the limits of effective action. At times these chapters will conclude with challenging policy recommendations with which many people may disagree. But conflict, controversy and debate are what this book is about. Sitting on the fence is most decidedly not what this book is about.

Chapter 1 looks at the rapidly changing world of illegal drugs both globally and nationally. Drawing upon data from the United Kingdom and other countries we see how in 40 or so years we have gone from a situation where we barely had a drugs problem worthy of the name to a global epidemic that leaves hardly any country untouched. In other areas of public policy we have come to realize that some of the biggest challenges we face can arise as a result of small changes in scale. We realize that a few degrees difference in average global temperatures can generate environmental problems that are previously beyond our imagination. In the case of terrorism we have come to realize that a small number of dedicated individuals can carry out actions that can change fundamental aspects of our everyday lives. In the case of illegal drugs we have an activity that in its most problematic forms rarely involves more than one per cent of a country's population, and yet which delivers to governments across the globe a seemingly limitless array of problems to do with health harms, criminal harms, corruption harms, child protection harms, economic and political corruption harms and environmental damage. So widespread and so intractable are those harms that it has become important to ask the question of how big a drug problem can any society contain? If the answer to that question is a drug problem only slightly bigger than the problem we are facing at the present time, then drugs may pose a threat to our society every bit as damaging as climate change and global terrorism.

The field of illegal drugs policy and practice has changed beyond all recognition over the last 30 or so years as a result of the influence of one idea more than any other, namely harm reduction. There has been no more controversial set of ideas and practices in the drugs field than those associated with the philosophy of harm reduction. Arising initially out of the concern in the 1980s to reduce drug injectors risks of acquiring and spreading HIV infection, harm reduction has gone on to become a global social movement. But is the harm reduction movement primarily focused on improving the health and welfare of drug users or a Trojan Horse for drug legalization? The controversies around harm reduction are the focus of Chapter 2.

Chapter 3 looks on the world of drug abuse treatment which, within the United Kingdom, is a one billion pound a year industry. For many years the mantra that "treatment works" has guided government policy on drugs. Recently however, confidence in that mantra has been eroded as hard questions have been asked as to whether drug abuse treatment is indeed worth the billions of pounds that is directed at it. Doubts have begun to surface as to the effectiveness of drug abuse treatment, its aims, its methods and the professionalism of its staff. Under concerted questioning from the media, from academics and from opposition politicians confidence in the belief that treatment works has been steadily eroded. Drug treatment services have been shown to be enabling only a tiny minority of drug users to become drug free. In countries across the world hundreds of thousands of drug users are being prescribed the opiate substitute drug methadone, but is this helping them to recover or locking them further into a state of continuing drug dependency? Can drug treatment services even cope with the numbers of addicts that are now seeking treatment or do those numbers inevitably result in poor-quality treatment and poor outcomes for addicts and their families? These are the controversies that are addressed in Chapter 3.

Politicians love to talk tough when it comes to illegal drugs – promising draconian measures targeted at those who are profiting from the drugs trade and forcing addicts to confront the reality of their addiction. To those who favour drug legalization, the activities of the drug enforcement agencies are often seen as part of the problem rather than part of the solution. But how successful are drug enforcement agencies at seizing illegal drugs, at arresting drug users and at dissuading drug use? If you are a drug user what are the chances of you being caught in possession of a controlled drug? Should drug enforcement agencies be trying to deter drug use or guiding drug users into treatment? Are the drug enforcement agencies in danger of becoming little more than an arm of the social work and drug treatment services? These are the controversies that are addressed in Chapter 4.

If there is one area of drugs policy that has suffered more than any other from confusion and political changes of heart it must surely have to do with cannabis – a drug which has been the subject of serial reviews by the UK Advisory Council on the Misuse of Drugs and a yo-yo movement in its classification within the Misuse of Drugs Act. But just how harmful a drug is cannabis? Should we even be attempting to place different drugs into different categories of harm and seriousness or does such an approach inevitably result in a fruitless and unending debate? Chapter 5 looks at the controversies and confusions that have swirled around the issue of drug classification and cannabis harm and which have resulted in a belief, in the minds of many young people, that the drug has already been legalized.

Chapter 6 looks at the harms to children from living with a drug-dependent parent. It has been estimated that within the United Kingdom alone there may be more than three hundred thousand children with one or both parents dependent upon illegal drugs. As a result of a number of high-profile cases of child neglect we have become more aware than at any time in the past of the enormous price that many of those children are paying for their parent's drug habit. But what should services do in the face of that knowledge? Should they be seeking to support those families for as long it takes or should they be forcing parents to choose between their children and their drug use? What does it mean to be a good enough parent, and when do addict parents cross the threshold into inadequate child-harming parents? The decisions that social work staff take on these issue are amongst the most sensitive that any professional will ever make in any area of their work and they are the threads upon which the lives of thousands of children hang. The controversy around parental drug use and child welfare is at the heart of Chapter 6.

No book looking at the controversies to do with illegal drugs could be complete without considering the issue of legalization. Does legalization amount to the magic bullet that seems to elude every other attempt at tackling the problem of illegal drugs? Or would it amount to a social policy in search of a disaster; leading in time to much wider patterns of drug use and much greater drug harm to individuals, families and societies? Should we be following the example of countries such as Portugal that have decriminalized drug use, or would we be better implementing the zero tolerance drug policies of Sweden? What does the international data tell us about the relative merits of liberalizing or toughening our drug laws? These are the issues that are addressed in Chapter 7.

Chapter 8 has a very different focus to all of the preceding chapters in looking at the experience of undertaking research into the drug problem and contributing to the debates around drug policies. Within the United Kingdom the sacking of the government drugs advisor Professor David Nutt, from his position as Chair of the Advisory Council on the Misuse of Drugs, has resulted in widespread discussion as to the relationship between academics and politicians and the interface of evidence and the political process. This chapter looks in detail at the experience of delivering unwelcome findings to those in authority, the reality of working with civil servants, and the price that can be paid for the freedom to follow the logic of scientific enquiry.

Chapter 9 concludes the book by addressing a question that is rarely asked, namely: where is the morality in drug policy? Over the last 15 or so years drugs policy and the drugs debate have been influenced by the concept of pragmatism. That concept is not easy to define but it consists in large part in an acceptance of the inevitability of illegal drug use and a determination to adopt measures that in various ways make drug use less harmful but which do not for the most part seek to address drug use as a behaviour that ought not to be occurring. The principle of pragmatism can in this sense be seen as the polar opposite of the view that sees illegal drug use as a moral issue. As a result of the pragmatism that has characterized our response to the drugs issue over the last few years, drug use itself has been placed in a kind of a moral vacuum. To observe that someone has a moral view of illegal drug use has become almost a criticism in its own right – as if we somehow should not have a moral view of the drugs issue. But how appropriate is it to adopt a position of moral neutrality on a behaviour that is causing so much harm to individuals, to families and to communities? And are we not in danger of creating a cultural environment within which drug use can continue to flourish by our very refusal to adopt any kind of moral stance in relation to the use of illegal drugs? Chapter 9 makes the case for rediscovering a sense of morality in how we are dealing with illegal drugs.

Chapter 1

The Rapidly Changing World of Illegal Drugs

Introduction

The world of illegal drugs is a domain of truly staggering statistics. Estimated to be worth some $400 billion a year, the drugs trade is second only to the arms industry in scale and outstrips the arms industry in terms of profitability. The United Nations Office on Drugs and Crime has estimated that in 2007 somewhere between 172 million and 250 million people had used illicit drugs in the last year; between 15 and 21 million are estimated to have used opiates; 16 and 21 million to have used cocaine; 143 and 190 million to have used cannabis and between 16 and 51 million to have used amphetamines (UNODC 2009). Within Europe it has been conservatively estimated that some €34B is spent each year tackling the problem of illegal drugs; since this figure relates to 2005, it is likely that the current figure is significantly higher (EMCDDA 2009).

Drug abuse is the archetypal business with a small number of producers, millions of dedicated, often addicted, consumers, small overheads and an impressive capacity to respond flexibly to a changing market and the attentions of enforcement agencies. The drugs trade also happens to be one of the greatest social, political and economic challenges we face today. This chapter looks at how rapidly the drugs problem has evolved, where that problem may be going and how big a drugs problem society can contain.

Illegal Drugs: A Global Business

Within Europe there are estimated to be something in the region of 74 million people who have tried cannabis at least once, and 22 million who have done so in the last year. Around 20% of all people starting drugs treatment in Europe report cannabis as their primary drug of use. In the case of amphetamines around 12.5 million Europeans are estimated to have used the drug at least once in their life with some 2 million estimated to have done so in the last year. Cocaine is the second most commonly used illegal drugs with some 13 million Europeans believed to have used the drug at least once in their life and 4 million having done so in the last year. In relation to the prevalence of heroin use this varies across different countries though the average figure Europe is estimated to be 4.6 per 1,000.

The level of drug use–related HIV infection across Europe varies widely with an average of around 4.7 cases per million head of population although some countries like Latvia are considerably higher than that with a rate in 2008 of 58.7 per million. Hepatitis C connected to drugs misuse in Europe ranges from a low of 18% in some countries to a high of 95% in others. Drug-related deaths are also a major concern in Europe with one recent study indicating that between 10% and 23% of deaths in the 15–49 age range can be attributed to drugs misuse in seven European countries (EMCDDA 2009).

As the drugs problem has expanded in Europe and globally over the last few years, growing concern has been directed at the development of new drugs, many of which are chemically very similar to the traditional drugs of abuse but which have been designed in such a way to take them outside of the orbit of existing drug laws. As the European Monitoring Centre on Drugs and Drug Addiction has observed, the Internet has fundamentally changed the marketing of these drugs, opening access to a much wider range of consumers and dramatically shrinking the time between the design of new drugs and their marketing and consumption:

The internet has emerged as a new market place for psychoactive substances, providing retailers with the possibility of offering for sale alternatives to controlled rugs to a large public. (EMCDDA 2009: 93)

In 1997 the EMCDDA set up a system to monitor the development of new drugs; since that system went live, some 90 substances have already been identified which gives an indication of the growing problem that we now face in regard to the production and marketing of new drugs.

Tackling Drug Production

Through the use of satellite monitoring and human intelligence a great deal is known about the production and the trafficking of illegal drugs. We know, for example, that Afghanistan is the major opium-producing country in the world, and we are able to calculate the acreage turned over to opium production within the various regions comprising Afghanistan. Turning that intelligence into effective means to stem opium production, however, is by no means straightforward. At the present time an alliance of national forces is engaged in military conflict within Afghanistan simultaneously battling the Taliban whilst at the same time working with the national government to build up the rule of law across the country. Combining the aim of developing a fledgling democracy with the fight against drug production, however, is far from straightforward given that many of the individuals who are leading lights in taking on local governmental responsibilities will be deriving profits from drug production. Perhaps the clearest example of the tension between the aims of building up local government structures and reducing drug production can be seen in the case of crop eradication through aerial spraying.

Since it is possible to identify the major areas of poppy production in Afghanistan through satellite technology, it would also be possible to overfly those areas using crop eradication chemicals. To impose aerial crop spraying on local farmers however can hardly be seen to be an effective means of winning local hearts and minds – rather it is a blunt technological solution, the use of which is likely to massively offend local people. The alternative approach is to try to negotiate with local farmers and influential local figures, to encourage them to shift from poppy production to cultivating entirely different crops. Unavoidably that process of negotiation will move at a much slower pace, and have a less dramatic impact on poppy production than aerial spraying, but it does at least mesh with, rather than undermine, wider efforts to build up local governmental structures. At the same time, however, one would probably have to say that the patience on the part of the international community to wait for a locally workable solution to the problem of poppy production is not limitless, and that over time without clear evidence that such measures are having an effect, there is likely to be growing pressure for the imposition of an external military solution to the problem of poppy production which may include much wider use of aerial spraying.

Whilst it may be possible for an alliance of Western democracies to use their personnel on the ground in Afghanistan to tackle the problem of poppy production, it is by no means the case that the same approach can be used in other areas of drug production. In the case of many of the new "legal high drugs" that are being produced there is increasing intelligence that their production is concentrated in China (ACMD 2010). Clearly, it would not be possible for those countries that have a growing consumer base of the legal high drugs to impose a solution to the production of the legal high drugs within China – indeed it may not even be possible to negotiate such a solution on the ground with local personnel. In this instance successful attempts to tackle the production of the legal highs will have to come about through careful negotiation with the existing national governmental structure within China.

As an alternative to such negotiations there have been very well funded aid programmes targeted at the major cocaine-producing countries such as Columbia, Peru and Bolivia. There are indication that these aid programmes, coupled with national and local security measures, have successfully reduced cocaine production with global production in 2008 reducing by 15% from 994 metric tonnes in 2007 to 845 metric tonnes in 2008 (UNODC 2009: 65). However, whether such aid programmes can continue to reduce global cocaine production is yet to be seen. At the same time one of the clear risks of targeting aid on drug producer countries is the possibility that other countries not presently involved in drug production see this as a route to secure major international aid to support their own economic growth.

The Rapidly Changing World of Illegal Drugs

Many of those working in the field of illegal drugs have a view that we have always had a drugs problem, that we will always have a drugs problem and that the scale of the problem we face now is broadly speaking the same as the problem we will face in the future. So focussed are we on the drugs problem that confronts us at the moment that we spend hardly any time looking at where that problem has come from and where it may be going in the future. If there is one thing that is certain about the trade and consumption of illegal drugs however, it is the capacity for rapid and widespread changes to occur.

If one were looking for an example of how quickly the world of illegal drugs can change there is probably no country that demonstrates that better than Scotland. In the late 1960s Scotland barely had a drugs problem worthy of the name and yet by the turn of the century it has become the drugs capital of Europe – a remarkable and in many ways shocking transformation. In 1968 the Scottish government organized a small group of experts to consider whether Scotland was experiencing anything like the drug problem that was taking off in London and the south of England in the mid-1960s. The report produced by the group opened with an emphatic answer to the question the group had been asked to consider:

> We agreed at the outset that in Scotland there was not a problem of drug mis-use comparable to that reported in London and the Home Counties. A few persons addicted to narcotic drugs were known to the Home Office though the inspection of pharmacy records; there were rumours and occasional factual reports of drug taking at parties or cafes or dance halls by young people. (SHHD 1968: 1)

The expert group offered a number of reasons why Scotland may have avoided the drugs problem that was becoming increasingly evident in the south of England:

> Scotland had no Soho and no place comparable to Picadilly Circus as a focal point of the drug world. Traditionally, the mood altering drugs of the Scots is alcohol and though as a nation they are possibly not misusing psychotropic drugs as widely as elsewhere, their record of chronic alcoholism is a sad tale of human weakness and of social disruption. This tradition of alcohol misuse may, however, have protected the young people in Scotland from following the cultural trend of those in England, and particularly in London, to take drugs as a source of kicks. (SHHD 1968: 2)

There were good grounds for the optimism of this committee. In the mid- to late 1960s in Scotland, for example, there were only a handful of people receiving treatment for their drug dependency. In the second quarter of 1968 there were only four people receiving inpatient treatment for a drugs problem and 13 people receiving treatment on an outpatient basis for a drugs problem. Whilst the committee were mindful of the possibility that drug misuse may take off within Scotland at some point in the future, it is doubtful that they were thinking along the lines of the drugs epidemic that would overtake the country within a small number of years.

The first published account that Scotland might have been starting to experience a drugs epidemic was provided by sociologists at the University of Glasgow; Jason Ditton and Kevin Speirits had looked at referrals to the two main drug treatment centres in Glasgow in 1981. What they found shocked them and others who went on to read their report – "The New Wave of Heroin Addiction in Britain" (Ditton and Speirits 1982). Ditton and Speirits had identified a 388% increase in the number of drug treatment referrals over the first 6 months of 1981:

> In our opinion the dramatic rise in clinic referrals reflects a rise in actual use ... A conservative estimate of the proportion of unknown heroin users to known heroin users in Glasgow is 10:1. Given 174 new referrals in Glasgow in 1981 it is reasonable to suppose that some 1470 individuals are involved in the latest wave of heroin addiction. (Ditton and Speirits 1982: 595)

On the publication of this report questions were asked in the Westminster Parliament about what action was being taken within Scotland to tackle this new and emerging problem (Hansard Deb, 22 October 1981, vol 10, pp. 500–512). Two years after Ditton and Speirits research the health researcher Sally Haw provided a further estimate of the scale of heroin use in Glasgow. Based on an analysis of routine data and fieldwork, Haw calculated that the total number of heroin addicts in the city had risen to some 5,000 by the mid-1980s (Haw 1985).

In the late 1980s all of the attention on drug abuse in Scotland was focussed on HIV infection. The general practitioner Dr Roy Robertson had tested drug users in contact with his surgery and found that 50% were HIV positive (Robertson et al. 1986). The fear was that Scotland was on the verge of an HIV and AIDS epidemic, the like of which had rarely been seen outside of Africa. The psychologist and epidemiologist Dr Martin Frischer undertook research to provide an updated estimate of the number of people injecting drugs in Glasgow. On the basis of this work Haw's figure of some 5,000 heroin users was revised up to over 9,424 (Frischer et al. 1991).

By the late 1990s fear of an imminent HIV epidemic in Scotland had received and attention switched back to getting a clearer picture of the scale of the drugs problem across the country as a whole. Dr Gordon Hay recruited a team of researchers at the University of Glasgow to provide national and local estimates of problem drug misuse prevalence in Scotland over the period 2000–08 (Hay et al. 2005, 2009). The most up-to-date estimate of problem drugs misuse prevalence in Scotland in 2008 puts the figure at some 55,328. Around 1,200 drug users begin a new episode of drug abuse treatment each year in Scotland (ISD 2009). The country that in the mid-1960s barely had a drugs problem worthy of the name now had a drugs problem greater than almost anywhere in Europe (ONDCP 2009).

Recent research has estimated that the heroin market alone in Scotland is worth around £1.4B a year whilst the social and economic cost of drugs misuse is estimated to be around £3.5B a year (Casey et al. 2009). There are estimated to be between 41,000 and 59,000 children in Scotland growing up with a drug-dependent parent – that figure represents between 4% and 6% of all children in Scotland (ACMD 2003). Whilst the level of HIV infection amongst injecting drug users in Scotland is estiamted to be around 1%, the level of Hepatitis C infection amongst injecting drug users is estimated to be around 40% and in some parts of Scotland (Glasgow) may be as high as 60% (Bloor et al. 2006, Health Protection Agency 2009).

In research that involved interviewing and drug testing of arrestees, 81% of those arrested reported to researchers that they had used illegal drugs in the past, and 63% that they had done so in the last 3 days. Fifty-two per cent of arrestees tested positive for cannabis and 31% tested positive for opiates (McKeganey et al. 2000). The level of opiate abuse amongst arrestees in Scotland was higher than that recorded in any US city in a similar programme of interviewing and drug testing arrestees (US Department of Justice 2000). Scotland also now has one of the highest drug-related death rates anywhere in Europe. In 1996 there were a total of 244 drug-related deaths in Scotland – by 2008 that figure had more than doubled to 574 (General Register Office 2009).

Research looking at the level of illegal drug use amongst schoolchildren has found a higher level in Scotland than virtually any other European country. The Scottish Schools Adolescent Lifestyle and Substance Use Survey has been run every 2 years in Scotland since 1998. In 2008, 25% of 15-year olds and 7% of 13-year olds had used illegal drugs. Twenty-two per cent of 15-year-old boys had used drugs in the last year compared to 19% of 15-year-old girls (Black et al. 2009). These statistics powerfully reveal how a country can go from barely having a drug problem worthy of the name to being virtually overwhelmed by its drugs problem within what in historical terms is little more than the blink of an eye.

The Normalization of Illegal Drug Use and the Growth of the Legal Highs

In the late 1980s the sociologists Howard Parker, Judith Aldridge and Fiona Measham used the term "normalization" to describe the growing cultural acceptance of illegal drug use which they saw as being part of the youth culture of the 1990s (Parker et al. 1998). Parker and colleagues thesis was not that all or even the majority of young people were regularly using illegal drugs, rather their thesis was about the changing place of some illegal drugs in the world of young people:

> Normalisation in the context of recreational drug use cannot be reduced to the intuitive phrase "it's normal for young people to take drugs"; that is both to oversimplify and overstate the case. We are concerned only with the spread of deviant activity and associated attitudes from the margins towards the center of youth culture where it joins many other accommodated "deviant" activities such as excessive drinking, casual sexual encounters and daily cigarette smoking. Although tobacco use is clearly normalised and most young people have tried a cigarette only a minority are regular smokers and even then their behaviour is only acceptable to their peers in certain settings. So normalisation need not be concerned with absolutes; we are not even considering the possibility that most young Britons will become illicit drug users. It is quite extraordinary enough that we have so quickly reached a situation where the majority will have tried an illicit drug by the end of their teens and that in many parts of the UK up to a quarter may be regular recreational drug users. (Parker et al. 1998: 22)

For Parker and his team the normalization of illegal drugs that they saw as occurring was a process that involved some drugs, particularly cannabis and ecstasy and to an extent LSD, being much more widely available than in the past, where more and more young people were at least prepared to try some forms of drug use, and in which there was an open-mindedness about illegal drugs and a cultural accommodation to at least some forms of illegal drugs use.

The phenomenon that Parker was charting has been described by him as the growth of an illegal leisure culture of recreational drug use. More recently however Parker and his team have seen the development of what they regard as a much more troubling small group of young people (often under age 18) who have developed a problematic style of combining alcohol cannabis cocaine and ecstasy (the so-called ACCE profile). For Parker these young people may in earlier decades have drifted into a form of heroin use; however, their negative attitudes towards heroin use has steered them away from the drug but it has not steered them clear of problems. In a way these young people are seen to be in even greater difficulty than their pervious heroin-using peers given that according to Parker government drug strategy and national resources have continued to be targeted on those using Class A drugs (heroin and cocaine) largely ignoring in terms of priorities those young people who have developed a harmful pattern of what may mistakenly now be called recreational poly drug use (combining alcohol cannabis cocaine and ecstasy) in a way that is often personally damaging for the young person (Parker 2007).

The penetration of illegal drug use into youth culture within the United Kingdom and elsewhere continues to evolve and is perhaps evident today in the growth of what have come to be called "legal highs", drugs that mimic the effects of some of the illegal drugs but which in terms of their chemical constituents are sufficiently different to their illegal counterparts as to be legally available within a wide range of countries. One of those drugs mephedrone that first came to attention in 2007 appears to have become the fourth most commonly used drug by young people in the United Kingdom despite evidence that it may have been associated with a number of deaths of young people (ACMD 2010). Mephedrone, however, is only one of what appears to be an unending sequence of drugs manufactured to get round country's drug laws, in this case sold under the guise of plant food but which is very plainly being promoted as a lifestyle drug producing a similar effect to that of ecstasy. Within little more than 2 years mephedrone has gone from being a drug that hardly anyone had heard of to being the fourth most widely used illegal drugs on the club scene (Winstock 2010), with some researchers suggesting that its appeal to clubbers has grown out of a dissatisfaction with the poor-quality cocaine that is now felt to be being sold in the United Kingdom (Measham et al. 2010).

The reality which we face is one in which drug use has expanded well beyond the familiar territory of cannabis, heroin, cocaine, LSD and such like to include a bewildering array of newly designed substances that within a matter of months appear to be widely available and consumed by young people. The speed with which these drugs are being developed and marketed presents a massive challenge to what by contrast seems the painfully slow process of drug assessment and classification by individual country's drug laws.

A Drug Tipping Point?

In response to the statement that illegal drugs pose a challenge to society every bit as great as global warming or terrorism there will be those who say that such a statement is at best incorrect and at worst alarmist. After all how can it be possibly the case that a problem which in its most chaotic form involves less than 1% of the adult population could possibly threaten the very sustainability of any society? Along with the view that we have always had a drugs problem, and probably always will, there is also a widely held view that society will always be able to cope with its drugs problem no matter what the scale of that problem actually is. But what if that optimistic view is incorrect and society can cope with a drugs problem only slightly greater than it is at present? If that is the case then a critical question comes into the foreground: where is the tipping point that shifts a drug problem from being something that society can cope with to being a problem that threatens the very sustainability of societies? If there is a tipping point between a country being able to cope with its drugs problem and having its very sustainability threatened by that problem, then that point is likely to vary from one society to another reflecting the different scale of the drugs problem in different parts of the world. But is the theory of a drugs tipping point itself sustainable? To answer that question it is necessary to take a concrete example – the United Kingdom.

Research within the United Kingdom has estimated that at the present time there are approaching 400,000 problematic drug users – these are individuals who are using heroin or cocaine at a high level and experiencing major problems as a result of their drug use. The figure of approaching 400,000 is a composite based on an estimate of there being around 327,466 problematic drug users in England (Hay and Gannon 2006), 55,328 in Scotland (Hay et al. 2009), 8334 in Wales (Wood 2000) and somewhere between 1,000 and 2,000 in Northern Ireland (McElrath 2002). These individual estimates produce a total for the United Kingdom of there being around 393,128 problematic drug users.

As a result of the fact that there have been only a small number of studies estimating the prevalence of problematic drug misuse within the United Kingdom and that those studies have reported prevalence measures on a small number of occasions, it is not possible to show the growth in annual prevalence of problem drug misuse over the last 50 years. What is evident however is that over that period the prevalence of problem drug misuse has increased from being counted in the hundreds to now being counted in the hundreds of thousands and that since the 1960s the prevalence of problematic drug misuse has either increased steadily and incrementally to its current level or more probably there have been periods of rapid expansion, for example, in the late 1980s.

Whilst it is not possible to know which of these two models of problematic drug use spread has occurred in reality (steady growth or rapid staccato expansion), the question arises as to whether that growth curve has reached a peak and will steadily reduce over time or whether the upward trajectory of that growth curve could continue. This issue is very much the territory of the Foresight Brain Science and Addiction project (McKeganey et al. 2002). There are a number of possible reasons why the curve of drug use prevalence in the United Kingdom might increase in the coming years. Firstly there are indications that the typical gender ratio of three males to every one female in the problematic drug-using group may begin to change as drug use in its various forms becomes increasingly common amongst females. If over the next few years the level of problematic drug misuse amongst females were to move closer to that amongst males, then the prevalence of problematic drug misuse could increase in England to around 488,702 and in Scotland to around 70,000, meaning that we would be heading towards 600,000 problematic drug users within the United Kingdom. That figure would only represent a doubling of the current estimate of problematic drug misuse prevalence which on the basis of past experience within the United Kingdom occurs over a 10–15-year period. Other notable developments that might lead to an increase in the prevalence of problematic drug misuse within the United Kingdom are increases in problematic drug misuse within the rural areas bringing their rate of drug use into closer alignment with that found within the urban centres and the reducing age of onset of illegal drug use which some researchers have drawn attention to (McKeganey et al. 2004).

But if the prevalence of problematic drug misuse were to double over the next 10–20 years, what would be the impact of that change. First we could see the United Kingdom coping with approaching 800,000 problematic drug users. Second, drug deaths in the United Kingdom, currently running at around 2,000 a year, could increase to around 4,000 deaths per year. In terms of Hepatitis C infection a twofold increase in drug user numbers could result in there being around 300,000 injecting drug users who were Hepatitis C positive. In terms of children affected by parental drug dependence a doubling in the numbers of problematic drug users could mean that there were around 700,000 children with drug-dependent parents. The social and economic cost of Class A drug use in England, currently estimated to be around £15B a year, could increase to around £30B a year.

In the event of a marked increase in drug user numbers it is likely that drug use itself would become more visible within publicly accessible spaces in the United Kingdom. At the present time it is possible to travel through most major UK cities without encountering the signs of serious drug use. An increase in drug user numbers could change that dramatically resulting in the visible signs of drug use and drug-related paraphernalia becoming much more common.

In terms of the possibility of society coping with a twofold increase in drug use prevalence it is important to consider the impact of such an increase on the criminal justice system. At the present time it is estimated that between 60% and 70% of crime is connected to the use of illegal drugs either being carried out by individuals under the influence of illegal drugs or in order to obtain money to buy illegal drugs. Crucially where research has looked at who is being arrested for crimes within the United Kingdom and who is being jailed as a result of those crimes it is very often the same people who are being repeatedly arrested and repeatedly jailed. To an extent this is not surprising since an individual who is committing crimes to fund a drug habit is unlikely to stop committing those crimes simply as a result of having been arrested and jailed; rather he or she is likely to continue to commit those crimes and to run the risk of further arrest and further jail sentences so long as they remain dependent upon illegal drugs. The result of this is that a very substantial proportion of police time is already being taken up with a small number of high-frequency offenders whose offending is directly connected to their drug use. In the event of a possible doubling in drug user numbers it is questionable whether either the police or the prison system could cope without a commensurate increase in their scale of funding.

With regard to the economic system, it is already known that the funds from the drugs trade are being systematically laundered through the legitimate economy. Much of the work of the Serious Organised Crime Agency in London, and the Scottish Crime and Drug Enforcement Agency in Scotland, is devoted to following the money associated with the drugs trade and identifying the multiple ways in which the proceeds of that trade are invested back into the legal economy. In the event of twofold increase in drug-related finances it is likely that more and more parts of the legitimate economy would come to be corrupted by the flow of that finance. One of the results of that development would be increasing numbers of people working within companies that unknown to them had connections to the drugs trade. Equally, the development of a larger drugs trade could also lead to an impact on the political system in the United Kingdom with those involved in the upper echelons of that trade possibly seeking to gain political influence as a way of protecting their huge financial assets. Within the United Kingdom the process of donations to political parties has already been identified as a potential weak point within the democratic system with a number of initiatives having been developed to try to ensure that those with a criminal connection are unable to direct funds to political parties (Winnet and Rayner 2007).

There will be those whose response to the suggestion of the drugs trade acquiring political influence in the United Kingdom as little more than alarmist fantasy. However, two events would lead one to question that optimistic view. One of those events occurred in 2002 and the other in 2010. In 2002 a fund-raising dinner for the Scottish Labour Party took place in Lanarkshire that was attended by some of the most senior members of the UK cabinet. That dinner was organized by one of Scotland's major drug dealers who within 2 weeks of the event was shot dead (Allardyce and McLeod 2002). It is impossible to know how many of those attending the dinner were aware of the drug connections of the event's organizer. However, to the extent that drugs money is able to successfully infiltrate the legal economy it is highly likely that there will be individuals who will be able to present themselves to political figures as legitimate and successful business people without ever giving any indication of the original source of their financial success.

The second event occurred in 2010 in Glasgow when the leader of the Labour council, Stephen Purcell, resigned spectacularly following revelation that his cocaine use (which he subsequently admitted to in a national newspaper) may have made him vulnerable to possible blackmail attempts by organized crime groups within the city, and that he had been interviewed in 2009 by police officers from the Scottish Crime and Drug Enforcement Agency in connection with his drug use and possible vulnerability to blackmail (Carrell 2010, Dinsmore 2010).

Looked at in these terms it is by no means certain that the United Kingdom could cope with even a relatively small increase in the number of problematic drug users (an increase from around 1% to 2%). What this powerfully reveals is that the problem of illegal drugs is not a problem to do with its large scale but a problem that arises from its small scale. Expressed in other terms what we are seeing at the moment is a situation in which many of the organizations that are responding to the drugs problem in the area of treatment enforcement education and social support are struggling to cope with a drugs problem at its present level. In the case of children living with drug-dependent parents, for example, it is clear that social work services are presently unable to cope with the number of children living within these circumstances and that as a result they have to prioritize their resources on the children at greatest risk and in greatest need. By definition this means that there are many children that support services would be able to help were they not devoting their resources to the children living in more harmful circumstances. If social works services are already unable to meet the needs of the number of children we estimate are living within these families, then there is simply no way in which they could cope with a doubling in the number of children involved.

Conclusions

Illegal drugs use is now a global economy delivering massive problems to societies around the world. For the most part our awareness of those problems has centred on the issues of drug-related crime and the need for treatment for those most affected by drug dependency and addiction. However, there are a multiple of other more hidden problems associated with illegal drug use ranging from the needs of children within drug-dependent families to the possible corruption of the economic and political systems by the drugs trade. These latter problems are more evident in countries that we regard as new democracies or as politically less stable than the Western democracies – however, there is no reason to assume that the problems of drug-related violence and corruption that has become evident in countries such as Mexico, Brazil and Argentina are somehow unable to become evident in the United Kingdom and other developed Western countries. Nobody knows where the drugs problem is developing although it is showing no signs of abating. It is now a massive industry in its own right with a level of financial worth greater than many small countries in the world, and it is second only in scale to the arms industry. It is for those reasons that the drugs problem may in due course come to be seen as a threat to society every bit as serious as global terrorism and climate change. As is the case with both of those problems the optimistic side of our nature may lead us to believe that we will identify and implement a solution to the drugs problem before that problem undermines the very sustainability of our society. That likelihood though is far from guaranteed.

KEY DISCUSSION QUESTIONS

1. Could the problem of illegal drugs challenge society to anything like the same degree as global terrorism and climate change or will society always be able to cope with its drugs problem no matter the scale of that problem?

2. How much more widespread could the problem of illegal drug use actually become?

3. With the increasing proliferation of legal highs and designer drugs, is the distinction between legal and illegal drug use increasingly redundant?

4. How far can one country intervene in another country to stem the production of illegal drugs?

Chapter 2

What's Wrong With Harm Reduction?

Introduction

The concept of reducing the harm associated with the use of illegal drugs has been the single most influential idea impacting upon the drugs field over the last 20 years. In that time harm reduction has gone from being a radical new idea challenging the established ideas of drug treatment to becoming a global social movement with its own distinctive set of ideas, evidence base, politics, professional practice, internal conflicts, international conference and academic journal. In addition to being hugely influential, harm reduction has also been hugely controversial seen, by some, as a Trojan horse leading ultimately to drug legalization.

On the face of it the question "what's wrong with harm reduction" may seem somewhat impertinent – after all what could possibly be wrong with a commitment to reduce the harms associated with individual's drug use? Harm reduction sits though, at the intersection of both public health protection and drug law reform and it is largely for that reason that it has generated such heated debate within the addictions field. Ethan Nadelmann, a prominent supporter of harm reduction and a long-time advocate for drug legalization, identified early on the convenient appeal of this new approach to tackling the drugs issue:

Who in their right mind could oppose the notion of reducing harm. It is easily embraced by government officials and others who favour less emphasis on criminal justice policies and more emphasis on public health approaches, and not readily disavowed even by those who prefer more punitive drug control measures. It is sufficiently vague that people with very different ideas about drug policy feel comfortable adopting it as their label. And it conveys a sense of British and Dutch sensibility that can prove irresistible to those who view the ideological excesses of drug war rhetoric with a sceptical eye. (Nadelmann 1993: 37)

It is easy to see the appeal of an approach to drug policy that seems to offer the opportunity of setting aside some of the old dividing lines between those who are "for drugs" and those who are "against drugs" and focussing instead on reducing the harm associated with individual's drug use. What, one may wonder, could possibly be wrong with that? As we will see in this chapter the harm reduction approach that was initially seen as having such universal appeal also had the capacity to resurrect some of the old conflicts between those who viewed drug use as something that needed to be stopped and those who saw it as a matter of free will for individuals to use whatever drugs they wished. Before looking at some of the ethical and moral dimensions underpinning harm reduction it will be useful to look at its origins.

The History of Harm Reduction: From Public Health to Drug Law Reform

Whilst the origins of the harm reduction approach have been traced back to concerns in the late 1980s with reducing the spread of HIV infection amongst injecting drug users, the addictions historian Virginia Berridge has suggested that the origins may lie in the Rolleston Report prepared for the UK government in 1926 (Berridge and Strong 1993, Berridge 1999). This report identified a role for doctors in prescribing heroin on a long-term basis to those individuals who were unable to cease or reduce their use of the drug and who had failed to benefit from any other forms of treatment.

Whilst the authors of the Rolleston report may have had a concern to reduce the harm associated with individual's continuing drug dependency, the key document that marked the beginning of what came to be known as the harm reduction approach to drug policy and drug practice was the 1988 report from the Advisory Council on the Misuse of Drugs titled "AIDS and Drug Misuse" (ACMD 1988). Contained within that report was a 15-word sentence that has been much quoted since, and which virtually overnight changed the entire direction of drug policy and drug treatment in the United Kingdom and in many countries across the world. That sentence boldly asserted:

> The spread of HIV is a greater danger to individual and public health than drug misuse. (ACMD 1988)

In the wake of the fear that large numbers of injecting drug users might become HIV positive, and might spread infection to the wider non-drug-injecting population, the focus of attention shifted from viewing drug use as a criminal justice matter or a matter of individual addiction to viewing it as a public health challenge. Within the latter perspective the primary object of policy had to do with reducing drug users chances of acquiring and spreading HIV infection. In the new climate of fear about the spread of HIV the Advisory Council on the Misuse of Drugs set out a hierarchy of aims for drug services and drug policies to:

1) Reduce the shared use of injecting equipment by drug users.

2) Reduce the incidence of drug injecting.

3) Reduce the use of street drugs.

4) Reduce the use of prescribed drugs.

5) Increase abstinence from all drug use.

It is interesting to note that the first detailed articulation of a distinctively harm reduction approach to drug policy combined the aims of reducing drug user risk behaviour and reducing the overall level of drug use. However, not all of those who were advocating the new approach of harm reduction were equally catholic in embracing the twin goals of risk reduction and drug use reduction. Gerry Stimson, for example, was quick to spot a potential conflict between the goals of drug use reduction and HIV-related risk reduction and to stress that it was the latter, not the former, that needed to be given priority:

> A key issue in shaping drug policies is the choice that has been posed between two targets: between the prevention of HIV transmission and the prevention of drug abuse. Preventing the physical disease of AIDS has now been given priority over concerns with drug problems. In this paradigm prevention takes

on a new meaning – the key prevention task is not the prevention of drug use, but the prevention of HIV infections and transmission. (Stimson 1990: 333)

As the harm reduction approach has developed, the degree to which it is committed to reducing the overall level of drug use in society has become one of the major fault lines in addictions policy. In 2009 the International Harm Reduction Association offered an updated definition of harm reduction within which the notion of reducing individual's drug use was barely even mentioned:

"Harm Reduction" refers to policies, programmes and practices that aim primarily to reduce the adverse health, social and economic consequences of the use of legal and illegal psychoactive drugs without necessarily reducing drug consumption. (IHRA 2009)

According to the International Harm Reduction Association the harm reduction approach is based upon seven key principles:

- Targeted at risk and harm
- Evidence-based and cost-effective
- Incremental
- Dignity and Compassion
- Universality and interdependence of rights
- Challenging policies and practices that maximize harm
- Transparency.

The principle of targeting "risk and harm" has to do with identifying the specific risks and harms experienced by drug users and working towards their subsequent reduction. The principle of "evidence based cost effectiveness" has to do with the claim that harm reduction interventions are typically low cost but are believed to have high impact. The principle of "incrementalism" refers to the idea that small changes in the behaviour of large numbers of people towards lower levels of risk taking are preferable to "heroic gains achieved for a select few". Although the idea of abstinence is seen as being desirable, the principle of incrementalism places greater emphasis on the goal of keeping drug users alive and preventing the irreparable damage that can arise from their drug use. The principle of "dignity and compassion" has to do with accepting people where they are and avoiding using what are seen as pejorative terms to refer to those using drugs. "Universality and interdependence of rights" has to do with the belief that individuals do not forfeit their human rights as a result of their drug use and that those rights include their right of access to high-quality health services. The principle of "challenging policies and practices" that promote harm includes the commitment to drug law reform and in particular to challenging the harms that are seen as arising from the fact that certain drugs are illegal. Finally, the principle of "transparency and accountability" has to do with the view that drug users themselves should be involved in the process of setting up interventions and shaping policies and that individuals are held to be accountable for their actions with regard to either reducing or increasing drug-related harm.

Within this array of principles and beliefs that characterize the harm reduction approach, abstinence has typically been seen as playing only a relatively minor role. According to Neil Hunt, a prominent UK harm reduction advocate, abstinence represents only a subset of the harm reductionists overall focus (Hunt et al. 2003: 4). For the Canadian Center on Substance Abuse, harm reduction

> Does not focus on abstinence: although harm reduction supports those who seek to moderate or reduce their drug use, it neither excludes nor presumes a treatment goal of abstinence. Harm reduction approaches recognise that short-term abstinence oriented treatments have low success rates, and, for opiate users, high post-treatment overdose rates. (CCSA 1996)

Despite the uncertainty as to the degree to which harm reduction includes a commitment to drug use reduction it would be hard to overemphasize the impact of these ideas on global drug policy and drug interventions. In the wake of the AIDS and Drug Misuse Report, for example, the conservative government in the United Kingdom made funding available for the development of an array of harm reduction focussed services. Needle and syringe exchange, methadone maintenance, outreach harm reduction and advice aimed at providing drug users with information on safer injecting techniques became the front line in the battle to reduce the spread of HIV infection. The urgency of the threat that HIV posed was nowhere more powerfully demonstrated than in the results of laboratory tests of blood samples taken from drug users attending a general practice surgery in Edinburgh, Scotland. Those tests demonstrated that in excess of 50% of drug users had already become infected with HIV (Robertson et al. 1986). If HIV infection could spread that widely in a major urban city there was a very real fear that this could occur in any city in any country and could lead in time to HIV becoming widespread within the non-drug-injecting population through the vector of sexual transmission.

Although subsequent research in Scotland identified that the level of HIV infection amongst injecting drug users in Edinburgh was less widespread than had appeared from the Robertson results, it was clear that HIV remained a major cause of concern (Davies et al. 1995) and the UK government remained committed to the development of a wide range of harm reduction initiatives aimed at reducing drug users risks of acquiring and spreading HIV infection. Within New York, whilst HIV spread rapidly amongst injecting drug users increasing from around 10% of injecting drug users in the early 1980s to around to 60% by the late 1980s the US government generally eschewed the deployment of harm reduction measures which it saw as coming close to condoning forms of illegal drugs use (Des Jarlais et al. 1989).

Although many of the harm reduction initiatives that were developed at that time, such as needle and syringe exchange, were seen as hugely controversial they have now become common-place in countries across the globe. Alex Wodak, for example, a prominent supporter of the harm reduction approach to drug policy and drug treatment has written that:

> Providing access to and encouraging utilisation of sterile needles and syringes for injecting drug users is considered a fundamental component of any comprehensive and effective HIV prevention programme. (Wodak and Cooney 2005: 231)

Within the United Kingdom the level of government support for harm reduction has been nothing short of remarkable. The updated national drug strategy published in 2002 underlined the government's commitment to harm reduction services:

> All problematic drug users must have access to treatment and harm minimization services both within the community and through the criminal justice system. (Home Office 2002: 3)

The updated drug strategy also gave an indication of the extent to which harm reduction had penetrated the world of drug treatment in 2002:

> Nearly all Drug Action Team areas (97%) have harm reduction services and 87% provide access to drug prescribing services. (Home Office 2002: 53)

Long-term maintenance prescribing of powerful drugs such as methadone came to be seen as one of the key means of attracting drug users into treatment and thereby reducing their HIV-related risk behaviour. Within England, the number of drug users in treatment increased from around 85,000 in 1998 to 207,580 in 2008/09 (NTA 2009). The National Treatment Agency has reported that out of an estimated 201,830 drug users in treatment in 2007/08, 146,999 (72.8%) were on a methadone programme (NTA 2008). Within Scotland the government has estimated that there may be around 22,000 heroin addicts on methadone out of a total estimated problematic drug using population of just over 55,000 (Scottish Executive 2005). Within the United States, the number of methadone prescriptions rose by nearly 700% from 1998 to 2006 while the amount of methadone provided increased from some 1,987g per 100,000 head of population in 1998 to 5,197g per 100,000 head of population in 2007 (US Department of Health and Human Sciences Substance Abuse and Mental Health Services 2009).

As the hysteria over the spread of drug injection–related HIV infection receded in many countries, the harm reduction movement has shifted its focus in two important respects. First, there has been an expansion in the definition of the harm that harm reductionists sees themselves as tackling, and second there has been a growing interest in the issue of drug user rights. These developments have led to discussions as to the level of importance that harm reduction has given to drug law reform:

> Over the last decade harm reduction has become much more than a public health approach. To an extent harm reduction has become an essential response to harm generating drug prohibition policies. (Moskalewicz et al. 2007: 505)

For Moskalewicz, "There is an intrinsic contradiction between drug prohibition and harm reduction" (Moskalewicz et al. 2005: 507). Other writers have also emphasized the drug law reform element of contemporary harm reduction policies and practices:

> I want to suggest that harm reduction is a movement within drug prohibition that shifts drug polices from the criminalized and punitive end to the more decriminalized and openly regulated end of the drug policy continuum. Harm reduction is the name of the movement within drug prohibition that in effect (though not always in intent) moves drug policies away from

punishment, coercion, and repression, and toward tolerance, regulation and public health. (Levine 2001)

The most detailed exposition of a harm reduction model of controlled drug availability has been outlined by David Burrows (2005). According to Burrows in a market where drugs are made available in a controlled way:

- Drug use and drug possession would be legalized.

- The regulated manufacture and supply of drugs would be allowed.

- There would be controlled availability of cannabis, heroin, amphetamines, ecstasy and anabolic steroids.

- These drugs would be available either on an over the counter basis or through prescription.

- The age limit for supplying these drugs to individuals would be the same as it is for alcohol.

- Prices would be calibrated in terms of the harms associated with different substances with the more harmful substances priced more highly.

- Drug users would be able to demonstrate a detailed knowledge of the drugs they were using.

- Education on the effects of the drugs being consumed would be readily available.

Van Ree (1999) has gone further than Burrows in proposing that drug use itself should be included within the Universal Declaration of Human Rights. According to Van Ree:

> Human rights concern forms of behaviour which we regard as positive and enriching for our lives to such a degree that we experience it as a violation of our personal dignity when we are forced to give them up. Drug use belongs in that category. Instead of being included in the category of murder and rape, drugs should be appreciated as a cultural asset similar to religion and art. (Van Ree 1999: 89)

In this version of harm reduction, drug use has shifted from being seen as a source of personal and social harm to being viewed as one of the highest forms of cultural expression. Seen in these terms it is difficult to understand why those who are using drugs should be regarded as vulnerable and in need of access to high-quality drug treatment and support services. Harm reduction, however, is a broad church and just at there are those who emphasize the centrality of drug user rights and drug legalization, there are others who are more cautious in taking up the banner of drug law reform. In a "harm reduction comes of age" editorial published in the *International Journal of Drug Policy*, the past Executive Director of the International Harm Reduction Association (Professor Gerry Stimson) has identified two key pillars of the approach – neither of which draws explicit attention to the right of the individual to use illegal drugs:

> Harm reduction has had two main pillars. First, it has been driven by pragmatic public health approaches emphasising the need for identifying specific harms, the need for interventions to be evidenced based and targeted at the need to adopt realistic goals – rather than pursue unattainable aspirational goals such as a drug free society. Many people involved in harm reduction have argued that it takes a morally neutral view on drug use, a position which is held in distinction to drug policies based in moral stands against drug use and drug users per se... The second pillar for harm reduction has been based in human rights, especially the right of drug users to life and security, to health protection against hurts from the community and state. (Stimson 2007: 68)

Neil Hunt, a prominent advocate of the harm reduction approach, has posed the question of which come first in harm reduction – public health or drug user rights? In answering that question Hunt has outlined what he sees as two versions of harm reduction and the drug user rights perspective (Hunt 2004). The first of these, labelled as the "weak rights version of harm reduction", focuses on reducing the health harms associated with individual's drug use. Within this version the right of the individual to use drugs of his or her choice is seen as secondary to the commitment to protecting individual and public health. By contrast, the "strong rights version of harm reduction" places primary importance on the rights of the individual to use whatever drugs he or she wishes and only secondarily attends to drugs harms. Within this version of the harm reduction approach it would be seen as a violation of the rights of the individual to seek to curb or reduce levels of drug use, even where there may be a public health case for doing so. According to Hunt the conflict over whether harm reduction is primarily a health optimizing movement or a rights-based movement is becoming more acute (Hunt 2004: 235).

In asking the question of which comes first "health or drug users rights", Hunt is calling for clarification of an issue that has remained unresolved since the very inception of the harm reduction approach. The claim that harm reduction is a Trojan Horse leading ultimately towards drug law reform can be seen as being rooted in precisely the ambiguity that Hunt has drawn attention to. However, it is by no means the case that all of those who would regard themselves as harm reductionists' would support Hunt's call for greater clarification as to the primary aims of the harm reduction approach. Craig Reinarman, a US academic supportive of the harm reduction approach, has cautioned against the urge on the part of some harm reductionists to clarify the extent to which the harm reduction approach is primarily about reducing harm or promoting drug user rights. For Reinarman there are real merits in fostering the kind of ambiguity that Hunt and others have been seeking to resolve:

> The (harm reduction) movement has succeeded where other attempts have failed partly because it blended human right and public health, not because it chose one as superordinate. Just as ambiguity is functional for nation states...ambiguity is functional for the harm reduction/drug law reform movement. Ambiguity helps create a large political tent under which our unwieldy coalition can fit, maximising our appeal, increasing membership, and allowing for local autonomy so that unique local conditions can be addressed.... The public health principles that under gird harm reduction practices have afforded much needed political legitimacy to controversial policies. This legitimacy is a precious resource, some of which might be jeopardized if the movement were to give loud primacy to the right to use whatever drugs one desires and to make legalization its principle policy objective. (Reinarman 2004: 240)

For those whose support of harm reduction is rooted in a concern to reduce the health harms associated with illegal drug use it may well strike a rather unsettling note to hear their concerns and commitments being characterized as a strategy for attaining "political legitimacy". Danny Kushlick and Steve Rolles from the Transform drug legalization lobby group have gone even further however, in calling for harm reductionists to set aside their preoccupation with individual and public health harms and focus instead on the goals of drug law reform:

> The question is not whether human rights or public health comes first. Rather it is whether we collude with a policy that invariably degrades and sometimes destroys our clients and the communities in which they

live, or whether we speak out against it, both as individuals and organi-
sationally . . . More important is the question of how organisations can most
effectively challenge the status quo, terminate prohibition and replace it with
a system that is effective, just and humane. (Kushlick and Rolles 2004: 245)

It is not solely in terms of legalization that the harm reduction movement has challenged some of the more conventional ideas about drug
use and drug policy. As a number of commentators have pointed out,
harm reduction places drug use itself within a kind of moral vacuum
in which it is seen as being neither "good" nor "bad" in itself but simply an act that is associated with various harms which, with the correct
policies and services in place, can be removed or reduced. The clearest expression of the moral ambivalence at the heart of harm reduction
was provided by John Strang, Professor of Addictions Psychiatry at the
National Addiction Centre in London. According to Strang:

> The true champion of harm reduction is not necessarily anti-drugs nor nec-
> essarily pro-drugs . . . A pre-determined position on drug use as intrinsically
> "bad" or "good" has no meaning in this context, where the response is deter-
> mined solely by the extent of observed or anticipated harm which results
> from drug use. Thus the champion of harm reduction is neither for nor
> against increased civil rights for users . . . neither for nor against the legali-
> sation or decriminalisation of drug use . . . except insofar as one or other of
> these choices influences the nature and extent of harms consequent upon the
> drug use. (Strang 1993: 3–4)

This view of drug use as essentially amoral has been similarly expressed
by Mugford in the following terms:

> Drug use is viewed as neither right nor wrong it itself. Rather, drug use is
> evaluated in terms of harm to others and, to some extent, harm suffered
> by users. The latter is regrettable, but acceptable if it arises from 'informed
> choice'. Laws are appropriate to prevent harm to third parties and to reduce
> exploitation of users by producers/sellers but not as primary barriers to
> informed use. (Mugford 1993)

Mugford's view resonates with that of the philosopher John Stewart Mill
who maintained that the state should only seek to curb the freedom
of the individual in circumstances where the actions of the individual
adversely affects other people. However, many people would argue, in
concordance with Mill's principle, that drug use is a classic case of

an individual behaviour that does indeed result in tremendous harms to others and for that reason alone (wholly aside from the harms to individual users) should be socially proscribed.

Within some forms of the harm reduction approach the two issues of drug user rights and drug user health have been combined in an analysis of what are seen to be the health harms associated with vigorous drug enforcement. From this perspective drug enforcement is seen as a potential source of further harm. Maher and Dixon (1999) have described how the street policing of local drug markets can have an adverse impact on the health of drug users, whilst Fitzgerald has characterized some forms of drug policing as being a "public health menace":

> Given our knowledge that aggressive styles of anti – drug policing contribute significantly to the spread of blood borne viruses it is not too extreme to say that aggressive anti drug street policing is itself a public health menace. (Fitzgerald 2005: 203)

Although harm reductionist's have criticized the actions of the police in targeting those who are using illegal drugs, it is not at all clear how the harm reduction approach would address the issue of drug dealing. According to Fitzgerald:

> A key problem for harm reduction is what to do with drug dealers in risk environments. The conventional approach is to arrest them and promote legal economies in marginalised communities. Providing harm reduction approaches when it involves drug users is relatively easy compared to trying to find solutions for drug dealers. (Fitzgerald 2009: 268)

Fitzgerald's recommendations for developing a harm reduction approach to drug dealing give a clear illustration of just how difficult it is for harm reductionists' to tackle the issue of drug dealing:

> Future harm reduction strategies, if they are truly to engage with the economic dimension of the risk environment, need to account for embodiment of the risk environment and to treat low level drug dealers as compassionately as they do drug users. (Fitzgerald 2009: 268)

What Fitzgerald is doing here is attempting to resolve the difficulty of identifying an appropriate harm reduction approach to drug dealing by focussing attention on that part of the drug dealing spectrum (low-level dealers) that comes closest to the activities of drug users.

However, that still leaves unresolved the much tougher question of what harm reductionists would see as being the appropriate response to those who are higher up the drug dealing chain. To the extent that the harm reduction approach supports the rights of the individual to use whatever drugs he or she wishes, it is hardly congruent with that view to then penalize the activities of those who are making those drugs available for others to use. Indeed if drug use itself is seen as a human right then the key harm which drug sellers may be seen to pose could have to do with the quality and price of the drug they are selling in a kind of Fairtrade sort of way. Alternatively harm reductionists might address themselves to the marketing techniques of those who are selling illegal drugs and seek to reduce the harms associated with specific drug markets, for example, drug market–related violence.

Recently the harm reduction–inclined UK Drug Policy Commission published the report "Refocusing Drug Related Law Enforcement to Address Harms" (UKDPC 2009) which sets out a distinctively harm reduction approach to drug enforcement. The thrust of the UKDPC's report is to encourage drug enforcement agencies to shift from the traditional terrain of drug seizures and drug arrests towards adopting an approach aimed at reducing the harm associated with drug markets. The principle underlying the approach advocated by the UKDPC, and derived from the work of US academics Peter Reuter and Jonathan Caulkins, is that drug markets differ in the level of harm they are causing to the surrounding community. For example, an open drug market operating in a residential area may be seen as causing more harm than a closed drug market operating from within a residential property. Equally, a drug market that is associated with high levels of violence can be seen as causing more harm than a drug market that is more consensually organized. The principle that drug markets differ in the level of their harm opens up the possibility of law enforcement agencies encouraging drug dealers to adopt a "less noxious form of selling", for example, encouraging a drug market to shift from its present location to an area of a city where its activities are less visible:

> Displacement might be actively sought to deliver a net reduction in harm to a community, for instance by displacing a market from a residential area to an industrial estate. Thus the focus is not so much on reducing the amount of drug dealing but rather on reducing the harms associated with the way dealing operates in this particular area. (UKDPC 2009: 50)

The idea of drug enforcement agencies seeking to shape local drug markets will be regarded by some as enormously controversial, whilst for others it might be regarded as a pragmatic response to the reality of different levels of harm associated with different ways of marketing illegal drugs. The UKDPC is well aware of the controversial nature of its recommendations in stating that:

> Adopting such an approach will be a challenge. Some of the more radical suggestions such as prioritising open markets and thereby "tolerating" other activities (e.g. closed dealing conducted away from residential areas) can be seen as letting dealers get away with crime. The current media and political climate would seem unfavourable to such an approach. However, where resources are finite, sometimes these sorts of decisions are made implicitly, and if they can be shown to reduce harms in the long term then attitudes might change. (UKDPC 2009: 62)

Part of the problem with this view of harm reduction–oriented drug enforcement is that whilst one might be sympathetic to the idea that enforcement agencies should prioritize those markets associated with the greatest harm, it is not at all clear what approach they should take towards the lower harm-causing drug markets. Following the logic of the UKDPC position, for example, it would be incongruous for enforcement agencies to tackle the low harm markets for fear of disrupting the very equilibrium those markets may have established. However, doing nothing about a low-level harm drug market on the basis that it is not seen as a high harm-causing drug market amounts to a form of decriminalization or legalization by the back door. A further difficulty with the harm reduction approach to drug enforcement has to do with the fact that the harms associated with illegal drug use are by no means confined to the drug market itself and how it is organized. A low harm drug market may well be causing enormous harms to individuals, to their families and to the wider community as a result of the adverse impact of the individual's drug dependency. For these reasons the development of a harm reduction approach to drug enforcement is likely to be no less controversial than within the field of drug treatment.

The Effectiveness of Harm Reduction Interventions

There are two ways in which the effectiveness of harm reduction initiatives can be assessed; the first is in terms of the evidence of effectiveness from the various evaluations of harm reduction services that have been carried out, and the second is in terms of the overall impact of harm reduction policies and initiatives at a national or a local level. It is important to recognize that these two things are by no means the same. An intervention may be evaluated as being effective in its own right but still not effect a change of such magnitude as to have a positive effect in reducing the overall level of risk behaviour and harm at the national level.

In relation to studies evaluating the effectiveness of harm reduction interventions there is now a substantial body of evidence demonstrating a range of positive outcomes associated with those interventions, for example, needle and syringe exchange, methadone maintenance, heroin prescription, safe injecting centres and the provision of naloxone to drug users to reduce their risk of experiencing a fatal drug overdose. The available research is strongest in relation to the evaluation of needle and exchange programmes and methadone maintenance programmes. There is strong evidence that the needle and syringe exchange services have had a beneficial impact on preventing the spread of HIV infection amongst injecting drug users and in reducing drug injectors HIV related risk behaviour. Many of these evaluations have contrasted levels of risk behaviour amongst needle and syringe exchange attendees and non-attendees (Donoghoe et al. 1989, Hartgers et al. 1992, Des Jarlais et al. 1994, 1996, Heimer et al. 2002). A recent review of the evidence on needle and syringe exchange services by the National Institute for Health and Clinical Excellence commented favourably on the capacity of those services to reduce HIV spread (NICE 2009). In the research which compared levels of HIV infection amongst injecting drug users in cities with or without needle and syringe exchange programmes MacDonald and colleagues concluded that:

> On average HIV seroprevalence decreased in studies of injecting drug users in cities with needle and syringe programmes, whereas in studies from cities without needle and syringe programmes HIV seroprevalence increased. (MacDonald et al. 2003: 356)

In contrast to those studies that have identified a positive impact on drug injectors risk behaviour associated with needle and syringe exchange attendance, Bruneau and colleagues found higher levels of HIV infection amongst needle and syringe exchange attendees than non-attendees (Bruneau et al. 1997). When these research findings were first published they shook the fledgling confidence in the effectiveness of needle and syringe exchange programmes, and raised the very real possibility that by bringing injecting drug users into closer proximity with each other (thereby potentially expanding drug injectors needle and syringe sharing networks) the new services might actually increase rather than decrease levels of HIV infection. The response to Bruneau's findings on the part of the harm reduction establishment was to point out that needle and syringe exchange services may well be attracting drug users with higher levels of risk behaviour, and higher levels of HIV infection, rather than actually causing such heightened levels of HIV infection (Wodak and Cooney 2005). Without detailed information on the precise point at which individuals became HIV positive, enabling one to determine whether it pre- or post-dated the contact with needle and syringe exchange services, it is impossible to tell which of the two explanations accurately accounts for Bruneau's findings.

Where research into the effectiveness of needle and syringe exchange programmes has really struggled is in determining how much of the service needs to be available to bring about sufficient change in drug injectors risk behaviour to have an overall impact on levels of HIV infection. If needle and syringe services were a drug the question would be how much of that drug is needed to have a maximum therapeutic impact. In other words, how many needles and syringes need to be given out, to how many drug injectors, to have an overall impact on reducing levels of HIV infection? Heimer and colleagues have raised some questions as to how big an effect any individually focussed harm reduction service can have in changing drug user risk behaviour:

> After more than a decade of studying these responses, it can be concluded that harm reduction interventions, which focus solely on the behaviour of individuals, can maximally reduce the risks of transmission by between 25% and 40%. Since this degree of reduced transmission seems unlikely to prevent the epidemic spread of HIV and hepatitis among injector and their intimate contacts other interventions have been proposed, implemented and evaluated. Some of these seek to act at the community level changing behavioural norms and consequently individual risk behaviour. (Heimer et al. 2002: 103)

Aside from the question of how big an effect needle and syringe exchange programmes can have, there are also questions as to the degree to which drug injectors themselves have remained supportive of these programmes. McVeigh and colleagues looked at data on the operation of needle and syringe exchange services in the north of England over an 11-year period and found that whilst the proportion of anabolic steroid injectors had increased over time (compared to heroin injectors) the number of attendees overall had fallen:

> The reduction in the frequency of client visits to agency based syringe exchange programmes by both opiate and anabolic steroid injectors is of additional concern, in particular the reduction in the frequency of visits and the increase in the number of clean syringes taken by opiate users may indicate that substantial numbers of these injectors are choosing to reduce their level of engagement with these services. (McVeigh et al. 2003: 4003)

Finally, in terms of the evidence from the various needle and syringe exchange evaluations that have been carried out, it is not at all clear how successful or otherwise these services have been at discouraging individuals from injecting. This is an important issue because we know that injecting is by far the riskiest form of drug use even where it is carried out with sterile injecting equipment. For example, there remains the risk of both overdose and of introducing serious life-threatening bacteria into the blood stream. Although injecting with sterile equipment reduces some of those risks, it does not reduce all of the risks. Whilst there is no evidence that needle and syringe services have led to an increase in the level of drug injecting, equally there is very little evidence that they have been associated with an overall reduction in injecting. There is a degree to which needle and syringe exchange schemes, by their very nature, may tend to reinforce injecting as a route of drug misuse. Despite such concerns the National Institute for Health and Clinical Excellence recently recommended much wider provision of needle and syringe exchange services to injecting drug users (NICE 2009).

In terms of sheer scale, the extensive body of research reporting on needle and syringe exchange services is matched only by that evaluating the effectiveness of methadone prescribing to drug users. The National Institute for Health and Clinical Excellence recently reviewed the effectiveness of methadone maintenance provided to drug users (NICE 2007). According to NICE, methadone maintenance is associated with improved rates of patient retention in treatment, with lower levels of illicit opioid use, and with lower levels of HIV-related risk behaviour compared with either no treatment or a placebo treatment. The NICE review also demonstrated that drug users who were not taking methadone, or who were discharged from services, were four times more likely to die than those receiving methadone. With regard to reductions in levels of criminal behaviour the evidence was less clear-cut. The review identified some studies that reported a significant positive effect of methadone maintenance on reduced criminality whilst in other studies there appeared to be little or no clear effect.

In terms of the amounts of methadone prescribed to individuals, the NICE review concluded that higher dosages of methadone were associated with a greater reduction in self-reported illicit opioid use than higher fixed dosages of buprenorphine. In summary, methadone has come to be seen as the most appropriate treatment for dependent opioid users and it is undoubtedly for this reason that such large numbers of drug users are routinely prescribed the drug as part of their treatment programme.

Where the research on methadone maintenance has been less impressive is in documenting the extent to which it is associated with successful recovery from dependent drug use – where success is defined not simply in terms of a reduction in the use of illicit opioids but in the cessation of drug using behaviour. This is an issue that is looked at in greater depth in a later chapter on drug abuse treatment services. It is sufficient to note here that there has been growing concern at the length of time some drug users are left on methadone (in some cases in excess of 20 years), raising the possibility that they may have become dependent on the drug itself in a form of treatment-acquired dependency. Recently too there has been growing concern at an increase in the numbers of deaths where methadone has been identified as one of the drugs being used by dependent drug users. In Edinburgh, for example, where methadone is widely used as a treatment for heroin dependency there are now more deaths associated with methadone than with heroin (GRO 2008). This is clearly a worrying development and raises the question of the appropriateness of long-term methadone prescribing in circumstances where drug users may be combining their prescribed methadone with other illicitly obtained substances, thereby increasing their risk of experiencing a drug overdose.

Heroin prescribing, as distinct from methadone prescribing, has been a feature of the British System of drug addiction treatment for many years although the number of drug users receiving heroin is tiny by comparison. According to Metrebian and Stimson there are only a handful of doctors within the United Kingdom licensed to prescribe heroin and less than 500 drug users who are being prescribed the drug (Stimson and Metrebian 2003). At the present time research is underway within the United Kingdom comparing the relative benefits of injectable heroin and injectable methadone prescribed to dependent drug users. There has been widespread media coverage of the results of this research within both the United Kingdom and the United States, which has included calls for heroin prescribing to be rolled out on a national basis (BBC 2009, Gardham 2009, Newsbusters 2009).

Despite the positive media coverage that the UK heroin trial has received, it is evident that not all sections of the medical profession are equally supportive of heroin prescribing to dependent drug users. The Royal College of General Practitioners, for example, issued the following statement setting out its view of heroin prescribing:

> It is the belief of the Royal College of General Practitioners that there would be no added value from general practitioners prescribing heroin to their patients. Heroin has a low therapeutic index (that is the difference between a safe dose and a toxic dose) and in a naïve user that has lost their tolerance it is rapidly fatal in overdose. (Dr Clare Gerada speaking on behalf of the Royal College of General Practitioners 2002)

Part of the concern with prescribing heroin has to do with the fact that it is between four to five times more costly than prescribing methadone. In addition, there are worries as to whether prescribing a highly addictive drug to individuals who have already become dependent upon that drug amounts to "treatment" in the normal sense of the term. There are concerns that within a national programme of heroin prescribing doctors might come under increasing pressure to prescribe the drug even in circumstances where they were reluctant to do so. Equally, there are concerns that once heroin became more widely available on prescription, pressure might start to mount to prescribe other Class A drugs, for example, cocaine to those who had become dependent upon the drug. Certainly it is easy to see how, once one has accepted the principle of prescribing what many people regard as the single most dangerous drug currently being abused by dependent drug users, there could be pressure to prescribe other drugs that are regarded as less harmful and for which there are at present no substitute drugs.

It is also easy to see the likely difficulties a doctor might face when he or she attempts to reduce the dose of the heroin being prescribed. Within such a situation the drug user may simply argue that any reduction in the amount of heroin they are being prescribed would result in a return to their past level of chaotic drug use. Faced with such a threat it is easy to see how a doctor who had already been prescribing heroin to the individual might simply continue that prescription as a way of coping with an individual determined to maintain his prescription drug supply.

In terms of research that has been carried out on heroin prescribing Nordt and Stohler have argued that this may have led to a reduction in the overall incidence of heroin use in Switzerland (Nordt and Stohler 2006). Other benefits that have been shown to be associated with heroin prescribing include reductions in levels of mortality compared to drug users participating in other maintenance treatment programmes, improved social functioning and improved psychological and physical health (Uchtenhagen et al. 1999, Van den Brink et al. 2003, Rehm et al. 2005). Within many of the evaluations however, it is difficult to know whether the apparent benefits are due to the heroin being prescribed or to other aspects of the treatment regime, for example, the intensive counselling that often accompanies heroin prescribing. One of the few UK studies, undertaken in the 1980s, found no health benefits associated with heroin prescribing and identified that one in ten of those who were being prescribed the drug were selling it on to other drug users (Hartnoll et al. 1980). The evidence in relation to heroin prescribing, whilst positive in certain respects, still leaves unanswered many of the ethical and practical questions associated with how and whether such a treatment should be made more widely available, and what the likely impact and cost of such a policy would be (McKeganey 2008).

Since the late 1980s there has been growing concerns within a number of countries at the rising number of individuals dying from a drug overdose. Within the context of those concerns there have been repeated calls to provide drug users and their families with the overdose reversal drug Naloxone (Strang et al. 1996, 1999, 2008). This drug is able to provide a short-term reversal of the depressant effects of heroin, and in the circumstances of a heroin overdose can save an individual's life. Part of the controversy around Naloxone has to do with the worry as to whether being in possession of such a drug may encourage a greater willingness on the part of some drug users to take risks with the quantity of the heroin they are using. There is a possible analogy here with the situation in which individuals may be more likely to engage in sexual risk taking when they are in possession of barrier contraception. At the present time we do not know whether providing drug users with a Naloxone-loaded syringe would encourage a greater degree of injecting risk behaviour than would otherwise occur. Within Scotland, Mcauley and colleagues have described the results of a small pilot in which 19 drug users and selected family members were trained in the use of Naloxone and then provided with the drug on a take-home basis (Mcauley et al. 2009). By the time of the 6-month follow-up, two of the study participants had administered the Naloxone in circumstances of an apparent drug overdose. The authors on this study report that there were no inappropriate uses of the drug during the pilot. Whilst the results of this study were seen as providing encouragement for a wider distribution of Naloxone, one of the key questions to be considered in relation to the pilot is whether the two overdoses that resulted in the administration of the Naloxone would have occurred had it not been for the fact that the drug users were in possession of the drug in the first place.

One way of considering this question is to look at the likelihood that two out of a sample of 19 drug users would have had a fatal drug overdose within a 6-month period. Fatal drug overdoses are very rare such that within Lanarkshire (the area in which the Naloxone pilot took place) there were only 44 drug-related deaths in 2008 not all of which arose as a result of a drug overdose (GRO 2009). Research into the prevalence of problem drug use within Scotland has estimated that in 2006 there were 6,261 problematic drug users within Lanarkshire. Combining the estimated total number of problematic drug misusers within Lanarkshire with the number of drug-related deaths in Lanarkshire, the average risk of a drug user in that part of Scotland dying from a drug-related cause over a 12-month period would be 7% and over a 6-month period would be 35%. The likelihood of a pilot study involving 19 out of a possible 6,261 drug users identifying two individuals who would have experienced a fatal drug overdose within a 6-month period had it not been for the availability of the Naloxone drug in the situation where they were overdosing seems unfeasibly small.

One possible explanation of the Lanarkshire study results is that the drug treatment agencies involved in the pilot were able to target the drug on those individuals who they correctly judged were at much heightened risk of experiencing a fatal drug overdose. If this is the case, and services are indeed able to identify which drug users will experience a drug overdose, one wonders whether there are other methods for reducing the individual's risk of overdose that do not carry a possible risk of inflating the drug user risk behaviour. Two other possible explanations, however, are (a) that individual drug users in possession of the drug were more willing to engage in a higher level of injecting risk behaviour than they might otherwise have been, and (b) that simply being in possession of the drug increases the likelihood of it being used in circumstances where the individual was not in fact experiencing what would otherwise have been a fatal drug overdose. The first of these two possible explanations would have far-reaching consequences for the wider distribution of the drug, whilst the second could fall under the heading of an inappropriate use of the drug.

Within the Lanarkshire pilot it is not clear whether the two administrations of the drug involved individuals who had been involved within the pilot or individuals who the study participants had come across in the midst of what might otherwise have been a fatal drug overdose. This latter possibility gives rise to a further ethical concern to do with the appropriateness of an individual, who has received only limited training, administering an injection to someone who they interpret as suffering from a possible drug overdose but who has not given any kind of informed consent to have the drug administered to them. Whilst the distribution of Naloxone is being widely promoted by harm reductionists, the evidence base for such a service is far from clear-cut and there is at least a possibility that provision of the drug on a take-home basis might in fact lead to an increase rather than a decrease in drug-related harm.

Research has been undertaken in a number of countries into the provision of safe injecting centres where drug users can inject illicitly obtained street-drugs under some level of medical supervision. The European Monitoring Centre for Drugs and Drug Addiction has undertaken a review of the evidence as to the effectiveness of safe injecting centres (Hedrich 2004). Similarly, the Joseph Rowntree Foundation in the United Kingdom undertook a detailed review of the arguments and the evidence "for and against" safe injecting centres (Joseph Rowntree Foundation 2006). Safe injecting centres have been found to be effective in facilitating drug users access into treatment (Kerr et al. 2007), in reducing drug injectors risk behaviour (Wood et al. 2007) and in reducing ambulance call-outs for drug overdoses (Salmon et al. 2010). Research has also shown, however, that high-risk injecting behaviour may continue to occur within a safe injecting centre. Kerr and colleagues reported on 336 overdose events that occurred between March 2004 and August 2005 within the safe injecting centre in Vancouver (Milloy et al. 2008).

Despite the evidence of their positive effect, safe injecting centres remain a highly controversial form of provision. The International Narcotics Control Board, for example, has repeatedly indicated that the provision of any kind of centre where individuals are allowed to use illicit drugs amounts to a breach of the international drug conventions which many countries have signed up to as part of their obligations in tackling the global drugs problem (INCB 2009). There are also concerns that just as with needle and syringe exchange, safe injecting centres may have the unintended consequence of further entrenching a risky form of drug use – resulting in the individual persisting with injecting for longer than they otherwise might have done.

Are Harm Reduction Interventions Able to Reduce Overall Levels of Harm?

In addition to evaluating individual services it is also important to consider the overall impact that harm reduction initiatives may have had in those countries where these methods have been widely applied. The United Kingdom is a good case study for such an examination because of the enormous investment that has been made in harm reduction services over the last 20 years. The question here then is not so much one of whether the individually evaluated harm reduction services are effective but whether there are clear indications that harm reduction services have had a beneficial impact overall.

Perhaps the clearest indication of a possible overall positive effect associated with the development of harm reduction interventions is the low level of HIV infection amongst injecting drug users in those countries that have developed a network of harm reduction services. The UK Harm Reduction Association has drawn attention to this as being one of the major achievements of the approach:

> Between 1987 and 1997 Britain led the world in developing a harm reduction approach to drug use. The clearest achievement was in the prevention of HIV infection among people who inject drugs (by heeding the advice outlined in the report of the Advisory Council on the Misuse of Drugs). UK has thus averted an epidemic of HV infection associated with drug injecting and there is evidence that harm reduction has resulted in lower rates of Hepatitis C virus (HCV) infection than found in comparable countries. (UKHRA 2001)

According to the UK Health Protection Agency (2009), by the end of 2008 there were a cumulative total of 5,023 diagnosed cases of HIV infection estimated to be associated with injecting drug use in the United Kingdom. The yearly total number of new diagnosed cases of HIV infection amongst injecting drug users in the United Kingdom has been around the 150 mark for the period of 1998 to 2006. The overall prevalence of HIV infection amongst injecting drug users for the United Kingdom is estimated to be around 1.6% (Health Protection Agency 2007). There is concern that the level of HIV infection amongst injecting drug users may be starting to rise within at least some parts of the United Kingdom. For example, it appears that at present one in 77 drug injectors are becoming HIV positive within 3 years of beginning injecting compared to 1 in 400 in 2002 (Health Protection

Agency 2009). Nevertheless, the overall level of infection remains low and nowhere near the apocalyptic predictions that fuelled the 1980s fears of an impending of HIV epidemic. It seems likely that the United Kingdom's avoidance of an HIV epidemic amongst injecting drug users may indeed have been due in part to the rapid development of harm reduction initiatives such as needle and syringe exchange:

> Other than an outbreak in Edinburgh in the early 1980's HIV infection amongst injecting drug users has remained relatively uncommon in the UK probably as a result of prompt community and public health response. (Health Protection Agency 2007)

Although harm reduction services may have reduced the spread of HIV infection amongst injecting drug users the same cannot be said about Hepatitis C infection which is also spread as a result of drug injectors using contaminated injecting equipment. According to the UK Health Protection Agency "Hepatitis C is currently the most important infectious disease affecting those who inject drugs" (Health Protection Agency 2009). Up to 80% of those who are Hepatitis C positive may go on to develop chronic infection and a significant minority are at risk of acquiring cirrhosis and liver cancer. By the end of 2008 there were a total of 69,864 diagnosed cases of Hepatitis C infection in England – over 90% of which are estimated to have been acquired as a result of injecting drug use. According to the Health Protection Agency around 40% of injecting drug users in the United Kingdom may now be Hepatitis C positive. In some cities the proportion of drug injectors who are infected may be higher still. In Glasgow, Bloor and colleagues found that 60% of drug users were Hepatitis C positive (Bloor et al. 2006). In London, according to the Health Protection Agency (2009) 56% of injecting drug users are estimated to be Hepatitis C positive, while in the North West of England the figure is estimated to be 58%.

Interestingly the overall level of Hepatitis C infection in England and Wales does not appear to have changed dramatically over the period from 1998 to 2008 with 41% of injecting drug users testing Hepatitis C positive in 1998 and 40% testing positive in 2008 (Health Protection Agency 2009). On this basis then it is hard to avoid the conclusion that the harm reduction services developed within the United Kingdom have had only minimal impact on reducing drug injectors risks of acquiring and spreading Hepatitis C infection.

With regard to the data on the prevalence of problematic drug use there is no evidence to suggest that harm reduction services have succeeded in reducing the overall use of illegal drugs. To an extent this is as one might expect given the fact that reducing the overall level of drug use is not a priority of harm reduction interventions even though this was included within the original hierarchy of aims outlined by the Advisory Council on the Misuse of Drugs in 1988. The fact that the United Kingdom has one of the highest levels of problematic drug misuse in Europe (EMCDDA 2009) is perhaps the clearest evidence for the lack of impact of harm reduction interventions on reducing the overall prevalence of problematic drugs misuse.

Within the last few years growing attention has been directed at the high number of drug-related deaths with a number of governments committing to reducing the overall scale of drug related mortality. Within the United Kingdom, for example, the government included achieving a 20% reduction in drug-related deaths as one of the goals of its first national drug strategy. Not only has that reduction not been achieved but we have actually seen an overall rise in the number of deaths in recent years. Within Scotland, there were a total of 244 drug-related deaths in 1996, 455 in 2007 and 576 in 2008 (General Register Office for Scotland 2009). The Office for National Statistics (National Statistics) regularly produces information on the number of drug-related deaths in the United Kingdom; in 1993 there were a total of 829 deaths amongst drug users in England and Wales with that figure rising in 2008 to 1,738 (ONS 2009). On the basis of these statistics it is hard to conclude that harm reduction services within the United Kingdom have had a positive impact on reducing drug-related mortality.

It is also important to consider the issue of drug user risk behaviour and in particular the extent to which harm reduction measures have resulted in a reduction in needle and syringe sharing amongst injecting drug users. Information on the levels of needle and syringe sharing amongst injecting drug users in the United Kingdom is obtained on the basis of the Unlinked Anonymous Surveillance Programme which has been monitoring drug injectors risk behaviour since the early 1980s (Health Protection Agency 2009). In 1991 the surveillance programme reported that 24% of injectors had shared needles and syringes in the last month, whilst in 2006 the percentage had reduced by a single percentage point to 23%. On this basis then one would have to conclude that, despite the enormous investment of resources and finances in distributing many millions of needles and syringes to injecting drug users within England, the proportion of drug users reporting recent sharing has changed very little. Even where needle and syringe exchange services are widely available this does not in itself rule out the likelihood that a significant minority of drug users will continue to share injecting equipment.

Finally, there is the question of whether harm reduction services have had a positive impact on reducing the harms caused by drug users rather than those experienced by drug users. It is difficult to quantify the harms caused by those using illegal drugs since very few countries have audited those harms. Within England, however, it has been estimated that the social and economic costs of problematic drugs misuse is approaching £15B a year (Gordon et al. 2006), whilst in Scotland the equivalent figure is estimated to be around £3.5B a year (Casey et al. 2009). In the absence of any time series data it is difficult to know whether these social and economic costs have been rising or falling in recent years but it is difficult to believe that over the last 20 years harm reduction measures have actually served to reduce these costs to their current level.

Much the same can be said about the statistics on the numbers of children that have at least one parent dependent upon illegal drugs. Within the United Kingdom there are estimated to be approaching 350,000 children with a drug-dependent parent (ACMD 2003). Although not all of these children may be experiencing harm as a result of their parent's drug use, the Advisory Council on the Misuse of Drugs has reported that out of 77,928 drug-dependent parents on whom they had data only 46% were actually living with their dependent children. These figures give an indication of the high rate of family breakdown in circumstances where parents have a serious drug problem and give indication of the harm to young children associated with parental drug dependency. Whilst there are no time series data with which to assess whether the harms to children have been increasing or decreasing over the last 15 or so years, it is hard to believe that harm reduction measures have succeeded in reducing that harm in part because harm reductionists have largely ignored the impact of parental drug use on children. The 2005 International Conference on the Reduction of Drug Related Harm, for example, had as its main theme "widening the agenda" with key presentations on topics ranging from young people, refugees and asylum seekers, human rights and US drug policy. There was though scant attention paid to the needs of children with drug-dependent parents and no mention at all of this topic in the published report based on the conference (Percy 2005).

The Harm Reduction Paradox

There is a paradox here. On the one hand there are studies of individual harm reduction interventions that have identified positive outcomes on the basis of evaluation research that has been carried out. On the other hand there are clear indications that, apart from in relation to HIV, harm reduction measures have not succeeded in reducing the overall level of drug-related harm even where they have been widely implemented. There are a number of possible explanations for that apparent paradox.

First, it may be that whilst the level of investment in harm reduction initiatives has been substantial it may still have been less than would be needed to have a major impact on reducing the overall level of drug-related harm, for example reducing the drug death statistics, reducing levels of Hepatitis C infection, reducing the numbers of children with drug-dependent parents and reducing the overall scale of the drug using population. Although this explanation is favourable to the harm reduction approach, in implying that harm reduction funding should be increased rather than decreased, the explanation itself has more to do with faith than science. Without a near religious belief in the benefits of harm reduction it is difficult to see how simply providing more funding to harm reduction interventions would result in an overall positive reduction in drug-related harm. The persuasiveness of this explanation is further undermined by the lack of any clear empirically based guidance as to the quantity of harm reduction input (e.g., the number of needles and syringes that would need to be provided) to bring about the level of reduced harm that would be required.

Second, it may be that the failure is not so much to do with the overall level of support that has been provided to harm reduction services but in the quality of the services themselves. The likelihood that this offers at least a partial explanation of the harm reduction paradox can be seen from a review of needle and syringe exchange services undertaken by Abuldrahim and colleagues in 2006 in the United Kingdom. This review found major shortfalls in the quality of the services offered by many needle and exchange clinics, for example, 16% of needle and syringe exchange clinics did not discuss issues to do with needle and syringe sharing, 30% did not discuss issues to do with safer injecting and 35% did not discuss issues to do with injecting hygiene (Abuldrahim et al. 2006). If these deficiencies are in any way reflective of the overall quality of harm reduction services it is little wonder that substantial levels of drug-related harm have continued even in the face of those services.

Third, it may be that whilst harm reduction services can facilitate improvements in individual's drug-related risk behaviour, the scale of that improvement is not sufficient to bring about a reduction in the overall drug-related harm. Whilst it may be possible to reduce the proportion of drug users sharing injecting equipment from a high of 60% down to a low of 20%, nevertheless that remaining 20% may still be sufficient to generate significant further spread of blood-borne infections amongst injecting drug users. The issue here may not be one simply of whether harm reduction services have an effect in reducing drug user risk behaviour so much as to the size of that effect and whether it is of a sufficient scale to bring about a reduction in overall drug harm.

Fourth, it may be that the effectiveness of harm reduction interventions is limited by the level of the individual's drug dependency. Whilst many drug users may be able to make positive changes in their behaviour, as a result of accessing harm reduction services, there may be many others who are in such a state of chaos in their lives, associated with their drug dependency, that they are simply incapable of benefiting from harm reduction interventions even where these are widely available locally. Whilst outreach harm reduction services have sought to access the most chaotic drug users it may be that there is a level of personal chaos associated with an advanced drug habit that will always be inimical to the kind of support that harm reduction services can provide.

Fifth, it may be that harm reduction services cannot attain the level of impact that would be required to reduce levels of overall drug harm so long as drug use itself remains illegal. This is clearly the view of some of those working within the harm reduction movement. Consider the case of needle and syringe exchange services. Within these services drug injectors are provided with sterile injecting equipment in exchange for previously used equipment. Those individuals are then required to leave the needle and syringe exchange clinic to inject the black market drugs they may have previously obtained. Crucially, the drugs the individual may be injecting could carry a serious health risk arising from the fact that they may have been produced, stored and transported in highly contaminated environments. This is likely to be the explanation for the outbreak of anthrax infection amongst drug users that have been identified in various parts of the United Kingdom in 2009 and 2010 (Health Protection Agency 2010). In addition to those health risks arising from the drugs themselves there are also a number of risks that are associated with the environments in which those drugs are being used, for example, derelict buildings, alleys, parks and toilets. Injecting drugs within those circumstances does not become safe simply as a result of using a sterile needle and syringe. To reduce these other health risks would require providing drug injectors not only with the means to inject their drugs and the setting where their injecting could take place under some level of medical supervision. It would also require providing drug users with the drugs they were using. In effect the government would have taken on responsibility for every facet of the individual's drug use thereby making drug use itself legal.

Conclusion

This chapter has been about the development of harm reduction ideas and practices within the addictions field. The notion of reducing drug-related harm has exerted an unparalleled influence on drug policy and drug services across the globe. Harm reduction has literally re-shaped how we think about the use of illegal drugs and how we respond to drug users. The harm reduction philosophy has created a distinction between the use of illegal drugs and the harm that flows from that use and it has held out the promise that it is possible to minimize drug harms whilst leaving the drug use intact. That vision may be little more than a chimera. Drug use and drug harm may be two sides of the same coin such that wherever the drug use is occurring there will be some level of drug-related harm that flows from it. The failure of harm reduction interventions to substantially reduce the overall level of drug harm may actually reveal a different truth entirely, namely: that it is only by reducing the overall level of drug use that we may be able to reduce the overall level of drug harm.

When in 1988 the Advisory Council on the Misuse of Drugs announced that "the spread of HIV is a greater danger to individual and public health than drug misuse" they may simply have been wrong. In the intervening years, when drug misuse has expanded beyond all expectation on a global scale we have come to recognize that it is drug use, not HIV, which has proven to be the bigger threat. If it is the case that drug use poses a greater threat than HIV then we need to focus our efforts first and foremost not on harm reduction but on drug use reduction. For this to occur will require a revolution in drug policy no less substantial than the revolution that ushered in the commitment to harm reduction.

But does this mean we should now dispense with harm reduction services and switch our commitment and funding to drug prevention? Such a shift would be both impractical and unethical given that there are large numbers of people continuing to use illegal drugs. The key question becomes one of how to achieve a balance between the aims of reducing drug-related harm and reducing drug use itself. For this to be achieved it will be necessary to dispense entirely with the notion that drug use is an activity that should be celebrated and encouraged. We need to see drug use for what it is – a profoundly harmful domain of human experience that threatens society in a multitude of ways. The challenge of combining the approaches of drug use reduction and harm reduction will be substantial. We have very little experience of drug use reduction services and harm reduction services working in concert with each other as opposed to operating in largely separate domains. In the case of methadone maintenance services, for example, the need will be to ensure that once those services have succeeded in developing a level of stability in individual drug users' lives that they are then able to refer those individuals on to services that can enable them to become drug free. Combining "harm reduction" and "drug use reduction" may well become then the greatest challenge that we face in drug policy and drug interventions over the coming decade and beyond.

KEY DISCUSSION QUESTIONS

1. Is it possible to substantially reduce the level of drug harm without also reducing the overall level of drug use?

2. Does drug use pose a greater threat than HIV and were the ACMD wrong to suggest the reverse?

3. How possible is it for services to combine the aims of harm reduction and drug use reduction?

4. Does harm reduction need drug legalization for it to work effectively and to what extent is harm reduction a Trojan horse for drug legalization?

5. What should be the balance between harm reduction and drug prevention?

6. Can there be such a thing as harm reduction focussed drug enforcement and if so what should be the drug enforcement approach to drug dealing?

Chapter 3

Drug Treatment: So What's All the Fuss About?

Introduction

If there is one statement that sums up the view of drug abuse treatment over the last 15 years it must surely be that "treatment works". So prevalent has been the notion that drug abuse treatment does indeed "work" that there has been an unparalleled growth in many countries in the funding for treatment and in the numbers of drug users in treatment. Within England, for example, over the 6 years from 2001 to 2007 there was a 70% increase in the numbers of drug users in treatment from 118,500 to 202,000. Over that period the funding for drug abuse treatment rose from around £390 million a year in 2002 to £800 million a year in 2007. The view that "drug abuse treatment works" was virtually unshakeable in the United Kingdom until around 2007 when the confidence in that statement evaporated virtually overnight and a definite sense of crisis descended:

> Is it fair to say our field is in crisis at this point in time? Unfortunately I believe it is. I believe that this is because of two things. First, I think

we are divided within. Second, increasingly there are attacks on drug treatment from outside – and these are becoming more virulent, sustained, and widespread. (Ian Wardle quoted in Great Debate 2009: 7)

Others expressed similar concerns at what they saw as a chasm that had opened up between the abstinence and harm reductions wings of the treatment industry. Richard Philips, contributing to a national debate on the nature and direction of drug abuse treatment, expressed his fears for the sustainability of addictions treatment in the United Kingdom:

There is the idea that a chasm is opening up between those who believe in abstinence and those who believe in harm reduction. But if this is allowed to become a binary debate it is going to be very damaging for us as a field. It will make us much less able to defend what has been achieved over the last few years in both harm reduction and abstinence. (Richard Phillips quoted in Great Debate 2009: 35)

This chapter will look at some of the controversies that encircled addictions treatment over the last few years. The questions that have come to the fore most recently are all to do with whether drug abuse treatment does indeed "work", whether it "fit for purpose", what its purpose actually is, and whether there needs to be a root and branch reconstruction of the entire approach to drug treatment. To understand how those questions have displaced the "treatment works" mantra it is necessary to look at the various contributors to the drugs treatments debate in the United Kingdom that has been raging over the last few years.

The Role of the Media and the Loss of Confidence in Drugs Treatment

One of the key factors in the loss of confidence in drug abuse treatment was a series of interviews on the BBC flagship current affairs "Today" programme between the BBC Home Affairs Editor Mark Easton and the Head of the National Treatment Agency Paul Hayes. In the first of three interviews Mark Easton reported that as a result of an additional £130 million spent on addictions treatment in England during the period 2004/05–2006/07 only 70 more people had become drug free (BBC 2007). On that basis, it was argued, each individual case of recovery had cost the taxpayer around £1.8 million – hardly evidence of a drug treatment system working in an efficient and cost-effective way. Immediately following the BBC broadcast the National Treatment Agency put out a press release claiming that the "BBC got its numbers wrong" and that in fact, out of 66,123 drug users who left drug abuse treatment in 2006/07, 5,829 or 8.8% were drug free (NTA 31 October 2007). The NTA press release also outlined that overall 180,000 drug users had been treated in the year 2006/07 which would mean on the NTA's own figures that only around 3.2% of those treated had indeed become drug free. In the light of the 3.2% figure, the NTA's claim that "Drug treatment in England offers a good return on investment" (NTA 2007) seemed at best rather hollow.

If the NTA felt that it had weathered some harsh criticism from the BBC over the low rate of recovery from dependent drug use it could hardly have expected that within a few weeks it would be called upon again to defend the drug treatment industry. The next item the BBC addressed had to do with the role of "contingency management" in the treatment of dependent drug users. In the simplest of terms contingency management refers to the practice of providing drug users with small rewards, for example, food vouchers, as an encouragement for positive changes in their drug use. Although the practice of contingency management had been positively evaluated by the National Institute for Health and Clinical Excellence (NICE 2007), a BBC report revealed that as many as one-third of drug agencies were rewarding drug users by providing them with additional amounts of the opiate substitute drug methadone. Having initially disavowed any knowledge of this practice occurring, the Head of the National Treatment Agency accepted that a report from his own agency had identified that the practice was widespread and that on reflection drug users should not be receiving drugs as a reward for behaviour change. Within the same interview the Health Minister Dawn Primarollo was more damning calling the practice "unethical" (BBC October 2007).

In a third item on the United Kingdom's drug treatment system, the Today programme contrasted the widespread use of methadone in England (prescribed to around 147,000 drug users in 2007) with the fact that only around 5,000 drug users (i.e., 2% of those in treatment) were provided with residential rehabilitation (BBC 2008). According to the National Treatment Agency the widespread use of methadone was entirely congruent with a recent National Health and Clinical Excellence review that had identified the benefits of methadone prescribing to dependent drug users (NICE 2007). Despite the NTA's reassurances as to the value of methadone the outcome of this series of interviews was clear for all to see – the UK drug abuse treatment

industry was in a state of disarray. Those charged with the responsibility for managing that system seemed unaware of unethical and
unprofessional practices occurring within treatment agencies, only a
tiny proportion of clients of those agencies were leaving treatment
drug free, and there seemed to be an over reliance on the use of
methadone at the expense of other treatment options including residential rehabilitation.

The Role of Research in Reassessing the Goals of Treatment

If the media questioning of the effectiveness of drug abuse treatment
took off in 2007 the climate of uncertainty as to the aims of drug abuse
treatment had begun 3 years earlier with the publication "What Are
Drug Users Looking for When They Contact Drug Abuse Treatment
Services – Abstinence or Harm Reduction?" (McKeganey et al. 2004).
That publication, based on the largest survey ever undertaken of drug
users in Scotland, involved asking the clients of drug treatment agencies what change or changes in their drug use they were looking to
achieve on the basis of having contacted the drug treatment agency.
In response to that question the research team found that across all of
the different treatment modalities studied – residential rehabilitation,
methadone de-tox, methadone maintenance, counselling – the majority
of drug users said that the one thing they wanted to achieve was to
become drug free. Hardly any of those interviewed said that they were
looking to drug treatment services for help in making harm reduction
type changes in their drug use. For example, whilst 57% of drug users
said that they were looking for help to become drug free, 0.7% said they
were looking for help in identifying safer ways of continuing to use their
drugs, 7.4% said they were looking for help to stabilize their continuing
drug use.

The publication of this paper raised the very real possibility that an
enormous gulf had opened up between what drug treatment professionals and policy makers saw themselves as providing through treatment
(harm reduction) and what drug users themselves were looking for from
treatment (abstinence). The publication of the research findings drew a
critical response from many of those at the heart of the harm reduction
establishment in Scotland and elsewhere. The Scottish Drugs Forum,
for example, described the research as "manipulative and unwelcome".
Robert Newman, a leading harm reduction physician in the United

States, questioned the wisdom of drug treatment services focusing on abstinence:

> Addicts who embrace an ultimate goal of enduring abstinence should be assisted in every way possible, but they must be advised with brutal frankness of the low prospect of success – and the grim, potentially fatal, consequences of failure. (Newman 2005: 266)

The Scottish Government, which at that time had been heavily influenced by harm reduction ideas in drug abuse treatment, observed in response to the findings that:

> It is high time we ended the unhelpful obsession in trying to prove whether abstinence or harm reduction strategies are best. The most effective treatment will always depend on the circumstances of the individual addict: there is no one size fits all solution. (Scottish Executive Spokesperson 5 September 2005)

The harm reduction organization Drugscope questioned how much weight should be given to the expressed wishes of drug users in shaping their drug treatment:

> A proper responsiveness to users of drugs and medical services is about hearing what they say and want as part of a process of discussion and negotiation that should be framed by the evidence base and the professional competencies of service providers and informed by the stated goals and desires of service users which are indispensable data but not unassailable prognoses. (Roberts 2005: 263)

Irrespective of the reactions of the various commentators to the research findings, the genie that drug users were looking to become drug free, rather than to receive harm reduction support, was very much out of the bottle and influencing public and professional debate on the direction of drug treatment.

The Contribution of the Think Tanks

The debate about the nature and effectiveness of drug treatment that began in 2004 with the publication of the "abstinence or harm reduction" report and which was amplified in 2007 by the media in the series of "Today" interviews between Mark Easton and Paul Hayes was further developed in the contribution from two of the leading UK think tanks – the right wing leaning Centre for Social Justice and the harm reduction leaning United Kingdom Drug Policy Commission. Within the Centre for Social Justice, Kathy Gyngell chaired a working group assessing the impact of the drugs problem and looking in particular at the failures of the drug treatment system and drug policies under the New Labour government:

> The last ten years of drugs policy under Labour have marked a fundamental shift in objectives. They have seen the introduction of an additional route into treatment, a new target population, and a doubling of the numbers in treatment. However, there has been no parallel shift in what is deemed appropriate and effective treatment. Under Labour, abstinence has been lost in the hierarchy of goals for treatment. Harm reduction and harm minimisation services, not recovery and rehabilitation, dominate national and local treatment provision. (Centre for Social Justice 2007: 25)

The group highlighted, amongst other things, the enormous growth in the use of methadone in the United Kingdom with the number of methadone prescriptions in England doubling from 970,900 in 1995 to 1,810,500 in 2004 – an increase of 86.5%. According to Gyngell the ubiquity of methadone as a treatment for drug addiction in the United Kingdom had been driven in large part by the performance measurement culture that had evolved under New Labour:

> Our analysis is not that methadone does not and cannot have a useful and positive role in the treatment of addiction. Its routine and mass prescription is hard to justify on either clinical or ethical grounds and is entrenching rather than solving addiction. The rapid expansion of its prescription appears to be as much an outcome of political pressure and target driven policy as of a dispassionate clinical response to the treatment needs of a particularly vulnerable population. We have found the current mass prescription of methadone to be the cause of deep disquiet amongst drugs workers and addicts alike. (Centre for Social Justice 2007: 25)

Following the concerns and criticisms over the widespread use of methadone by the Centre for Social Justice, the National Treatment Agency issued a press statement marshalling the views of leading figures and organizations from within the drug treatment field in an attempt to stifle what it saw as the growing and politically motivated criticism of methadone (National Treatment Agency 2008). Within the NTA press release, Michael Farrell, consultant psychiatrist and Reader in Addiction Psychiatry at the National Addiction Centre in London, stated that:

> Methadone is a useful treatment for heroin addictions and works in complimentary fashion to other forms of treatment. Methadone and other related types of medication make an important contribution to the improvement and well-being of people who are addicted to heroin. (National Treatment Agency Press Release 2008)

Paul Hayes, Chief Executive of the National Treatment Agency, commented that:

> Methadone is the first line treatment for opiate dependency because that is what NICE guidance and expert clinical guidelines recommend. (National Treatment Agency Press Release 2008)

And Drugscope, a major charity in the drugs field commented that:

> Drugscope supports the availability of the widest possible range of interventions including the prescribing of methadone and the provision of rehab. While we do need more investment in rehab services, we must be careful not to treat them as a silver bullet for addiction recovery, ignoring the demonstrable benefits of methadone treatment in the process. (National Treatment Agency Press Release 2008)

Even in the face of such reassurance it was clear to virtually all with an interest in these matters that all was not well in the garden of drug abuse treatment. There is no doubt that the heat in the debate around the goals and mixed achievements of drug treatment in the United Kingdom was substantially increased by the awareness of an approaching general election and the possibility that a rejuvenated conservative party and future government might usher in a very different set of goals for drug abuse treatment services.

Within Scotland the leader of the Scottish Conservatives (Annabel Goldie) coined the term "parking" to express her and others dissatisfaction at the length of time some drug users were being left on methadone without any clear expectation that they would indeed become drug free:

> It is a well known fact that methadone is more addictive than heroin, yet this is virtually the only option open to many drug addicts across Scotland. Every

pound spent on this so-called harm reduction route is a pound not spent on rehabilitation and the real fight against drugs. (Annabel Goldie quoted on BBC Monday, 14 November 2005)

Other commentators claimed that the United Kingdom was witnessing the growth of a new militant abstentionism that was seeking to threaten the harm reduction achievements of the last 15 or so years. Mike Ashton, a respected commentator on drug-related matters in the United Kingdom, produced an extended essay, circulated to those working in the drugs treatment field, lamenting what he saw as the rise of the "New Abstentionists" (Ashton 2008):

> The new abstentionists were on the march and the statistics seemed to be with them. But their attacks and the defences put up against them were based on questionable assumptions and misinterpreted or just plain mistaken figures. (Ashton 2008: 1)

Within the context of what it saw as an increasingly polarized debate the United Kingdom Drug Policy Commission sought to bolster confidence in the achievements of drug treatment:

> In recent months an increasingly polarized debate has developed in the UK, which has tended to portray abstinence and maintenance approaches to drug treatment as an either/or issue. At its most extreme the debate appears to suggest that substitute prescribing is incompatible with recovery. The UK Drug Policy Commission felt that this debate was becoming increasingly divisive, with little reference to the evidence on treatment effectiveness, which indicates a treatment system should be composed of a range of different services to meet different needs. It appears to be diverting attention away from more legitimate questions, such as whether individuals in need of drug treatment have enough choice, particularly with respect to residential rehabilitation, the variability in quality of services of all types and if there has been too much focus on numbers in treatment and retention rates rather than outcomes ... There was also concern that the debate risk undermining the wider public message that drug treatment (generally) is a good thing that should be supported and properly funded. (UKDPC 2008: 2)

To stem what it saw as the alarming loss of confidence in drug treatment, the UK Drug Policy Commission (UKDPC) convened a panel of experts and gave them the task of producing a consensus definition of "recovery". If it were possible to produce such a definition, the UKDPC theorized, then it might be possible to knit together the two wings of the drug treatment debate (those who stressed abstinence and those who stressed harm reduction) under a single umbrella notion of "recovery". The crucial question was whether the group could indeed come up with a definition that embraced both sides of the drug treatment debate. The result of the group's deliberation was to define recovery in the following way:

> The process of recovery from problematic substance use is characterized by voluntarily sustained control over substance use, which maximizes health and wellbeing and participation in the rights roles and responsibilities of society. (UKDPC 2008: 6)

Whether intended or not the definition bore all the hallmarks of the harm reduction orientation of the UKDPC. To define recovery in terms of the possible continued use of substances, and to place such emphasis on the issue of controlled use, demonstrated that at heart the definition was rooted in the view that drug use itself was not the problem so much as the lack of control over that use. Recovery, in these terms, did not necessarily require the individual to cease his or her drug use but only to regain control over that use. As a result of this notion of "controlled drug use" the consensus which the UKDPC had hoped would dissolve the differences between the abstentionists and harm reductionists failed to materialize with various commentators claiming that the recovery definition was little more than an attempt to re-badge the ideology of harm reduction–oriented treatment in the increasingly fashionable language of recovery (Boyd 2008, McKeganey 2008).

The Political Sea Change in Drug Abuse Treatment

Whatever the rights and wrongs of the debate on the direction of drug abuse treatment it would be hard to overestimate the political impact of that debate. Faced by the prospect of a loss of public confidence in the drug treatment industry, government ministers and key officials in the United Kingdom have virtually tripped over themselves to stress that the goal of drug abuse treatment is indeed to enable people to become drug free. In England the Minister of State for Public Health underlined the importance of abstinence as the goal of treatment in her address to the 2008 national conference on injecting drug use:

I want to be clear that the primary objective of any treatment has to be abstinence. We want as many users as possible to be permanently drug-free and a positive influence in their families and communities. These objectives drive our whole drug strategy. (Speech by Rt Hon Dawn Primarolo MP, Minister of State for Public Health, 28th October 2008: National Conference on Injecting Drug Use)

Paul Hayes, Chief Executive of the beleagued National Treatment Agency, performed a remarkable U-turn in embracing abstinence as the key challenge facing drug treatment services having been highly critical of what he saw as the politically motivated attacks of the "new abstentionists":

> In the year ahead all of us in the field face this challenge to focus our efforts on the outcomes of treatment, to enable more addicts to become drug free. (NTA 2007/08)

Within Scotland, the nationalist government announced a new drug strategy that for the first time contained a clear commitment to ensuring that drug treatment services were indeed working towards individual's becoming drug free:

> In the governments view recovery should be made the explicit aim of services for problem drug users in Scotland. What do we mean by recovery? We mean **a process through which an individual is enabled to move on from their problem drug use, towards a drug free life as an active and contributing member of society.** Furthermore it incorporates the principle that **recovery is most effective when service users needs and aspirations are placed at the centre of their care and treatment.** In short an aspirational, person centred approach. (Bold text in original – Scottish Government The Road to Recovery 2008: 23)

Drug Abuse Treatment Services and Drug User Abstinence: A Goal too Far or an Achievable Aspiration?

But how near or far are drug abuse treatment services in the achieving the goal of enabling dependent drug users to become drug free? In answering that question it is useful to look at the results of the various treatment outcome studies that have been undertaken within the United Kingdom and elsewhere.

Within England, the major study evaluating the impact of drug abuse treatment services is the National Treatment Outcome Research Study (NTORS). This study employed the design of recruiting a large sample of drug users starting a new episode of drug abuse treatment and following those individuals over an extended period of time to measure what improvements they made in their life as a result of the drug treatment services they had received. The longitudinal treatment cohort design employed in the NTORS project has become the most widely used approach for assessing the impact of drug abuse treatment services. For example, the approach has been used in Australia (Darke et al. 2007a, 2007b), England (Gossop et al. 2001), Scotland (McKeganey et al. 2009), Ireland (Comiskey et al. 2009) and the United States (Simpson 2003, Simpson and Flynn 2008).

The NTORS study defined "drug free" or "abstinent" in terms of the non-use of six substances over the last 90 days: illicit heroin, non-prescribed methadone, non-prescribed benzodiazepines, crack cocaine, powder cocaine and amphetamines. An individual using methadone or smoking cannabis during the last 90-day period would still be regarded as drug free within the NTORS study definition so long as he or she was not also consuming one or more of the six listed drugs. At the 4/5-year follow-up point 38% of the drug users within the NTORS study were abstinent in terms of that definition. Because the NTORS study recruited from different treatment modalities it was possible to compare the abstinence rates of those individuals who had received residential rehabilitation with the abstinence rate of those who had been treated in the community. In terms of the drug users recruited from residential rehabilitation services 47% were drug free at the 4–5 year follow-up point. By comparison, among those drug users who were recruited from methadone prescribing community based services 35% were drug free at the 4–5 year follow-up point (Gossop et al. 2001).

The equivalent of the NTORS study within Scotland is the Drug Outcome Research in Scotland (DORIS) study. In this research just over a thousand drug users were followed over a 33-month period. Abstinence within the DORIS study was defined in terms of the cessation of all forms of drug use other than alcohol and tobacco. Within the Scottish definition, drug users who were continuing to use methadone (whether prescribed or not) or who were smoking cannabis would not have been regarded as drug free. At the 33-month follow-up interview only 8% of drug users in the Scottish study (5.9% of females and 9.0% of males) had been drug free for a 90-day period in advance of being interviewed. In relation to those drug users in the Scottish study who had been recruited from a residential rehabilitation centre 24.7% had a 90-day drug-free period in advance of their 33-month follow-up interview. By contrast, only 6.4% of those who were recruited from community-based treatment agencies had a 90-day drug-free period in advance of their 33-month follow-up interview (McKeganey et al. 2006).

The Scottish research was able to look at the possible impact of the treatments individual drug users had received following on from the initial treatment agency where they had been recruited into the DORIS study. In the case of those drug users who had received methadone maintenance at some point over the 33-month follow-up, 3.4% had a 90-day drug-free period, whereas amongst those drug users who had received residential rehabilitation at some point over the last 33 months, 29.4% had enjoyed a 90-day drug-free period.

Within Ireland, the equivalent of the DORIS and NTORS studies is the Research Outcome Study in Ireland (ROSIE) in which 404 opiate users were re-interviewed over a 3-year period with information provided on their drug and alcohol use over a 90-day period (Comiskey et al. 2009). In this study, 29.4% of the sample were not using any illicit drugs at the 3-year follow-up point. In the case of those who were continuing to use cannabis, but who had not used any other illicit drug, the percentage who were drug free at the 3-year follow-up point was 42.9%. The proportion that were neither using any illicit drug nor continuing to use methadone at the 3-year follow-up point was 19%.

On the basis of these studies the proportion of drug users who were able to become entirely drug free at or approaching 3 years following their initiation of a new episode of drug abuse treatment ranged from a low of 8% in Scotland to a high of 19% in Ireland. These figures would mean that somewhere between 81% and 92% of drug users in these studies had not been able to become entirely drug free on the basis of their contact with drug treatment services. Should we regard those proportions as a measure of treatment failure or as an indication of the difficulties of enabling dependent drug users to become drug free? In answering that question it is important to consider the results of other drug abuse treatment outcome studies.

One key study in this regard has been reported by Thomas McLellan and colleagues in the United States and relates to the outcome of substance abuse treatment provided to physicians (McLellan et al. 2008). In this study McLellan and colleagues looked at the treatment outcomes of 904 doctors admitted to one of the 16 physician health care programmes in the United States. Just over half of the doctors participating in this research had a primary alcohol problem (50.3%) with over a third (35.9%) reporting a problem with opiate drugs. Seventy-eight per cent of the physicians entered a residential facility for an average of 72 days followed by outpatient treatment over a 6–9-month period. Twenty-two per cent of the physicians were treated on an outpatient basis. The vast majority of the doctors received an abstinence-focused treatment:

> Regardless of the setting or duration most treatment (95%) comprised 12-step, with the goal of total abstinence from alcohol and other drugs of misuse. The physicians were expected to attend Alcoholics Anonymous or other 12 step groups (92%). (McLellan et al. 2008)

In total, 647 physicians (80.7% of the original sample) completed their treatment. On the basis of urine testing 126 (19%) of these physicians were identified as having relapsed in their drug or alcohol use over the 5-year period of the study. By contrast 521 (81% of those completing their treatment) remained drug or alcohol free over the study period. On the basis of this study a very different picture emerges of the effectiveness of drug misuse treatment services.

There is an immediate caveat that should be added to the comparison of the McLellan study results with the NTORS, DORIS and ROSIE study results, which has to do with the different samples participating within these studies. The doctors within the McLellan study had a very strong incentive to engage in treatment and to become drug and alcohol free. Indeed their continued capacity to work as physicians was dependent to a large extent on the positive outcomes of their treatment. By comparison the drug users within the NTORS, DORIS and ROSIE study had very little in employment terms that was hanging on the outcomes of their drug treatment. On that basis one might be inclined to say that part of the explanation for the low success rate of the UK drug treatment outcome studies may have to do with the fact that we have simply not made abstinence or becoming drug free a valued outcome of treatment. The performance measures that the government has applied to the drug treatment sector in the United Kingdom have focused only upon increasing the numbers of drug users in treatment. There has been no requirement on the part of drug treatment services either to assess the quality of the services on offer or to increase the proportion of drug users becoming drug free. In this sense we have not actually highlighted abstinence or becoming drug free as a valued outcome of treatment and it may well be as much for that reason as any other that very few drug users leave treatment in the United Kingdom having ceased their drug use.

But to what extent could drug abuse treatment services enable a more conventional addict population to attain a higher abstinence rate? In answering that question it is interesting to consider the results of the Australian Treatment Outcome Study which, like the NTORS, DORIS and ROSIE, involved following up drug users in treatment over an extended period of time (36 months). Of the 429 heroin users recruited into the study at baseline 86% had been abstinent from heroin use for the preceding month and 40% had been abstinent from heroin use for the preceding 12 months at the 36-month follow-up (Darke et al. 2007). The Australian study has identified much higher levels of sustained abstinence than has been reported for any of the UK studies and on that basis there would appear to be some legitimate concern at the relative lack of effectiveness on the part those services within the United Kingdom.

A recent publication reporting on drug treatment services in England has presented a more positive view of those services. The publication from Marsden and colleagues reported outcome data from the National Drug Treatment Monitoring System on 18,428 drug users in contact with drug treatment services in England between January 2008 and November 2008 and who had received at least 6 months drug treatment (Marsden et al. 2009). The results of this study, reported in the *Lancet* medical journal, and announced at a press conference (Laurance 2009), were nothing short of remarkable:

> For clients analysed at the study endpoint, 4996 (34%) were abstinent from both drugs in the 28 days before review. 13542 (92%) clients analysed were heroin users, of whom 5016 (37%) were abstinent from heroin in the 28 days before review; 7636 (52%) clients analysed were crack cocaine users of whom 3941 (52%) were abstinent from crack cocaine in the 28 days before review. (Marsden et al. 2009: 1266)

Perhaps unsurprisingly, given the hard time that the National Treatment Agency felt they had received at the hands of the BBC, they were eager to trumpet the results of the Marsden study. A press release from the National Treatment Agency commented that:

> The largest ever study of heroin and crack cocaine treatment programmes in England has shown that the first six months of treatment leads to large

proportions of addicts of one drug or the other abstaining. (NTA 1 October 2009)

Colin Bradbury, Head of Delivery at the National Treatment Agency, commented that:

> Drug treatment has been greatly expanded in the last few years and so it is very encouraging that this study of the most commonly available treatments in England shows that even those with entrenched addiction to heroin and crack cocaine respond well to treatment. Whilst users are in treatment, we know that their drug use declines and that crime significantly reduces, which is positive for their health and for communities which suffer from the harms caused by drug addiction. "The goal of all drug treatment is for the user to overcome their addiction, and this study shows that although that may take time, it is possible to tackle the harms caused by drugs by investing in drug treatment". (NTA Press Statement 1 October 2009)

Recovery from dependent drug use, however, is about sustained not temporary abstinence and it is striking that whilst Marsden and colleagues refer to individuals being abstinent from heroin and crack "in" the 28 days before review, the paper does not report how many days these individuals were free of all forms of drugs misuse over the 28-day period. Obviously individuals can be free from any specific drug, on any specific day whilst continuing to use a variety of other prescribed and non-prescribed drugs. There are other reasons why one may need to be cautious about the results of this study. Research is at its best when it is dispassionate from any specific set of industry or professional interests. It is striking that the Marsden paper should include the following statement under the sub-heading "role of the funding source":

> Employees of the study sponsor, the NTA, contributed to the study design, data analysis, data collection, data interpretation, and writing of the report. The corresponding author (Marsden) had full access to all the data in the study and had final responsibility for the decision to submit for publication. (Marsden et al. 2009: 1265)

The NTA is the agency responsible for funding the majority of drug abuse treatment in England and for overseeing the effectiveness of the drug treatment provided. It is remarkable that the organization should have been so deeply involved in all aspects of this effectiveness assessment. Finally, both the initial assessments of drug use behaviour and the follow-up assessments, upon which the analysis of treatment effective-ness is based, were collected by drug treatment agency staff themselves. Those staff will have had a particular interest in the results of this study and it would be naïve not to consider the possibility that this interest may have impinged upon the data they were collecting. In this respect the Marsden et al. paper contrasts markedly with that from McLellan and colleagues (2008) in reporting the results of random urine testing of the participating physicians over the study period.

So What's Wrong With Drug Abuse Treatment?

There are a variety of possible reasons why drug abuse treatment services appear to be enabling only a small proportion of individuals to become drug free.

Disagreement Over the Aims of Treatment

As debate over drug abuse treatment has raged over the last few years, one of the main areas of contention has had to do with the aims of treatment and whether drug abuse treatment are about enabling drug users to become drug free. As a result of the impact of harm reduc-tion ideas over the last 20 years many drug treatment services would not necessarily see themselves as working towards drug user abstinence. Rather, those services would see themselves as addressing a much wider set of issues to do with individuals rehabilitation, for example, help-ing resolve drug users housing problems, debt problems, helping drug users to find employment and so on. Indeed some professionals working within addiction services are of the view that abstinence is itself a risky goal for services given the possibility that success in helping drug users reduce their drug intake might actually increase their risk of experienc-ing a fatal drug overdose in the event that they were to resume their previous pattern of drug use:

> Addicts who embrace an ultimate goal of enduring abstinence should be assisted in every way possible, but they must be advised with brutal frank-ness of the low prospect of success – and the grim, potentially fatal, consequences of failure. (Newman 2005: 266)

Some of those working within drug treatment services would regard methadone prescribed to the drug users as the equivalent of insulin prescribed to the diabetic, that is, as a medication that the individual will require for the remainder of their life. Part of the reason why drug treatment services seem to be enabling only a small proportion of drug users to become drug free may then have to do with the fact that abstinence itself has not been identified as an important goal of treatment.

The Problem of Numbers

If there is one aspect of the treatment system that has been trumpeted more loudly than any other over the last few years it is the marked increase in the numbers of drug users in treatment. The current UK drug strategy, for example, notes that:

> More people are receiving treatment with the number in contact with treatment services increasing from 85,000 in 1998 to 195,000 by 2006/07 with the target to double the numbers in treatment achieved two years early. (Drugs Protecting Families and Communities – The 2008 Drug Strategy: 28)

In Scotland the minister responsible for drug-related matters has been similarly upbeat about the increase in the numbers of drug users accessing drug treatment services:

> One simple statistic, which I have, is that the number of people in contact with services has almost doubled – let me say again that the number of people in contact with services has almost doubled and that is something to take great pride in, and we want to see that success continue. (Fergus Ewing 2007: 16)

And in England, Paul Hayes, the Chief Executive, opened the 2007/08 Annual Report of the National Treatment Agency with the statement that:

> With our record of achievement in the past we welcome the prospect of greater scrutiny in the future. The treatment system did what it said on the tin, the number in treatment more than doubled, waiting times fell dramatically and progressively more drug users were successfully retained in treatment programmes. The latest official statistics confirm that there were more than 202,000 people in treatment in 2007/08 – 138 per cent of our original target – and treatment worked for more than three quarters of our clients. (Paul Hayes 2007: 5)

Whilst there has been much celebration over the increase in the numbers of drug users in treatment, it is important to ask whether the focus on increasing the numbers of drug users in treatment is compatible with the commitment to ensure that services are working towards enabling individuals to become drug free? In one sense these aims are fundamentally incompatible. Research which I and James McIntosh carried out for our book *Beating the Dragon: The Recovery from Dependent Drug Use* (McIntosh and McKeganey 2002) showed that the process of recovery from dependent drug use entailed individuals building up a new non-addict identity for themselves. They needed to see their drug use, and that of those around them, in a new light – not as something they did for pleasure or as a way of enabling them in their eyes to function normally, but as something that was causing serious harm to themselves and those around them. They needed to build up a new set of relationships. On occasion this could involve moving to a new area where they were not known as someone who had a drug problem. They needed to be able to fill the time they had previously devoted to tracking down and using drugs, they needed to build up a sense of the person they could become rather than the person they had been throughout the years of their involvement with illegal drugs. They often needed to reflect back on the things they had done to the people they loved most over the years of their addiction. They needed, on occasion, to recapture a sense of the person they felt they might have become had they not gone down the road of protracted and chaotic drug use.

The addict's journey of recovery and identity reconstruction was not a process of fast turnaround and large numbers but of long-term, intensive work, of two steps forward and one step back, of talk-based counselling, appropriate medication and real practical help in terms of housing and employment support. As a result of increasing the numbers of drug users in treatment the government may have inadvertently driven down the quality of the drug treatment services offered to clients. It may be impossible to provide high-quality, recovery-oriented drug treatment to large numbers of drug users. With an estimated 220,000 drug users in treatment in the United Kingdom the pressure of that number may mean that it is simply inevitable that drug services will be unable to provide the intensive, high-quality treatment that a commitment to recovery would require. The small proportion of drug users who are able to leave treatment drug free may be a reflection of the political priority that has been given to increasing the numbers of drug users in treatment.

The Failure to Provide Services that are Focused on Abstinence

Whilst harm reduction ideas have influenced the provision of drug treatment in the community (most notably in the growth of community-based substitute prescribing services) there has been no parallel growth in the abstinence-focused, residential rehabilitation sector. Over the period when community-based drug treatment services have expanded and the numbers of drug users in contact with those services have increased there has been a notable contraction of the residential rehabilitation sector within the United Kingdom. The *Addiction Today* magazine, widely circulated to those working in the drug treatment field, has been maintaining a regular tally of the number of residential rehabilitation centres that have closed within the United Kingdom over the last few years. That number presently stands at 20 (Boyd 2008, Lakhani 2009).

The lack of provision of high-quality residential rehabilitation services within the United Kingdom is all the more striking when one recalls that both the NTORS study and the DORIS study identified the greater rate of recovery (abstinence) on the part of the residential rehabilitation services compared to the community-based drug treatment services. Within the DORIS study, for example, 6.4% of those drug users treated within the community were drug free for the 90-day period compared to 24.7% of those who were treated in a residential rehabilitation centre (McKeganey et al. 2006). It is hard to avoid the conclusion that within the United Kingdom the drug treatment service that is provided with the least frequency is the one that is most closely associated with addicts becoming drug free. By comparison, the treatment that has the lowest rate of success (methadone maintenance) in terms of addicts becoming drug free is the one that is provided with the greatest frequency. By comparison the treatment that is most widely provided (methadone) is associated with the lowest likelihood of drug users becoming drug free.

Whilst methadone is perceived to be a much cheaper treatment than residential rehabilitation, it is questionable whether the economics are quite so favourable to prescribing if after long-term methadone provision the vast majority of drug users remain drug dependent. Within Scotland it has been estimated that the methadone programme may be costing the Scottish government in excess of £40 million a year but enabling less than 5 per cent of addicts to become drug free. On that basis the programme would need to be running for 5 years to attain the recovery rate being achieved within the residential rehabilitation sector (in excess of 25%). The accumulated cost of the methadone programme over that length of time would be £200 million which is a figure that would certainly sustain the development and funding of substantial residential rehabilitation provision. What may appear to be the cheaper treatment option (methadone) may actually turn out to be the more expensive option when one figures into the equation the very small percentage of drug users who will be enabled to become drug free on the basis of the treatment provided.

The other attraction that methadone has over residential rehabilitation is in the numbers of drug users that can be treated. Whilst it is possible to prescribe methadone to hundreds of thousands of drug users, residential rehabilitation is never going to be able to work with anything like that number. In a situation where priority has been placed on increasing the numbers of drug users in treatment, with no equivalent priority being given to the proportion of drug users leaving treatment drug free, it is perhaps inevitable that methadone maintenance will be the favoured treatment over residential rehabilitation.

The Quality of Drug Treatment Staff

Another reason why drug treatment services may be enabling only a small proportion of drug users to leave treatment drug free could be the quality of staff working within the treatment sector itself. If you need to visit a doctor in the United Kingdom you can rest assured that the person you will be seeing has had a medical education lasting many years. If you want to buy a house you know that the solicitor you will be dealing with has been educated to degree level and if you need to contact a social worker you know that the person you will be seeing will in all probability have had a university education. If you need to take your much loved cat or dog to a vet you know that the person you will be seeing is one of the most highly trained professionals around. If, by contrast, you need to contact a drug worker you will in all probability be seen by someone who has not been to university, who may not have a professional or a postgraduate qualification, and who may have only entered the field in the last few years. None of this is to suggest that they will not be good at their job, but if the same standard applied in each of the other areas of professional work mentioned above you could be forgiven for sleeping a little less comfortably in your bed at night.

The reason why social workers, lawyers, doctors, teachers and other professionals take so long to train is because the knowledge base in their area of work is so large and the consequences of poor practice are so serious. But much the same could be said of work within the addictions. In terms of the knowledge base, for example, there are university libraries sinking under the weight of information on the genetics of addiction, the biology of addiction, the psychology of addiction, the economics of addiction and the sociology of addiction. For the most part, however, the knowledge contained within that list of "ologies" passes the average drug and alcohol worker by with only the briefest of engagement.

Working with addicts in recovery is by no means a straightforward process. Addiction workers need to understand the nature of drug dependency and the opportunities for recovery; they need to know when to confront their clients and when to offer supportive encouragement. Increasingly they need to assess the impact of parental drug use on children; balancing the needs of the child and the needs of the adult in a way, which does not do more harm than good for either the adult or the child. These are complex matters on which individuals lives can hang by a thread. In that sense the consequences of poor professional practice in the drug and alcohol field are no less serious than in other areas of medicine or the law.

There will be those who say that there is no need for the effective drug and alcohol worker to have received a university education or to have access to specialist knowledge and that it is sufficient for the individual to be committed to their work and empathic in their contact with their clients. But why should one assume that such commitment and empathy could not be beneficially combined with greater academic training to the benefit of those clients with a drug dependency problem?

Within the United Kingdom it is likely that somewhere in excess of £900 million is being spent each year on drug dependency treatment. On the basis of that level of financial support it is reasonable to expect that the drug treatment workforce would be every bit as well educated, well paid, well trained and well supported as the doctor, the solicitor and the social worker. If we are to effectively tackle our substance abuse problems and to ensure that drug treatment services are better equipped to enable individuals to recover then we need to ensure that those who are working within those services are appropriately trained. If we fail in this then drug treatment services will continue to fall short of what they should be achieving, and short of what their clients rightfully expect them to achieve.

The Failure to Assess and Monitor Drug Abuse Treatment Services

On the basis of the various governmental statements about the drug abuse treatment sector in the United Kingdom one might have the impression that this is a very closely regulated domain. In reality, however, as successive enquires have revealed, the opposite is the case and the world of drug abuse treatment is subject to only minimal regulation and government intervention. Audit Scotland recently reviewed drug abuse treatment within Scotland and identified a realm that seemed largely bereft of any government commitment to monitor or assess what services were actually doing. The Audit Scotland report noted that:

> There is no direction from the Scottish Government on what the money for drug treatment and care services should deliver. (Audit Scotland 2008: 2)

> Public bodies do not routinely evaluate the effectiveness of drug and alcohol services. Less than one per cent of total spend by NHS boards and councils on drug and alcohol services is used for research and evaluation purposes. (Audit Scotland 2008: 24)

> There is no consistent understanding of what the money spent on drug and alcohol services bought. (Audit Scotland 2008: 22)

> Funding for drug and alcohol services does not have clear aims or explicit outcomes attached. (Audit Scotland 2008: 25)

On the basis of these comments it is hard to avoid the view that drug abuse treatment services within Scotland have been left drifting for many years, with little clear guidance being given as to what those services are expected to be doing and very little assessment of what they are doing. Within England a review of the drug treatment sector undertaken by the Audit Commission identified similar failures and poor practice:

> (C)urrent assessment practices often do little to secure either rapid access or appropriate treatment. Multiple assessment is common, as few areas have developed a common screening and assessment framework or arrangements for passing information between providers. This not only leads to increased costs and delays but also means that many clients face unnecessary repetition of a lengthy, and often personally distressing, process. In many cases, assessments are undertaken by a single member of staff and may be focused

narrowly on a client's suitability for one specific intervention – such as maintenance prescribing or residential rehabilitation. This means that the client's options may be limited by the personal preferences or treatment philosophy of the individual undertaking the assessment and/or the eligibility criteria for a particular type of service. (Audit Commission 2002: 34)

A later review of drug treatment services undertaken by the Audit Commission in England identified similar poor practice particularly in relation to the degree to which service providers were using evidence of the effectiveness of drug treatment services to guide their day-to-day decision-making:

Although national research exists into 'what works', there is little evidence locally of commissioning decisions being based on proven effectiveness and value for money. While some local drug partnerships are making excellent progress in working with providers, users and carers to redesign and improve treatment services, many are struggling. Senior managers responsible for local drug partnerships need to take stock of existing treatment provision and judge its fitness for purpose against current and projected demand, using nationally available research to inform their assessments. (Audit Commission 2004: 40)

On the basis of these critical assessments of drug treatment services in Scotland and England it may be all too predictable that only a small proportion of clients are able to become drug free.

Conclusion: A Drug Treatment Revolution

The world of drug abuse treatment faces a massive and to an extent unparalleled challenge. Part of that challenge has to do with the problem of working out how to deliver intensive, high-quality treatment to a very large number of drug users. Without a major change in addictions treatment that challenge will not be successfully met. There are a number of possible ways that challenge may be met, each of which involves a major reorganization of drug treatment services. First we need to look again at the number of drug users in treatment. If the sheer weight of numbers of drug users in treatment has resulted in a downward pressure on the quality of treatment then whether we like it or not the issue of numbers has to be addressed. There will be few governments that would comfortably countenance reducing the numbers of drug users in treatment. However, unless there is a reduction in treatment numbers it is difficult to see how services will be able to provide the intensive support that addicts require to become drug free. Second if it is not possible to reduce the number of drug users in treatment then we may need to find some way of differentiating between those drug users in treatment for whom intensive support may enable them to become drug free and those drug users who presently at least do not stand any reasonable prospect of becoming drug free and for whom maintenance may be a more appropriate goal. However, differentiating the treatment population in this way will be far from easy. Moreover, as a solution to the problem of large numbers the differentiating solution relies entirely on the belief that the number of drug users who could become drug free would be a good deal smaller than the current large number of drug users in treatment. If this were not the case then simply differentiating the treatment population in this way would not resolve the problem of there being too many drug users in treatment in the first place.

Third we may need to become much clearer about the aims of drug treatment. At the present time we tend to think that any individual who expresses a wish for treatment should have access to that treatment even if they are in no way committed to the cessation of their drug use. Our acceptance of these individuals into treatment is largely based on the assumption that even modest improvements in their circumstances that can be facilitated by drug treatment are worth working towards. To an extent this view is also rooted in the notion that whilst an individual in treatment may not wish to cease or overcome his or her drug use nevertheless there may be societal benefits associated with reductions in their criminality, which mean that there is merit in providing them with drug treatment services.

There is an issue here that needs clarification – are we providing drug treatment services in order to enable drug users to become drug free or to reduce some of the adverse impacts of drug abuse on society? If it is the former then we may conclude that there is little point in attracting more individuals into drug treatment who are not committed to their recovery and we may seek instead to limit access to treatment services to those who are serious about their recovery. If by contrast we say that there is merit in retaining individuals in treatment even where they are not committed to their recovery then we may need to identify a form of drug support service that is differentiated from the treatment services and which has a set of goals that are framed in accordance with reducing some of the costs of drug use to society rather than being framed in terms of drug users recovery.

Fourth we may need to be much clearer about the responsibilities that attach to those entering drug dependency treatment. At the present time drug treatment services rarely specify the responsibilities that attach to drug users availing themselves of those services. This may need to change and drug users may need to commit to qualitative and quantitative changes in their behaviour towards their eventual recovery to justify their continued engagement with no cost (to them) drug treatment services. Related to this we may need to cap either the length of time an individual can be engaged with services or cap the number of drug users who are involved in drug treatment. In the former case we may need to set a time limit of, for example, 2 years for the provision of methadone on the basis that beyond that time period the individual is moved into a drug free programme. The benefit of this would be that it would counter against the idea of individuals participating in limitless treatment over many years without clear indications of the progress they are making towards their recovery.

Fifth we may need to ensure that the professional drug treatment sector is able to work much more closely with the self-help recovery movement illustrated by such organizations such as Alcoholics Anonymous and Narcotics Anonymous. To date the self-help treatment groups have been rather marginalized from the realm of professionalized addictions treatment. Whilst the world of professionalized drug treatment is rediscovering the goal of drug user abstinence, the self-help recovery movement by contrast never lost sight of abstinence as the goal of treatment. The experience of the self-help organizations needs to be integrated with the world of professionalized drug treatment if we are to ensure the wider delivery of high–quality, abstinence-oriented treatment.

These are major changes to the world of drug abuse treatment but they are the sorts of changes that will need to be implemented if we are to move from a situation in which hundreds of thousands of drug users enter treatment but only a few thousand leave treatment drug free. Without these changes there is a very real possibility that current poor practices within drug treatment agencies will continue, that the vast majority of drug users in treatment will remain drug dependent, and the vision of recovery set out within the national drug strategies will remain at the level of political rhetoric divorced from the reality of addictions treatment.

A Radical Alternative

Drug abuse treatment within the United Kingdom and other countries is a multi-million pound industry that has grown massively over the last few years on the basis of a belief that treatment works; that all treatment is good and that more treatment is better. Recent research and critical comment has raised serious doubts, however, about how effective drug treatment services are – particularly with regard to enabling drug users to become drug free. Doubts have begun to emerge about the professionalism and effectiveness of drug treatment services, about the goals of services and about the capacity of services to enable individuals to become drug free. There are few people who would now argue that the drug treatment sector should not change in at least some respects even if they may disagree as to the specific changes they would like to see come about.

Like many industries there is a degree to which the drug treatment industry may be more focused on meeting its own needs for continued funding than on the needs of its client base. If this is the case then it is likely that any proposed changes to the world of drug abuse treatment will be resisted to some extent by services who wish to continue operating in the way that they have done for many years, for example continuing to provide a harm reduction focus even where there is an expectation that they will be delivering an abstinence-based intervention. One might describe this as the operation of a certain conservatism on the part of those working within the drug treatment sector. One of the challenges that any incoming government might face then is how to ensure that radical changes to the world of drug treatment are enabled to take place rather than impeded. One way of doing this would be to entirely change the basis upon which drug treatment services are funded and purchased.

At the present time within local areas across the United Kingdom there are a range of key individuals who make decisions as to what drug treatment services should be available in their area. These individuals are commissioning a range of services which are then provided free of charge within a local area. This system of commissioning places the purchasing power entirely in the hands of a small number of key individuals in any area. As an alternative to this model it might be more desirable to provide drug users and their families with a set of vouchers, which could be used to purchase local drug treatment and support services. Clearly there would be a need to ensure the continuation of some element of central funding for services to ensure that a variety of services were available to drug users and their families to purchase. However, the greatest part of the cost of those services would be met through the process of drug users and their families redeeming their vouchers. There could be a number of benefits associated with this system of accessing drug treatment services.

First, through a voucher system drug users and their families would be able to exercise much greater choice about which services they wished to purchase and use. This would be one way of reducing the power of the small group of service commissioners who presently exercise enormous power in determining what services are provided locally. A voucher system could shift the purchasing of drug treatment services much closer to the experience of those using services.

Second a voucher system could operate in such a way as to integrate family members into the process of recovery. At the present time individuals engaging with drug treatment services may find their families somewhat marginalized from those services. A voucher system could help to ensure that local services were much more closely engaged with family members responding to the needs of families and working to enhance the family contribution to supporting an individual's recovery.

Third, a voucher system could be one way in which ineffective services could be rapidly identified and either closed down or helped to develop a higher quality of service. The anxiety here might be that an effective but challenging service may draw less support from its clients than a service that was more accommodating of clients but less effective in moving clients along the road to recovery. However, there is no reason to suppose that drug users and their families would wish to redeem their vouchers in return for ineffective services and it seems more likely that there would be a pressure for services to improve the quality of their work with clients rather than to reward poor service.

Fourth a voucher system could be useful in placing a financial cap on the costs of drug treatment services and in this way might counter against the presumption that presently exists in the minds of many people that drug treatment can be provided to anyone who wishes to avail themselves of it for a limitless period of time. Given that drug treatment services are largely funded from the public purse the reality in fact is that there is a limited budget for treatment which only appears to be limitless because the individuals taking the decisions as to which treatments to buy and provide locally are very far removed from the front line of service delivery. A voucher system could be helpful in bringing into much closer alignment the decisions on which services to purchase and the actual use of those services by clients.

If these are some of the potential benefits of a voucher system one would have to say that any proposal to develop such a system would in all probability be vigorously rejected by those who are presently key in determining the current range of services that are provided in any area. A voucher system shifting power from the small group of service providers and commissioners to the larger group of service users and their families would in all probability be seen as an unattractive option by those who presently have the power to determine which services are commissioned. However, to facilitate a major shift in the direction of drug treatment services from maintenance to abstinence and recovery may well require a fundamental reorganization in the way in which drug treatment services are purchased and provided. A voucher system may well be one way of bringing about that order of change and ensuring an overall improvement in the functioning of those services bringing them into much closer alignment with drug users' and their families' wishes.

KEY DISCUSSION QUESTIONS

1. To what extent can drug treatment services shift from a focus on maintenance to a focus on abstinence and recovery?
2. Should there be a cap placed on the length of time an individual can be prescribed substitute medication?
3. Should drug treatment be seen as a graduate entry profession?
4. Why are drug treatment services presently only enabling a small proportion of drug users to become drug free?
5. What are the obstacles to facilitating a closer working relationship between the voluntary sector projects like Alcoholics Anonymous and Narcotics Anonymous and the professional drug and alcohol treatment services?
6. Is there a need to reduce the numbers of drug users in treatment or can the world of drug treatment provide a high-quality service to drug users irrespective of the number of drug users in treatment?
7. Would a voucher system offer a preferable model for determining local service delivery?

Chapter 4

Drug Enforcement: A World of Myth and Reality

Introduction

If there is one abiding image of the application of the drug laws it must surely be the sight and sound of splintering door jams and stunned residents as another early morning drugs raid takes place. The fact that such events are held in vivid detail within the popular imagination, and yet rarely if ever actually witnessed, stands as a testimony to the fact that when it comes to drug enforcement, appearance and reality are often very far from being the same thing. Politicians love to talk tough about illegal drugs, reassuring a concerned public that robust action is being taken and that they are working determinedly to tackle the drug problem. The current UK drug strategy is no exception in its stated commitment to "present drug misusing offenders with tough choices to change their behaviour or face the consequences of it" (Home Office 2008: 16). The strategy promises to:

> Send a clear message that drug use is unacceptable; that we are on the side of the community; that we demand respect for the law and will not tolerate

illegal or antisocial behaviour; that we will provide help for those who are trying to turn their lives around, to get off drugs and into work to ensure that drug problem are not handed on to the next generation. (Home Office 2008: 7)

The tough actions set out in the drug strategy includes a commitment to:

- Identify drug dealers and their markets.

- Disrupt open markets and close crack-houses and cannabis factories.

- Seize drug dealers cash and assets.

- Reduce the supply of drugs into and within the country.

- Tackle drugs that cause the greatest harm – heroin, cocaine and crack.

- Monitor emerging drug threats such as cannabis factories and methamphetamines.

Enforcement has long been a key pillar of the UK drug strategy and on the face of it this list amounts to a range of tough actions designed to tackle the drug problem. It is noticeable, however, that reducing the actual use of illegal drugs is not one of the priorities listed. But just how committed is the government to drug enforcement? In a recent report Kathy Gyngell from the Centre for Policy Studies looked at government spending on drugs and the proportion of that funding allocated to drug enforcement across a number of European countries (Gyngell 2009). The results of her analysis are striking. Whilst the Netherlands allocates 0.43% of its gross domestic product to tackling the problem of illegal drugs and Sweden allocates 0.46%, the UK government allocates just 0.13% of its gross domestic product to tackling drugs misuse. With regard to the allocation of funds within the drugs budget there are further interesting comparisons between these countries. The Dutch government allocates 75% of its drugs budget to enforcement compared to 49% in the United Kingdom. In the case of Sweden, which is known for its zero tolerance approach to illegal drugs, the government allocates 60% of its drugs budget to health and social care compared to 51% in the United Kingdom (Gyngell 2009). The UK government allocates fewer resources to drugs enforcement than the Netherlands (widely known for its liberal approach to drugs misuse) and less funding for health and social care than Sweden (widely known for its zero tolerance approach towards illegal drugs). Ministerial statements about being tough on drugs do not necessarily mean that drug enforcement agencies will receive the funding they may require to deliver on those statements.

The Mystery of Drug Arrest and Drug Seizure Statistics

To get a clearer picture of the government's commitment to drug enforcement it is interesting to look at the UK crime statistics in relation to drug offences. Hoare (2009) has summarized the data on changes in crime rates for the years from 2007/08 to 2008/09. Whilst there are notable reductions in the rates of certain crimes, for example, violence against the person was down 6% in 2008 compared to 2007, and criminal damage was down 10%, drug offences were up 6% from 2007 to 2008. In relation to the trafficking in controlled drugs, there were a total of 23,153 offences recorded in England and Wales in 1997. By 2008/09 that figure had increased to 29,644 – a 28% increase over an 11-year period. Possession of controlled drugs other than cannabis however increased from 32,603 in 2004/05 to 44,310 in 2008/09 – an increase of 36% over a 4-year period. On the face of it then, despite government stated priority to tackle drug dealing, the rate of increase in those offences over an 11-year period is less than the increase in drug possession offences over a 4-year period. These statistics are not quite what one would expect on the basis of a stated commitment to be tough on those dealing drugs.

A similar picture emerges from the UK government data on drug arrests. In 1999/2000 there were a total of 105,400 drug arrests in England and Wales with this figure dropping to 77,100 in 2006/07 (Ministry of Justice 2008). On the basis of these data then the picture in relation to drug arrests within the United Kingdom is again not quite what one would have expected on the basis of government statements about being tough on drugs and drugs dealing.

Drugs Seizure

The seizure of illegal drugs is a key part of most countries drug enforcement activities with large seizures often being presented to the media as a powerful illustration of the successes of enforcement agencies. But how successful are drugs enforcement agencies in seizing illegal drugs? The UK government produces a regular update on drug seizures with the data on this summarized in Table 4.1:

Table 4.1 Quantity of Drugs Seized in England and Wales (kgs)

Drug	1998	1999	2000	2001	2002	2003	2004	2005	2006	2007
Cocaine	881	1,415	3,897	5,211	3,497	6,813	4,571	3,765	3,191	3,433
Crack	27	41	26	55	54	251	133	49	58	35
Heroin	457	1,440	3,329	3,996	2,615	2,657	2,109	1,864	1,003	1,041
Methadone	83	179	376	100	49	58	59	–	–	–
Cannabis	1,590	19,281	44,914	59,526	41,414	69,029	–	–	–	–

Source: Smith and Dodd (2009)

Two things are immediately apparent from this table. First, is the fourfold increase in the quantity of cocaine being seized over the period from 1998 to 2007 and second is the threefold reduction in the quantity of heroin seized from 2001 to 2007.

There is a difficulty of interpreting information on drug seizures as contained within the official statistics which has to do with the absence of any information on the quantities of illegal drugs entering the country. As a result it is impossible to know whether an increase or decrease in the quantity of drugs seized reflects a shift in the operational effectiveness of enforcement agencies or a change in the quantity of drugs being targeted at a country. It is possible however to analyse the data on drug seizures in the light of information on the amount of drugs being consumed and to calculate drug seizures as a fraction of drugs consumed. To undertake that analysis it is necessary to combine information on the number of individuals consuming a particular drug with information on the amounts of the drugs seized and the likely number of days individuals are consuming particular substances.

Based upon their prevalence estimation research, Hay and colleagues have calculated that there were 273,123 opiate users in England in 2007/08 (Hay et al. 2008). To estimate the amount of heroin being consumed in England it is necessary to estimate the average numbers of days individuals are using heroin and the average quantity of heroin consumed on those days. Gossop and colleagues estimated that 70% of opiate smokers used less than 0.5g of heroin per day, 19% used between 0.5g and 0.75g per day, and 11% consumed in excess of 0.75g per day (Gossop et al. 1988). More recently the DORIS study, which surveyed over 1000 drug users, identified that addicts consumed around 0.88g of heroin per day on an average of 261 days per year (McKeganey et al. 2009).

On the basis of these figures the estimated 273,123 opiate users in England would be consuming around 218.4kgs per day and 57,002kgs per year. It is possible to combine this information on heroin consumption with the published data on heroin seizures for England and Wales over the period from 2003 to 2007 to get an idea of the proportion of seized to estimated consumed heroin. For the year 2003 drug enforcement agencies seized a total of 2,657kgs of heroin. That quantity, however, represents only 4.6% of the total amount of heroin estimated to have been consumed by addicts in the same year. In 2007 a total of 1,041kgs of heroin were seized by agencies representing as little as 1.8% of the total amount of heroin consumed in that year. On the basis of this analysis enforcement agencies are seizing only a tiny fraction of the heroin that is available on the streets of the United Kingdom. According to the United Nations Office on Drugs and Crime enforcement agencies would need to be seizing around 75% of the available drugs to have a notable impact on drug consumption rates. Clearly seizing between 1.8% and 4.6% of the available heroin is so far below that threshold as to lead one to wonder at the effectiveness of drug enforcement agencies.

In Scotland a similar picture emerges from the analysis of seized to consumed heroin. According to Hay and colleagues there were an estimated 51,582 problematic drug users in 2003 (Hay et al. 2005). The definition of problematic drug use in this study relates to the use of opiates and benzodiazepines, rather than referring specifically to heroin. To estimate the proportion of the overall 51,582 problematic drug users using heroin it is necessary to combine information from the Hay et al. study of problem drug use prevalence in Scotland with information on drug consumption obtained in the course of the DORIS study. Overall, 90.5% of those interviewed in the DORIS research reported having used heroin within the preceding 90 days. Extrapolating that percentage to the wider problematic drug using population (e.g., taking 90.5% of the estimated total 51,582 problematic drug users within Scotland) would produce an estimate of there being 46,687 heroin users within Scotland in the year 2003. On average DORIS respondents reported having used heroin on 64 of the preceding 90 days. Extrapolating that figure over a 12-month period would indicate that problem drug users in Scotland were consuming heroin on 261 days per year. With regard to the amounts of heroin used DORIS respondents reported consuming on average 0.88g per day.

Combining the information from DORIS on the number of days heroin was consumed over a 12-month period with an estimate of their being 46,687 heroin users within Scotland would produce a total heroin consumption figure over a 12-month period of 10,705kg or 10.7 tonnes. Again it is possible to look at that figure in the context of the amount of heroin reported as being seized by enforcement agencies in Scotland. In 2000/01, 49.0kgs of heroin were seized by Scottish police forces representing just 0.45% of the total amount of heroin consumed in that year. In 2007 Scottish police forces seized a total of 97.5kgs of heroin with that figure representing only 0.91% of the total amount of heroin consumed in that year.

For those with an interest in drugs enforcement these are depressing totals indicating that enforcement agencies may be unable to seize even 1% of the heroin that is available on the streets within Scotland. Again it is hard not to wonder at the effectiveness and cost-effectiveness of drugs enforcement if these are the sorts of amounts of heroin being seized relative to the amount being consumed by addicts in Scotland.

Explaining the Modesty in Drugs Seizures

But why might enforcement agencies being seizing such a small percentage of the available heroin? One possible answer could lie with the issue of purity. We know that imported heroin will be cut by drug dealers intent on maximizing their profit – increasing the quantity of the drug they are selling by the addition of certain bulking agents. If it were the case that the heroin being seized by enforcement was all high purity and the heroin being consumed on the streets was all low purity, this might explain why the proportion of seized to consumed heroin is so low. Information on drug purity is available from the government and published along with the data on the quantity of drugs seized. In the case of heroin the average purity for the year 2006/07 was 43% whilst for the period 2007/08 it was between 51% and 54% (Hand and Rishiraj 2009). Assuming that the entire seized heroin was at the 100% purity level, and the entire consumed heroin was at the 50% level, this would only lead to a doubling of the percentage of seized to consumed heroin. Purity then cannot be an explanation of the low percentage of seized to consumed heroin.

Another possible explanation may lie in the targeting and tactics of the drug enforcement agencies themselves. Recently there has been much discussion within enforcement circles as to the importance of what is called "upstream disruption" (Serious Organised Crime Agency 2008). In essence this involves targeting enforcement resources closer to the drug production sites as opposed to the drug consumption sites within countries. Such a re-deployment switches the focus of interdiction efforts on to countries such as Afghanistan and Colombia in an attempt to seize or destroy drugs well before they reach the borders of consumer countries. An unintended consequence of this focus may well be a diminution of the resources targeted at drug seizure and interdiction within consumer countries and a corresponding decrease in the quantity of heroin seized within a country's borders.

Another possible explanation for the low proportion of seized to consumed heroin may be the shift away from drug seizures on the part of enforcement agencies. A recent Home Office report outlining the government's approach to tackling serious and organized crime illustrates the increasing emphasis being given by enforcement agencies towards reducing the harms associated with drugs misuse rather than reducing the availability of illegal drugs:

> Harm reduction, rather than quantities of drugs seized or individuals convicted, is a more useful way of prioritising activities to improve the lives of citizens in the UK. Harm reduction was specifically written into SOOCA objectives...now all law enforcement agencies are developing matrices to assess the different types of harm caused by organised crime. (Home Office 2009: 24)

The adoption of a harm reduction agenda by enforcement agencies, in which drug seizure and drug interdiction are regarded as less important than they were in the past, is another example of the gulf that has emerged between the public rhetoric of being tough on drugs and the reality of a systemic acceptance of the inevitability of some level of drug use and drug dealing within communities.

The Penalties for Drug Supply

In the minds of many people there is an important distinction between the supply of illegal drugs and the use of those drugs. Whilst we may typically think of those using illegal drugs as requiring help and support, we regard those who are supplying illegal drugs in a very different light. The difference between drug dealing and drug using is formalized in the criminal law in terms of the different penalties that are associated with the two acts. Drug dealing is very much the familiar territory of tough talking politicians who frequently emphasize the harsh penalties that will be meted out to those involved in supplying illegal drugs. The statistics on drug selling offences, and their punishment, presents a rather different picture. In 2007 more than a quarter (28%) of those found guilty of supplying Class A drugs were given a community sentence, fine or suspended sentence (Home Office Criminal Statistics for England and Wales supplementary tables 2007). In the case of Class B drugs the proportion of offenders receiving a non-custodial sentence increased to 66%. Within the United Kingdom then being found guilty of supplying a Class A or Class B drug is by no means guaranteed to result in a custodial sentence. In the light of those statistics it is worthwhile asking how illegal are illegal drugs?

How Illegal is Drug Possession?

The question "how illegal are illegal drugs" may seem non-sensical. Within the United Kingdom the possession of heroin is a criminal offence punishable by a maximum sentence of 7 years in jail and/or an unlimited fine. On that basis one might say that heroin possession is a serious criminal offence. But how likely is it for someone in possession of heroin to be arrested as a result of that possession? It is possible to produce an approximate answer to that question by comparing the statistics on drug possession offences with research that has been undertaken estimating the total number of problematic heroin users within England.

On the basis of figures provided by the Ministry of Justice (2009) there were a total of 242,907 offences in relation to controlled drugs in England and Wales in the year 2008/09. That figure was slightly up on the previous year total of 229,903. The majority of those offences involved cannabis. For the year 2008/09 there were a total of 167,840 cannabis offences and 44,310 offences related to the possession of other illegal drugs. Assume for the moment that all of the 44,310 recorded offences related to the possession of heroin (in reality some of those offences would relate to a range of other controlled drugs).

Research has estimated that there were 328,767 problem drug users in England in 2006/07, of whom 273,123 were estimated to be opiate users (Hay et al. 2008). On the basis of the DORIS study, problematic heroin users are consuming heroin on an average of 261 days per year. Over a 12-month period that would mean the offence of heroin possession is occurring at minimum on at least 71,285,103 occasions per year (assuming that each individual user is using heroin only once per day). On only 0.06% (44,310) of those occasions does heroin possession result in a recorded offence. Whilst heroin possession remains a serious criminal offence within the United Kingdom, the likelihood of an individual being arrested as a result of that possession is very small indeed.

The analysis of the likelihood of being prosecuted for heroin possession, much like the analysis of the quantity of heroin seized, illustrates the gap between appearance and reality when it comes to drug policing. Whilst politicians may talk tough about drug use – especially Class A drug use – the reality is that only a tiny proportion of those using heroin come to the attention of the police and only a tiny fraction of the heroin that is available on the streets is being seized by police.

There is a paradox here. On the one hand Class A drug possession is a serious criminal offence whilst on the other hand only a tiny proportion of those committing the offence are coming to the attention of the police. The answer to that paradox lies in the priority that the government has given to reducing the harms associated with illegal drug use in preference to reducing drug use itself. Since 2002, the UK drug strategy's primary aim has been to reduce the harm that drugs cause to society (Home Office 2002). The public service agreement targets for the drug strategy underline the priority that is being given to reducing drug-related harm with Public Service Agreement 25 being to "reduce the harm caused by alcohol and drugs". This target is operationalized within the drug strategy in terms of increasing the number of drug users in treatment, reducing the rates of drug related offending and reducing the percentage of the public who perceive drug use or drug dealing to be problematic in their area. In terms of government policy drug enforcement agencies are being encouraged to move away from the realm of traditional policing (reducing the number of individuals using and supplying illegal drugs) into the much more nebulous realm of reducing drug-related harm. Given that shift, it is perhaps less surprising than it might otherwise be to realize just how modest are the achievements in seizing drugs and punishing those who are involved in drug use and drug supply.

The Impact of Drugs on Prisons

If drugs and drug policy are having an enormous impact on the world of enforcement, their impact on the world of the prison is scarcely any less significant. Working in a UK prison 30 years ago it is highly unlikely that one would have come across more than the occasional drug-related offender. The 1970s British television comedy "Porridge" has been described as a reasonably accurate portrayal of life within prisons in the United Kingdom (James 2005). Within that series there was not a single reference to an addict prisoner. If one were going to write a drama about prison life today it is hard to see how drug abuse would be anything other than a daily occurrence.

A report prepared by David Blakey for the UK government acknowledges the impact of drugs on prisons reflecting the growth in the use of illegal drugs within the wider society:

> Prisoners going into prison have been taken from a world where the use of illicit drugs is endemic. Many, probably a majority, will be problem drug users. Drugs may well be the reason, or one of the reasons why they are incarcerated. They will view the use of drugs to "relieve boredom" or "cope with stress" as normal. It would be remarkable indeed if they did not attempt to bring their "normality" into prison. (Blakey 2008: 7)

In his report Blakey acknowledges the change in attitudes towards illegal drugs within prison that has occurred over the last 20 years:

> Some staff with long experience in the (Prison) service accepted that decades ago the smell of cannabis throughout a prison on a Friday evening might have suggested a quiet weekend for the staff. But if those days ever existed then they are long gone. Today, most types of drugs in prisons cause trouble. They affect behaviour, usually for the worst and they increase bullying and assaults, as drugs need to be paid for. (Blakey 2008: 7)

Liriano and Ramsay have provided an indication of the extent of illegal drug use on the part of those entering prisons in outlining the results of a survey of 1884 male prisoners in England and Wales (Liriano and Ramsay 2003). Dividing their sample into two age cohorts "17 to 24" and "25 to 59", Liriano and Ramsay report that 80% of the younger males and 54% of the older males had used illegal drugs in the 12 months before their incarceration. Cocaine had been used by 37% of the younger age group in the last 12 months and by 28% of the older group. Crack cocaine had been used by 33% of the younger group and by 29% of the older group and heroin had been used by 32% of the younger prisoners and by 31% of the older inmates (Liriano and Ramsay 2003).

With regard to illegal drug use occurring within prisons Bullock (2003) has drawn on the same survey to report that 30% of prisoners had used cannabis within prison on at least a weekly basis; 16% had used cocaine; 11% had used crack; and 36% had used heroin (Bullock

2003). Within Scotland, the 2008 Scottish Prison Survey reported that a quarter of prisoners (26%) had used drugs in the month prior to the survey while in prison and one-fifth had committed their offence to fund a drug habit (Scottish Prison Service 2008). In Scotland's sole female-only prison (Cortonvale) it has been estimated that around 98% of inmates have a serious drug problem (Scottish Government 2005).

As the proportion of prisoners with a drug problem increases it brings with it a number of notable challenges. In any situation where a significant proportion of one's residents are dependent on illegal drugs, it is inevitable that attempts will be made to smuggle drugs on to those premises irrespective of the level of security in operation. The methods of smuggling drugs into prisons are many and varied. In his report Blakey (2008) identified the various means through which illegal drugs may be smuggled into prisons:

- Visitors

- Over the wall

- Post and parcels

- Reception and remand prisoners

- Staff.

Illegal drugs can be smuggled into prisons by relatives visiting inmates, they can be thrown into prisons hidden within various projectiles (tennis balls, dead birds etc.), they can be smuggled into prisons with the active or passive collusion of prison staff whose involvement may have been secured on the basis of financial gain or intimidation and they can be concealed within packages sent to prisoners. Smuggling, however, is only one of the problems that drugs pose for prison staff and inmates. Clearly, where drugs are circulating within prisons they can undermine prisoner's efforts to benefit from any drugs treatment services, they can undermine efforts to maintain control over prisoners, they can lead to intimidation of prisoners and their visitors and they may form part of an underground black economy within the prison.

Stopping Drugs from Entering Prisons

In the minds of many people it is hard to understand why it should be so difficult to stop drugs from entering prisons given the level of control prison authorities exercise over inmates. However, tackling the availability of drugs within prisons is by no means a simple matter. Take, for example, the fact that it is known that a proportion of visitors will be attempting to smuggle drugs into prison. One response to that might be to insist that all visits involve prisoners being separated from their visitors by a physical partition. To impose such a condition would effectively penalize those prisoners and their relatives who are not seeking to smuggle drugs into prisons and could severely disrupt the relationships between staff and inmates.

Similarly, whilst it is known that a proportion of prison staff may be involved, directly or indirectly, in supplying drugs in prison, the level of surveillance that prison managers would need to exercise over prison staff to tackle that problem would be so great as to make it all but impossible to recruit staff to work within the prison setting in the first place. Equally, of course, those carrying out the surveillance of prison guards could also be corrupted by the offer of financial gain or by threats of violence to either them or their family members.

There is another massive challenge that the drugs problem poses for prison staff, which has to do with the need to provide drug treatment services to prisoners. As McIntosh and Saville (2006) have pointed out:

> As far as treatment is concerned, the opportunity that prison provides for intervening with problem drug users is potentially so valuable to the individuals and to society as a whole, that it would be remiss not to attempt to exploit it as far as possible. (McIntosh and Saville 2006: 240)

The challenge of providing drug abuse treatment within a custodial setting is substantial. First, there are the difficulties that arise from the fact that prisons are first and foremost custodial rather than therapeutic settings. On the basis of their qualitative study looking at the challenges presented by prison-based drug treatment, McIntosh and Saville point out that:

> It was evident from our observations and our interviews with staff members that the prison regime has a significant effect upon the delivery of treatment. Prison does not constitute a dedicated therapeutic environment as far as drugs are concerned. Treatment for drug use is very much a secondary function of prisons and has to defer at all times to the primary function of maintaining a secure environment. The custodial function, in turn, means that the prison environment is highly controlled by means of rules and procedures that dictate the prisoners' patterns of movement and

behaviour. The highly regimented nature of this regime has important practical consequences for the implementation of drug treatment within the prison environment. Most significantly, it leads to a restriction in the amount of time available for this activity. (McIntosh and Saville 2006: 235)

McIntosh and Saville also pointed out that the attitudes of prison offices towards treatment could present a major challenge. Some of the prison staff they interviewed were sceptical of the motivation of prisoners involved in drug treatment – perceiving that their real motivation had more to do with relieving the boredom of prison life rather than a genuine commitment to address their drug problems. Some staff saw themselves as prison officers first and drug treatment workers second, and as a result had only a limited interest in developing a therapeutic relationship with inmates:

Although drug service officers had specialist roles in relation to treatment provision, all of those who were interviewed identified their primary responsibility and function as that of maintaining a secure environment. As one officer explained:

"First and foremost I always see myself as a prison officer. My discipline duties will always come first." According to the officers, this latter priority applied boundaries to the extent to which they could develop therapeutic relationships with prisoners. It also meant that drug service officers had to strike a difficult and delicate balance between being supportive and sympathetic on the one hand and maintaining order and discipline on the other. (McIntosh and Saville 2006: 239)

Although on the face of it one might assume that the same range of treatment and support services that are available within the community should be available within prisons, the reality is more complex. Take, for example, the case of needle and syringe exchange services. As a result of concerns over the escalating numbers of injecting drug users who are Hepatitis C positive, there are moves currently being discussed to provide prisoners with access to sterile injecting equipment. Whilst needle and syringe exchange schemes have become commonplace within the community their development within the prison environment is highly controversial with some prison staff being understandably concerned that injecting equipment provided to prisoners could be used as a weapon with which to attack or threaten staff and other inmates (Williams 2009).

There are also questions about how far methadone should be made available within prisons. The controversy surrounding methadone in prisons reached a high point in 2006 in the UK when a small group of prisoners initiated legal action against the Home Office for having been denied access to methadone and forced to experience the discomfort of drug withdrawal. The legal counsel representing the prisoners maintained that the refusal to provide methadone amounted to a breach of the prisoners' human rights, and a failure on the part of prison medical staff, to follow appropriate clinical guidelines. As the case progressed the Home Office decided to settle and agreed to make a payment of £6,000 to each of the 198 prisoners covered by the legal action (Ford 2006).

This case is interesting in what it revealed about the issue of providing drug addiction treatment within the context of a prison. Whilst it is true that methadone is recommended as the appropriate treatment for opiate dependency, the clinical guidance around methadone is based entirely on evaluations of the effectiveness of prescribing methadone within community-based settings rather than custodial settings. As a result, it is far from clear that the same arguments that support methadone prescribing within the community apply with equal force where one is considering the applicability of methadone within the setting of a prison. Within the community methadone prescribing has been shown to be effective in enabling individuals to develop a level of stability in their lives, in reducing individual's use of street drugs, in reducing the level of the individuals involvement in crime to fund their drug use and in reducing the level of injecting. Each of these benefits, however, can be seen to be a feature of the prison environment itself and as such could be seen as weakening the case for providing methadone within prisons. Being resident within a prison is likely to result in the individual using fewer drugs, in injecting less frequently, in committing fewer crimes and in enabling the individual to develop a level of structure and stability in their day-to-day lives. On this basis it is not necessarily the case that prison medical staff should feel that there is an equivalent need to prescribe methadone within the setting of a prison even where they may accept the value of such prescribing within the community. Very recently the Department of Health and the National Treatment Agency have released new guidance to prison medical staff stressing that where prisoners are on a sentence of longer than 6 months methadone should not be used on a maintenance basis rather the prison treatment services need to be working towards such prisoners becoming drug free (Department of Health 2010).

Just as there have been discussions surrounding the issue of methadone within prison there have also been discussions around the question of where one should draw the limits of prison authorities' responsibilities for inmates' health and welfare. On the face of it one might say that the responsibility begins and end at the prison gate. In reality however, the matter is rather more complex. Research has shown that drug-using prisoners are at heightened risk of experiencing a fatal drug overdose within a relatively short period following their release where they resume their previous pre-incarceration pattern of drug consumption (Seaman et al. 1998). Other researchers have identified that within the week following their liberation drug using prisoners are 40 times more likely to die than the general population (Singleton et al. 2003). In view of the heightened risk of suffering a fatal drug overdose on liberation from prison some areas have developed what has been termed a "retox programme" (MacDougall 2002). Retox programme involve re-introducing prisoners to opiate-based medication in the latter stages of their sentence so as to increase their drug tolerance and thereby reduce their chances of experiencing a fatal drug overdose on release. There is of course some logic to that position if one concedes that prison authorities have a responsibility for inmates' health after their release into the community. However, the idea of deliberately building up an individual's tolerance to opiates prior to release when that individual may have successfully reduced his or her drug intake whilst within a prison is frankly bizarre. Clearly if prison-based medical services are going to reintroduce prisoners to opiate-based drugs prior to their release it hardly makes any sense to have been seeking to reduce their drug intake during the period of their incarceration. And yet to give up on trying to help prisoners overcome their drug problem during the period that they are incarcerated is to waste an opportunity that may be of substantial benefit not only for the drug user and his or her family but to the wider community.

Within a context in which drug use is having an increasing impact on prisons there is a need to be much clearer about how far we are expecting prisons to adopt a treatment focus in their work with prisoners, what treatments should be available to dependent drug users within prisons, and how far prison staff are responsible for prisoners health and welfare post their liberation. In addition, there is a need to determine what aspects of prison life can be maintained in the face of the growing impact of drugs misuse both within prisons and within the wider society.

At the moment there is very little attempt within prisons to segregate drug-using and non-drug-using prisoners. However, there may well be circumstances in the near future when a non-drug-using prisoner initiates legal action against prison authorities as a result of having started to use illegal drugs within the prison because of being forced to live in close proximity to other inmates who were using illegal drugs. In due course prison authorities may come to reconsider the appropriateness of housing drug-using and non-drug-using inmates in such close proximity where they are unable to stem the flow of drugs into prisons. Such a development would have an enormous impact on the social organization of the prison estate as well as its financial cost.

There is though likely to be a growing need to consider whether prison is the appropriate place to send an individual whose offending is directly related to their drug dependency. It could be argued that it would be more appropriate to ensure that drug-using offenders are provided instead with access to effective drug treatment within the community. To do this though would be to create a two-tier criminal justice system within which those individuals whose offending was not related to their drug dependency would be given a custodial sentence, whilst those whose offending was related to their drug dependency would be placed within a treatment setting. It is easy to see how such a system could come to be abused by individuals falsely claiming to be drug dependent as a way of avoiding receiving a custodial sentence.

Surveillance – Where Are the Limits?

The growth of drugs misuse within society and the increasing focus of attention on the criminal justice agencies has given rise to questions as to how far we are prepared to accept the intrusion of drug enforcement agencies into our everyday lives? Within the context of escalating fears over terrorism we have come to accept the need of the security services to closely monitor our movement as we go about our daily lives. That acceptance is rooted in a view that each and everyone of us could be caught up in a terrorist incident and in this sense it could be said that we have collectively come to "own" the threat of a possible terrorist attack. In the case of illegal drugs there is still a sense in which the problem is perceived as largely involving "other people" rather than ourselves, and for that reason alone there might be considerable reluctance to see an increasingly intrusive role on the part of drug enforcement agencies. The routine searching of individuals and property for the evidence of drug possession or drug usage, the routine use of drug dogs at major transport hubs or the wider use of swabbing door handles in public and private buildings to identify possible drug usage could be regarded as an intrusion too far. However, if the scale of our drug problem were to increase much beyond its current level then these intrusions might come to be accepted as the price for effectively tackling our drugs problem.

Conclusions

The world of drugs enforcement is a curious mixture of myth and reality. Within the United Kingdom, for example, whilst successive governments have talked tough on dealing with the drugs problem the reality is very different. Drugs possession as distinct from drug dealing is an activity that only rarely attracts the attention of the police. Indeed the UK drugs strategy itself gives surprising little attention to reducing the overall scale of drug consumption, focussing rather more on reducing the harms associated with drugs misuse. The lead agency charged with responsibility for tackling serious organized crime and drugs misuse has had its remit framed rather less in terms of drugs seizures and drug arrests and more in terms of reducing the harms to communities arising from drugs misuse. The remit of enforcement agencies has come to merge increasingly with the world of drugs treatment and support with prisons themselves increasingly becoming an arm of the drugs treatment industry.

For those of a liberal persuasion the gradual extension of the world of treatment into the domains of drug enforcement is likely to be very welcome. An important question remains though, whether any country can tackle a growing drugs problem without robust drugs enforcement? If drug use and drug possession come to take on the character of accepted behaviours, which draw only minor penalty, then in a way we are creating a cultural climate within which drug use itself is almost destined to increase.

Within the United Kingdom and in other countries we may need enforcement agencies that are focussed first and foremost on reducing the availability of illegal drugs on the streets of our communities and on identifying those who are using and those who are selling illegal drugs and ensuring that wherever possible they are dealt with in terms of the existing criminal law covering drugs possession and drug dealing.

To propose tough drug enforcement, however, is to propose something that goes against the drift of a cultural movement towards increasing normalization and acceptance of illegal drugs. It may well be that without a clear penalty being attached to the use and the sale of illegal drugs, that the drugs trade itself will flourish and may in time acquire such acceptance, and such financial resources, that it shifts beyond the regulatory power of the state. Countries that fail to draw an appropriate balance between the carrot and the stick in their drugs strategies may run a very real risk of becoming the narco-states of tomorrow.

KEY DISCUSSION QUESTIONS

1. If drug enforcement agencies are only able to seize less than 5% of the drugs that are being used on the streets, can drug enforcement be seen as an effective use of resources?
2. If the risks of being arrested for drugs possession are as low as they appear, is there a sense in which we have already effectively decriminalized drug possession within the UK
3. Is it possible for any government to effectively tackle the drugs problem whilst adopting a more liberal approach to drug possession as opposed to drug dealing?
4. Should prisons determinedly seek to create a drug-free environment around prisoners even where this presents massive challenges to the prison authorities?
5. Is there a case for offering prisoners a reduction in their sentence where they remain drug free during the period of their incarceration and similarly is there a case for increasing the length of sentences where individuals are found to have used illegal drugs during the period of their incarceration?
6. How far should states intervene in the lives of its citizens to tackle a growing drugs problem?

Chapter 5

Cannabis and the Classification Mystery

(or How to Make a Hash of the World's Favourite Illegal Drug)

Introduction

No book on controversies in drugs policy and practice could be complete without a discussion of cannabis. Cannabis is the world's favourite illegal drug, with the United Nations Office on Drugs and Crime estimating that in 2007 somewhere between 145 million and 190 million people used it at least once (UNODC 2009). As well as being the world's favourite illegal drug, cannabis is also the drug that excites more polarized debate than any other. On one side of the debate are those who regard cannabis as a relatively innocuous substance, with few adverse effects and unlikely to produce any long-term harm. For those who hold that view, cannabis should not even be classified as an illegal drug given that, in their view, it is associated with less harm than the currently legal drugs of alcohol and tobacco. On the other side of the debate are those who regard cannabis as a harmful substance that has acquired an entirely misplaced reputation as a soft or recreational drug, and which remains rightfully included within the illegal drugs legislation of countries across the globe.

Disputes over the characterization of cannabis as a soft or hard drug are by no means the preserve of the mass media. An editorial published in the *Lancet* medical journal in 2007 commented that:

> In 1995 we began a Lancet editorial with the since much quoted words "The smoking of cannabis, even long term is not harmful to health." Research published since 1995 ... leads us now to conclude that cannabis use could increase the risk of psychotic illness. . . . Governments would do well to invest in sustained and effective education campaigns on the risk to health of taking cannabis. (Lancet 2007: 370)

Governments too have demonstrated a remarkable capacity to change their minds on just how harmful a drug cannabis actually is. Antonio Maria Costa, head of the United Nations Office on Drugs and Crime, opened the 2006 World Drugs Report with the statement that:

> National policies on cannabis vary and sometimes change from one year to the next. With supply virtually unlimited and demand subject to the vagaries of government policy, traffickers have invested heavily in increasing the potency – and therefore the market attractiveness – of cannabis. The result has been devastating: today, the characteristics of cannabis are no longer that different from those of other plant-based drugs such as cocaine and heroin. With cannabis-related health damage increasing, it is fundamentally wrong for countries to make cannabis control dependent on which party is in government. Policy swings or reversals leave young people confused as to just how dangerous cannabis is. The cannabis pandemic, like other challenges to public health, requires consensus, and a stable and consistent engagement across society at large so countries can take appropriate and long-term remedial action. (Maria Costa 2006: 2)

Despite Maria-Costa's comments that the pandemic of cannabis use will only be effectively tackled to the extent that countries develop a "stable and consistent engagement" with the drug, this is perhaps the one thing that has been absent in some countries policies regarding cannabis. There is no country that demonstrates the confusion over cannabis more clearly than the United Kingdom where the drug has been subjected to serial investigations by the leading drugs advisory committee and swung like a yo-yo between different classes within the Misuse of Drugs Act.

The Cannabis Classification Mystery

In 2001 the British Home Secretary, David Blunkett, announced to the media that he was "minded" to reclassify cannabis from Class B to Class C within the UK Misuse of Drugs Act:

> It is time for an honest and common sense approach focusing effectively on drugs that cause most harm. Given this background, and the very clear difference between cannabis and Class A drugs, I want to consult the medical and scientific professionals on re-classifying cannabis from Class B to Class C. (David Blunkett quoted in the Independent Newspaper 23 October 2001, BBC 2001)

The "medical and scientific professionals" mentioned in the Independent article was the Advisory Council on the Misuse of Drugs (ACMD). Established in 1971 under the Misuse of Drugs Act, the ACMD is charged with providing independent, scientific advice to ministers about developments in the drugs field. Following the Home Secretary's announcement, the advisory council undertook the requested review and in March 2002 the chair of the council (Sir Michael Rawlins) wrote to the Home Secretary informing him of the outcome of the council's deliberations:

> The council recommends the reclassification of all cannabis preparations to Class C. The council believes that the current classification of cannabis is disproportionate in relation to its inherent toxicity, and to that of other substances (such as amphetamines) that are currently within Class B. (Rawlins 2002)

In 2004 the reclassification of cannabis from Class B to Class C that the Home Secretary had indicated he had been minded to undertake came into effect. Within 12 months however, with a new Home Secretary in place (Charles Clarke), the experts on the Advisory Committee were asked to undertake a further review of the harms of cannabis. In 2005 the Chair of the Committee Sir Michael Rawlins wrote to the Home Secretary to advise him of the council's recommendation:

> After a detailed scrutiny of the evidence, the Council does not advise the reclassification of cannabis products to Class B; it recommends they remain within Class C. While cannabis can, unquestionably, produce harms, these are not of the same order as those of substances within Class B. (Rawlins 2005)

By June 2007, with a third Home Secretary (Jacqui Smith) installed in as many years the advisory council were asked to undertake a third review of cannabis to consider whether the drug should be moved back from Class C to Class B. Delivering what by then had become a rather familiar trope, Sir Michael Rawlins wrote to the Home Secretary in 2008 setting out the council's latest recommendations:

> After a careful scrutiny of the totality of the available evidence the majority of the Councils members consider – based on its harmfulness to individuals and society – that cannabis should remain a Class C substance. It is judged that the harmfulness of cannabis more closely equates with other Class C substances than with those currently classified as Class B. (Rawlins 2008)

In advance of having received that advice there had been a flurry of media articles anticipating a possible change in the cannabis laws and claiming that the Home Secretary herself had formed the view that cannabis ought to be moved back to Class B. On receiving the advice from the ACMD, the Home Secretary duly informed journalists that she would be recommending to cabinet colleagues that cannabis was indeed moved from Class C back to Class B and in 2009 Prime Minister Gordon Brown announced the decision to parliament.

There are three questions that come to the fore in the wake of the twists and turns in the cannabis story: first how robust is the drug classification system at the heart of drug policy; second just how dangerous a drug is cannabis, and third what does this story reveal about the interface between science and drug policy?

The Classification of Individual Drugs

In the minds of many people the idea of an expert committee spending an inordinate amount of time serially deliberating whether a given drug should be in one category or another within a 1970s piece of drugs legislation will have had an almost surreal quality to it. The classification and regulation of certain substances as "dangerous drugs" and their subsequent regulation have been a feature of UK drug policy and practice since the Defense of the Realm Act of 1916 and the Dangerous Drugs Act of 1920, which sought to limit the availability of opium and cocaine within the United Kingdom. It was only with the 1971 Misuse of Drugs Act that individual drugs were placed within one of the three classes (A, B or C). Class A contains such drugs as Heroin, Ecstasy, Cocaine and Magic Mushrooms; Class B covers such drugs as Amphetamines, Cannabis and Ritalin; Class C covers such drugs as Ketamine, Diazepam and most of the anabolic steroids. As well as dividing these drugs across three classes, the Misuse of Drugs legislation also set out the legal penalties associated with each class with the harshest penalties for those using and selling the Class A drugs.

As the cannabis story makes painfully clear, the placement of any individual drug within a specific class or category is by no means a straightforward matter. The controversy around cannabis has led to increased attention being focused on the drug classification system itself. Whilst the classification of Heroin and Cocaine as Class A substances may seem straightforward enough, given what we know about how addictive these substances are, the placement of ecstasy and magic mushrooms alongside heroin and cocaine seems puzzling to many people. According to Professor David Nutt, who succeeded Sir Michael Rawlins as the Chair of the Advisory Council on the Misuse of Drugs, the classification system underpinning the Misuse of Drugs Act itself is fundamentally flawed. According to Nutt that system had:

> Evolved in an unsystematic way from somewhat arbitrary foundations with seemingly little scientific basis. (Nutt et al. 2007: 1047)

In response to what he saw as being the limitations of the existing system, Nutt and colleagues proposed an entirely different assessment that ranked 20 drugs in terms of the level of their relative harm. Importantly, the Nutt ranking combined both the legal and illegal drugs and in doing so dissolved a distinction that has been at the heart of UK drug laws since the 1920s. The ranking that Nutt and colleagues have proposed is set out below with the current class each drug is placed within noted in the brackets:

1. Heroin (Class A)

2. Cocaine (Class A)

3. Barbiturates (Class B)

4. Street methadone (Class A)

5. Alcohol (Not controlled)

6. Ketamine (Not controlled)

7. Benzodiazepine (Class B)

8. Amphetamine (Class B)

9. Tobacco (No class)

10. Buprenorphine (Class C)

11. Cannabis (Class B)

12. Solvents (Not controlled)

13. 4-MTA (Class A)

14. LSD (Class A)

15. Methylphenidate (Class B)

16. Anabolic steroids (Class C)

17. GHB (Class C)

18. Ecstasy (Class A)

19. Alkyl nitrates (Not controlled)

20. Khat (Not controlled).

Whilst heroin and cocaine sit at the most harmful end of the Nutt schema, ecstasy shifts from being classified as one of the most harmful substances (within the Misuse of Drugs Act) to being the third least harmful substance within the Nutt schema. Similarly, alcohol and tobacco (which are excluded from the Misuse of Drugs Act classification) appear within the Nutt schema as the fifth and ninth most harmful substances listed. According to Nutt and colleagues the results of their research:

> Do not provide justification for the sharp A, B, or C divisions of the current classifications in the UK Misuse of Drugs Act. Distinct categorisation is of course convenient for setting priorities for policing, education, and social support as well as to determine sentencing for possession or dealing. But neither the rank order of drugs nor their segregations into groups in the Misuse of Drugs Act classification is supported by the more complete assessment of harm described here. (Nutt et al. 2007: 1051)

It is worthwhile looking at the process through which the Nutt schema was produced to get a clearer idea of the pitfalls of ranking drugs in terms of their individual harm. The process which Nutt and his colleagues followed entailed asking a range of addiction experts to rank a list of drugs along three separate dimensions, for example physical harm, dependence and social harms. These three dimensions of harm were further divided with, for example, the dimension of physical harm being differentiated in terms of whether the harms were acute, chronic or associated with the way in which the drug was administered, for example by injection. The dependency dimension was based upon judgements as to the level of pleasure associated with the drug coupled with the level of psychological and physical dependence associated with its consumption.

On the face of it the Nutt schema involved a pretty inclusive set of judgements and on that basis might be seen as more robust than the three-class classification within the Misuse of Drugs Act. However, even within the Nutt schema we may puzzle about the judgements of the experts whose views were consulted. In total 77 consultant psychiatrists were asked by Nutt to provide their ranking of the various substances listed. Only 29 of those approached actually provided an assessment (a response rate of only 37.6%). Following this initial assessment a further series of assessments were undertaken by a number of experts from a diverse range of medical specialisms, with the resulting numerical values across each of the dimensions of harm being combined to produce a single rank order of the 20 drugs listed.

There is no question that the Nutt schema is more transparent than the ABC classification currently contained within the Misuse of Drugs Act although that is not saying a great deal since the thinking behind the ABC classificatory system itself has never been spelt out in detail. But how sensible is it to try to rank substances in terms of their individual harm. The present three-class classificatory system produces a rather curious set of judgements in which attention is not so much focused on the harms of any particular drug so much as whether the various substances within the same class share a similar level of harm. The judgement of where any individual drug should be placed is one of assessing relative rather than absolute harm. This was evident in the 2008 letter from the Chair of the ACMD to the Home Secretary:

> After a careful scrutiny of the totality of the available evidence the majority of the Councils members consider – based on its harmfulness to individuals and society – that cannabis should remain a Class C substance. It is judged that the harmfulness of cannabis more closely equates with other Class C substances than with those currently classified as Class B. (Rawlins 2008)

The widespread and often heated debate around the issue of whether cannabis should be placed within Class B or Class C can be seen to be a largely synthetic product of the classificatory schema itself. The judgement ACMD is being asked to make is not about whether cannabis is harmful or harmless but about whether the level of harm associated with cannabis is sufficiently close to the other drugs in the class for which it is being considered. In effect then the classificatory schema is producing the very debate that the ACMD is seeking to resolve through its own deliberations and in that sense producing a potentially endless cycle of assessment and reassessment.

The placement of individual drugs in different classes is further compounded by the politics that inevitably impacts upon the judgements as to where different drugs should be placed. In the case of cannabis, part of the concern surrounding the decision to move the drug from Class B to Class C had to do with the perceived message that would inevitably be conveyed by the act of downgrading. The degree to which consumers (and potential consumers) of any individual drug might be influenced by the drug classification system is, of course, a moot point. However, the message that is undoubtedly conveyed by any decision to downgrade a drug is that the substance is regarded as less harmful than was previously thought, and that users of the drug can consume it with fewer adverse consequences on their health than was previously believed to be the case.

Within the Nutt schema there is a further unfortunate message wrapped up in the ranking of relative harm that has to do with the incorporation into the ranking of tobacco and alcohol. That message is you can use all of the illegal drugs ranked lower than position nine (tobacco) with lower levels our harm than any of the legal drugs you may presently be consuming. Whilst the Nutt schema cannot be interpreted as recommending a form of drug use it does have the potential to reassure any smoker that they have already attained a level of harm threshold greater than would be associated with their possible future use of such drugs such as ecstasy, anabolic steroids, cannabis, LSD, solvents and Buprenorphine.

There are though other reasons why the attempt to classify individual drugs in terms of their overall level of harm may be flawed which has to do with the fact that many individuals consume a number of different drugs rather than limit their consumption to a single substance. Within the last 20 years we have seen the growth of a poly-drug-using culture described by Parker as a "pick-n-mix" approach to drug consumption on the part of consumers (Parker 2009). Within a cultural context in which individuals are consuming multiple substances, the idea of ranking specific drugs in terms of their individual level harm can be seen as increasingly misplaced. In addition, of course, the level of harm associated with any individual substance more correctly needs to be assessed in terms of a whole host of contextual considerations such as the age of the drug user, the quantity of the drug consumed and the setting in which the drug taking is occurring. Cannabis use on the part of a 10-year old would ordinarily not be seen as involving the same level of harm as cannabis use on the part of an individual in his or her mid-20s. Similarly, the occasional cannabis cigarette consumed on the part of someone in their mid-teens would ordinarily not be regarded as involving the same level of harm as the establishment of a pattern of daily consumption of the drug. The level of harm associated with any given drug then may have more to do with these contextual dimensions of use than with the nature of the specific substance involved.

What Do We Know about the Harms of Cannabis?

Despite being the most widely used illegal drug, research on cannabis is by no means extensive. Within the United Kingdom there has not been a single longitudinal study into the effects of cannabis consumption. Similarly, although there has been much recent concern at changes in cannabis strength, with particular interest in the consumption of what has been termed "skunk" cannabis, there are very few databases that have systematically recorded changes in cannabis strength over time. Where research on cannabis has concentrated is in identifying the possible adverse health effects associated with the drug. Huber and colleagues have shown that cannabis consumption can have an impact on the respiratory and cardiovascular systems, increasing an individual's heart rate and risk of heart attack (Huber et al. 1988, Herning et al. 2001). Other researchers have looked at the impact of cannabis on co-ordination and various motor skills including driving (Robbe 1994), at the possible link between cannabis consumption and the risk of developing various cancers (Mehra et al. 2006); at the impact of cannabis on the immune system (Zhu et al. 2000), at the development of a pattern of cannabis dependency (Gardner 2003), at the impact of cannabis on educational performance (Fergusson et al. 2003, Lynskey et al. 2003) and on the link between cannabis and suicide (Andreasson et al. 1990). By far the largest portion of this research effort has focused on the extent to which cannabis use is associated with various mental health problems.

With regard to the research assessing the mental health harms of cannabis use the key studies are those that have followed groups of young people over an extended period of time to record both the onset of any mental health problems and the possible prior use of cannabis. It is these studies that have held out the prospect of identifying whether cannabis use actually causes various mental health problems as opposed to simply being associated with those problems. Studies using this approach have been carried out in New Zealand, the Netherlands, Sweden, Australia and the United States. Simple cross-sectional surveys of cannabis users which report various mental health problems clearly cannot resolve the causality issue since it may well be that it is the mental health problem themselves that are causing the cannabis consumption rather than the other way round. However, in the absence of a detailed understanding of the mechanism through which cannabis harms may be occurring, even the longitudinal studies are limited in their capacity to identify a causal pathway through which the actual harms associated with cannabis may be occurring.

In a systematic review of the strongest studies reporting on the mental health harms of cannabis use, Moore and colleagues concluded that:

> We found a consistent increase in incidence of psychotic outcomes in people who had used cannabis ... The pooled analysis revealed an increase in risk of psychosis of about 40% in participants who had ever used cannabis. However, studies tended to report larger effects for more frequent use, with most studies showing a 50–200% increase in risk for participants who used most heavily. A dose response effect was observed in all studies that examined the relation to increasing cannabis exposure. (Moore et al. 2007: 325)

On the basis of their review the authors of this article provide clear guidance to policy makers on what they saw as the implications of their analysis:

> We believe that there is now enough evidence to inform people that using cannabis could increase their risk of developing psychotic illness later in life... Although individual lifetime risk of chronic psychotic disorders such as schizophrenia, even in people who use cannabis regularly is likely to be low (less than 3%), cannabis use can be expected to have a substantial effect on psychotic disorders at a population level because exposure to this drug is so common. (Moore et al. 2007: 327)

Whilst there is a growing consensus that cannabis consumption can have an adverse impact on increasing individual's risk of developing specific mental health problems, dispute has arisen in relation to the size of the effect involved and the proportion of mental health problems within a population may be attributable to the drug:

> Current estimates of lifetime cannabis use among young adults in the UK are around 40%. If there is a true causal relation the increased risk of 40% would mean that 14% of psychotic outcomes in the UK might not occur if cannabis was not used. This finding has tremendous implications for young people, their families, and society. (Lancet 2007)

The *British Medical Journal* reported research in 2002 that identified an even larger cannabis effect with regard to the likelihood of individuals developing mental health problems:

> The shown dose response relation for both schizophrenia and depression highlights the importance of reducing the use of cannabis in people who use it. It was estimated that lack of exposure to cannabis would have reduced the incidence of psychosis requiring treatment by as much as 50% in a Dutch cohort and is similarly reflected in the Swedish cohort showing that the use of cannabis increased the risk of schizophrenia by 30%. (Rey and Tennant 2002: 1184)

According to the advisory council the additional mental health risk associated with cannabis consumption may be as little as 1% (ACMD 2005: 11). In contrast, other researchers have suggested that the magnitude of the cannabis effect may be considerably greater:

The population attributable fraction for the Dunedin study is 8%. In other words removal of cannabis use from the New Zealand population aged 15 years would have led to an 8% reduction in the incidence of schizophrenia in that population. (Arsenault et al. 2007)

The "population attributable fraction" refers to that proportion of schizophrenia cases within the population that may have been caused by cannabis use. Alongside the studies that have attempted to measure the size of the possible "cannabis effect", research has also been undertaken to address the question of whether the prevalence of psychotic illness in the population has increased over the period that the prevalence of cannabis use itself has been rising. Frisher et al. (2009) looked at general practice data on almost 600,000 patients in England, Wales and Scotland between the period 1996 and 2005 and found no evidence of an increase in the incidence or prevalence of schizophrenia in the general population. Although the results of this study have been interpreted as posing a question over the strength of the cannabis–schizophrenia link, general practice records are not necessarily an accurate measure of the level of psychiatric morbidity within the population. As a result it is possible that there could have been an increase in levels of schizophrenia within the community that has not as yet at least been picked up by general practice data.

In its assessment of the harms associated with cannabis, the advisory council accepted the thrust of the various studies identifying the possibility of a link between the use of cannabis and the later development of schizophrenia in some individuals, although they framed this more in terms of an association than a causal connection:

Collectively, the weight of evidence from these studies suggests an association between cannabis use and the development of psychotic symptoms which is consistent between studies and which remains after adjustment for confounding factors. While bias and residual confounding factors cannot be entirely excluded, these are unlikely fully to explain the findings. (ACMD 2005: 11)

By the time of its 2008 review the ACMD was prepared to go further in accepting the possibility of a causal relationship between the use of cannabis in adolescence and the later development of schizophrenia:

The Council concluded that the evidence supports a causal association between the use of cannabis, in adolescence, and the later development of schizophrenia; although the evidence for this relationship is clearly more complicated than when it considered this previously. The Council also considered that the evidence supporting a dose-response relationship was more persuasive than previously. (ACMD 2008: 18/19)

In the light of such a statement one may wonder at the ACMD's advice to ministers that cannabis should remain a Class C drug. However, the key to understanding that advice lies in the unique judgement that the ACMD was being asked to make which had to do with assessing the relative not the absolute level of harm associated with the drug:

> Decisions about advising on classification must, ultimately, be based on the Council's collective judgment about the relative harmfulness of substances within, and between, classes. On balance, taking into account the totality of the relevant issues and very mindful of the actual and potential harms, the majority of the Council advises that cannabis and the cannabinols remain in Class C. Although the majority of members recognise the harms caused by the use of cannabis to individuals and society, they do not consider these to be as serious as those of drugs in Class B. (ACMD 2008: 34)

Oddly, given the relative nature of the ACMD's advice, the series of reports to ministers on cannabis classification make no mention of having undertaken any equivalent assessment of the harms of the other drugs in either Class C or Class B against which to make the relative case for cannabis. It is difficult to see what measure of relative harm the council's experts were using when they offered their advice that the harms of cannabis were similar to those associated with the drugs in Class C but less than those associated with the drugs in Class B. On that basis one would have to conclude that the classification of substances, including cannabis, within the Misuse of Drugs Act still remains something of a mystery locked it seems within the heads of politicians and their experts.

Politicians and their Experts

In November 2009, following the serial reviews of cannabis, the Home Secretary Alan Johnson announced that he had sacked Professor David Nutt who, by then, had taken on the role of Chair of the ACMD. It is difficult to imagine that the key players in the dispute could have anticipated the media storm that followed this announcement. Within hours, the sacking of Professor Nutt was a front-page national news story and within days it was a global news story with in excess of 1,200 articles spread across the world's media.

In the days following the sacking there were accusations from Professor Nutt about the competency and rationality of the Home Secretary and the Prime Minister, there were claims that ministers were pandering to popular media opinion, ignoring the advice of experts and threats of a possible mass resignation on the part of the advisory council. The Home Secretary was asked to provide an explanation to parliament about the reasons for his decision to sack Professor Nutt, four members of the Advisory Council resigned, two enquiries were initiated relating to the ACMD and the use of independent scientific advisors, and the Home Secretary met with the remaining ACMD members to reassure them that he welcomed and respected their advice but that he had personally lost trust in his former chief drugs advisor. In the weeks that followed an agreed protocol was produced which set out government responsibilities with regard to receiving scientific advice and the obligations upon scientists taking up advisory positions to make it clear that when they were commenting on matters of drug harm and drug policy whether they were doing so in their capacity as independent scientists or as government advisors. By March 2010 the rumblings of dissatisfaction on the council were still much in evidence with two further members resigning – stating in their resignation letters to the Home Secretary that they had continuing concerns over the degree to which ministers were prepared to be guided by the advice of its expert committee or were responding to media headlines in announcing, most recently, that the drug mephedrone would be banned (BBC 2010a, Hough 2010).

As in any dispute it is extraordinarily difficult to distinguish the elements of the original conflict between participants from the positions that the key players in the dispute came to take up as the arguments unfolded in the full glare of the media. In the view of the Home Secretary Professor Nutt had gone well beyond his advisory role in continuing to make the case for returning cannabis to Class C long after ministers had taken the decision to move it to Class B. It was also clear however that ministers had been irritated by an academic paper which Professor Nutt had published before taking on the role of chair of the ACMD, in which he argued that ecstasy use was less dangerous than horse-riding (Nutt 2009). Further comments from Professor Nutt that many of the illegal drugs currently covered by the Misuse of Drugs Act were less harmful than alcohol also stoked the flames of what had become a very fragile relationship between the government's chief drugs advisor and senior ministers.

As the arguments raged over the days and weeks following, Professor Nutt's sacking the terms of the dispute increasingly crystallized around the issue of the relationship between government and its independent scientific advisors. Sense about Science, a charity that promotes the use of science in public policy, released a statement signed by 75 leading scientists setting out the possible terms upon which independent scientific advisors might engage with ministers and other government officials. The principles included the responsibility on the part of government to give due consideration to advice from expert advisors and a recognition that reporting research findings critical of government policy should not be grounds for terminating the contract of any advisor.

Professor Nutt's sacking, and the subsequent machinations, provide a powerful illustration of the uneasy relationship that can exist between independent scientists and politicians on matters that are as highly charged as drugs policy. This case showed also the central role that the media can play in shaping policy debate. When David Blunkett, as Home Secretary, announced to the media that he was minded to move cannabis from Class B to Class C he was inviting the ACMD to confirm a political decision he was already inclining towards. Similarly when Jacqui Smith as Home Secretary let it be known to the media that she was minded to move cannabis back to Class B from Class C, she too was using the media to shape drug policy. There is a degree to which the use of the media in this way, to trail political decisions in advance of the evidence, is almost guaranteed to create tension between government advisors and their ministers.

A Radical Suggestion: Do Away with Drug Classification

If there is one thing that comes through more clearly than any other in the cannabis story it is that the classification of drugs in terms of their individual or relative harm is a system that is virtually guaranteed to produce limitless debate and disagreement. The capacity for that disagreement has been demonstrated most recently in the case of the so-called "legal" high mephedrone with the current chair of the ACMD indicating that the drug should be placed within Class B under the Misuse of Drugs Act (BBC 2010b) and the previous chair of the ACMD David Nutt suggesting that the drug should be made available in small quantities to young people in clubs throughout the United Kingdom (Syal 2010).

An alternative to the present classification system would be to simply differentiate between the legal and the illegal drugs and then leave it to the courts to undertake a detailed consideration of the individual circumstances of drug use or drug selling in individual cases and determine the appropriate punishment. In forming that judgement a court would pay attention to such matters as the age of the user, the circumstances in which the drug was being used or sold, the quantity of the drug involved and the history of past use. The aim would not be to produce a scientific ranking of individual substances but a detailed assessment of each occasion of drug use or drug selling on the basis of which the court could determine an appropriate penalty. This system would avoid the pitfalls of the present three-class classification as well as the problems associated with the Nutt schema.

Conclusions

The story of cannabis within UK drug policy is a very British farce with the drug "yo-yoing" between classes within the Misuse of Drugs Act. Although there are humorous aspects to this story it is important to remember that we are dealing here with the illegal drug that is used more widely than any other. If one was going to make a "hash" of classifying any particular drug, you would not want that drug to be the one used more widely than any other. And yet that is exactly what has happened in relation to cannabis. Perhaps the greatest harm associated with cannabis, and its greatest impact, lies not in the mental health harms associated with its use but the cloak of cultural acceptability that it has acquired and which has resulted in it being seen by many young people as barely an illegal drug at all. Cannabis may not be a gateway drug in the conventional sense of the word but it may have played an important function in furthering the normalization of illegal drug use on the part of young people. It is perhaps in this sense that the harms of cannabis use are ever bit as great as the harms of heroin use.

KEY DISCUSSION QUESTIONS

1. Does it make sense to differentiate between different drugs in terms of their individual harm in a context in which different drugs are often combined in their use?
2. What should be the right balance in drug policy between science and politics?

3. Is cannabis a drug associated with only minimal adverse effects or a drugs whose harmful effects have been under appreciated?

4. What weight should be given to government classification of individual drugs in terms of the judgements of those using illegal drugs?

5. To what extent has cannabis use become a normal part of youth culture?

6. What would be the merits of dismantling the present classificatory system and replacing it with a simple division between the legal drugs and the illegal drugs?

Chapter 6

Meeting the Needs of the Children of Drug Addicted Parents

Introduction

Over the last 10 years a revelation has taken place in the drugs field. That revelation consists in the realization that dependent drug users have children. Hardly a shattering realization you might think but there it is in all its predictable simplicity. The realization that drug users do indeed have children, and that many of those children suffer multiple harms as a result of their parent's drug use, seems to have eluded drug policy for most of the last 50 years. Within the United Kingdom the first national drugs strategy "Tackling Drugs to Build a Better Britain", published in 1998, talks at length about drug prevention, about treatment, about reducing drug users' rates of re-offending and about reducing the availability of drugs on the streets. All but the most alert of readers of that document will probably have missed the single, passing reference to the importance of meeting the needs of children with drug-dependent parents.

By the time of the second national drug strategy, published 10 years later, the realization that drug users do indeed have children and that many of those children suffer serious harm had struck at the very heart of government. Titled "Drugs: Protecting Families and Communities" the 2008 drug strategy stated in the clearest of terms that:

> Drug misuse can prevent parents from providing their children with the care and support they need and greatly increases the likelihood that their children will grow up to develop drug problems themselves. (Home Office 2008: 8)

The drug strategy set out a clear commitment to target services on drug-using parents and their children and to ensure:

> Prompt access to treatment for drug-misusing parents with treatment needs and particularly those whose children are at risk, with assessments taking account of family needs, and providing intensive parenting support alongside drug treatment; and ensure drug-misusing parents, and other at-risk parents, including offenders and their partners, are a target group for new parenting experts and in plans to develop Family Intervention Projects. (Home Office 2008: 70)

Within Scotland guidance provided by the Scottish Government in 2003 for services working with drug-using parents and their children was framed in terms of the rather optimistic view that "being a problem drug using parent does not necessarily mean an inability to parent" (Scottish Government 2003). Four years later a joint statement from the Ministers for Justice, Health and Education took a much tougher line:

> However our view is that serious and chaotic drug abuse is incompatible with effective parenting. Sadly, serious drug addiction can be so powerful that it takes priority over the most basic parental responsibilities. It can and does expose children to behaviour that put them in real danger and can have long lasting consequences. For very young children this can have such a devastating impact that, by the time they go to school, the prospect of fully repairing the damage is limited. (Ministerial Statement Hidden Harm Next Steps, Scottish Executive 2006: 1)

The shifting priority that government has accorded the importance of meeting the needs of children and parents within drug-dependent families gives a clear indication that this is an area where there are shifting views, complex ethical issues, and uncertain professional practice. Part of the problem here has to do with the difficulty of establishing a measure of what constitutes "good enough parenting" and by implication the point at which parents fall below that measure requiring the state to intervene within their family life. Along with the uncertainty as to what constitutes good enough parenting there is also a reluctance to judge other people's parenting. That hesitancy has held us back from responding to the multiple ways in which dependent drug use can fundamentally undermine parents' abilities to look after their children and it has almost certainly added to the burden upon those children.

The notion of "good enough parenting" cannot be defined in simple, quantitative terms, for example, in the number of hours spent with a child, or the number of school parent evenings attended. The notion of good enough parenting can however be understood in terms of the willingness of the parent to subject his or her needs to the needs of their child. It is in this sense that we intuitively recognize what it means to be a good enough parent even if we are hesitant about calling ourselves good parents. Where a parent is dependent upon illegal drugs, the impact on that person's capacity to meet their children's needs can be profound. The daily needs of the child for love, safety, support, food, education, stability and socialization can all fall a long way behind the overwhelming need to source and use illegal drugs. Drug policy is slowly beginning to recognize that fact and to commit itself to meeting the needs of children living with drug-dependent parents.

The commitment to meet the needs of children within drug-dependent families gives rise to some of the most challenging and ethically complex issues that professionals are likely to face in their work. For example, how long should children be left in the care of drug-dependent parents where there is evidence that they are being harmed? How much harm should a child be expected to endure as a result of his or her parent's drug misuse? Do all children living within drug-dependent households suffer harm to some extent or is it only a minority who are suffering the most extreme harm? How do we ensure a balance between the rights of the child and the rights of the parent within the circumstances of a parent's dependent drug use? Is dependent drug use fundamentally incompatible with the demands of providing a safe and nurturing environment for children to grow up within? Equally, to what extent are services able to repair the damage to children from growing up within drug-dependent households? Finally, should we be trying to reduce the number of children born to drug-dependent parents and if so how? The answers to these questions are the threads upon which the lives of hundreds of thousands of children hang. They are also the controversies that we must face if we are to deliver on the promise of meeting the needs of some of the most vulnerable children within our society.

The Scale of the Problem

In 2003, the Advisory Council on the Misuse of Drugs reported the results of its 2-year "Hidden Harm" enquiry into the impact of parental drug use on children. As part of that enquiry, the council sought to provide the first estimate of the number of children in the United Kingdom living with drug-dependent parents. Drawing upon a range of data, the ACMD estimated that there were between 205,300 and 298,900 children in England and Wales with a drug-dependent parent. Large as that figure may seem, the authors of the report cautioned that:

> In the light of the assumptions we have made, we believe that these are very conservative estimates and the true figure may well be higher (ACMD 2003: 25).

The figure of between 205,300 and 298,900 represents between 2% and 3% of all children in England and Wales under 16 year of age in 2000. In Scotland, it has been estimated that there may be between 40,800 and 58,700 children, or between 4% and 6% of all children aged under 16 with a parent who is a problem drug user (ACMD 2003).

If these figures give an indication of the numbers of children in the United Kingdom with a drug-dependent parent, it is important to get an idea of how many of these children are actually being looked after by their parents? To answer that question the ACMD drew upon information from the National Drug Treatment Monitoring System on 77,928 drug-using parents in England and Wales. Overall, 46% of the parents had dependent children living with them and 54% had children living elsewhere. According to the ACMD, the proportion of drug users who do not have their children living with them has increased from 51% in 1996 to 57% in 2000 (ACMD 2003). In Scotland it has been estimated that only 37% of drug-dependent mothers and 13% of drug-dependent fathers are actually living with their dependent children (ACMD 2003).

These figures give a clear indication of the very real likelihood that parental drug dependence will be associated with family breakdown.

As we have become aware of the adverse impact on children of growing up within drug-dependent families, there has been a growing realization of the importance of listening to, and hearing, the voices of the children within these circumstances. As important as the injunction of listening to the children undoubtedly is, it is important to recognize the difficulty of trying to unlock the often deeply painful experiences of children living within addict households.

The Impact of Parental Drug Use: The Voices of Young People and Drug-Using Parents

Interviewing young children about the impact of their parent's drug use presents a massive challenge to social science researchers. At the University of Glasgow researchers have undertaken a series of studies that have entailed lengthy interviews with children growing up within drug-dependent households as well as with their drug-dependent parents. These studies have been amongst the most challenging that the Centre has undertaken over the 16 years of its existence. Building the level of trust that can enable a child to talk in detail about some of the most frightening aspects of their lives is no easy matter. These are children who are understandably wary of questions from outsiders and who fear what may happen if they reveal the details of their lives. They are, for the most part, the invisible victims of their parent's drug addiction.

Children within these circumstances will often answer "fine" or "its O.K" to questions about the impact of their parent's drug use on their lives. Where a level of trust has been established, and the child is willing to talk about the circumstances within their family, the picture that emerges is deeply shocking. One of the children interviewed by researchers from the University of Glasgow had been dangled over the balcony of a multi-storey flat by a dealer demanding repayment of a drug debt. Another had a gun pointed at his head whilst drug dealers ransacked the family home in search of drugs that had been hidden within the premises. Another woke next to the corpse of his father who had overdosed in the night as the two slept side by side.

When these children do speak, their words often reveal a world that is about as far from any notion of a normal childhood as it is possible to get. The interview extracts below provide a glimpse into that world and are taken from research undertaken by Professor Marina Barnard and Joy Barlow from the Centre for Drug Misuse Research. The research aimed to describe the worlds of the children living in the midst of their parent's drug habit. Some of the children interviewed by Barnard and Barlow spoke about the violence that they were exposed to on occasion as a result of their parent's involvement in the world of illegal drugs:

> That was scary because there were guys who used to buy stuff off my uncle and they all burst in and were holding knives to our throats and asking for the drugs and the money. There were saying they would cut our throats if they did not give it to them.

The reaction of young people to such incidents could be completely different to what one might have expected. A young girl interviewed by Barnard described an incident in which a local drug dealer had ransacked her home, searching for drugs that had been stored in the house. The frantic search ended with the drug dealer, holding a gun to the child's head, demanding that the mother tell him where the drugs were hidden. The mother insisted she had no knowledge where the drugs were hidden but when the dealer left the flat she produced the drugs from her jeans pocket. In recounting that incident the child did not express anger or shock at the risk she had been exposed to by her mother. Rather, she said, she realized, for the first time, how much her mother needed her drugs (Barnard 2007).

The young people in Barnard and Barlow's study spoke about how, while they knew their parents loved them, they also knew that in their parent's eyes they frequently came second to the drugs:

> I knew they loved me but the just didn't care that I was there and I needed stuff as well. I needed things and they were just away taking drugs and stuff.

On occasion the young people were angry and deeply resentful at how their lives had been affected by their parent's drug habit:

> Well I used to feel angry, like when my mum was on drugs, cause I used to think how could this have happened to me? It was just sad all the time and then I would get angry and we would have arguments all of the time.

> She was always dead moody, she was always in her bed and she would never go out and buy food and she would never have money to go out and get it.

The lack of food and money was something that many of the young people drew attention to as being the obvious signs of their parent's drug habit:

> "We didn't have any routines really everything revolved around the drugs always". I asked about food being available "no there wasn't much food about, maybe the day they got paid there would be a dinner and maybe the day after but then there would be nothing again." "Actually" she said "if it was a choice of being hungry or using the money for drugs it was better if they used the money for drugs then at least they would leave you alone".

> I remember the mornings when they didn't have anything. My mum would be sitting and you knew not to talk to her and the house would be still. We'd all be waiting for my dad to wake up. You could hear every creak, every tiny noise. When he did wake up you knew there'd be trouble, see drugs made my dad terrible.

As difficult as things often were in their home the young people interviewed by Barnard and Barlow were clear about the dangers of telling other people what was happening within their family home. The young people had often been exhorted by their parents to never talk about their home life for fear of revealing the details about their parent's drug use:

> There were so many things I had to keep quiet about, so I just didn't bother to say anything in case I let something slip out that I shouldn't have done. So whenever they started talking about things I'd just say I didn't know.

Some of the young people talked about the fear that their parents might suffer a drug overdose:

> Sometimes I'd see her and she'd be pure white, just like a pure ghost, it was frightening. I'd go like that "Mum what's wrong with you? And she say nothing, just leave me alone the now and she'd go out." And then she'd come back and she'd go like that "I'm sorry hen" and she be all nicey nice. That must've been after she had her hit or whatever.

Within Scotland the vulnerability of young children living with a drug-dependent, single parent became a matter of widespread concern when a 3-year-old child sat for between 4 and 6 weeks next to the decomposing body of his mother who had died from a drug overdose. The child survived by scavenging scraps of food from around the tenement flat he had shared with his mother (Summerhayes, 2006). Such incidents revealed more powerfully than research could ever do the vulnerability of children living within these circumstances and the failure on occasion of services to truly know what is going on within addict households.

In their research into the impact of parental drug use on children, Brynna Kroll and Andy Taylor have written powerfully about the nature of that impact:

> The young peoples' data reflect the long shadow cast by the emotional and physical impact of parental drug misuse and its consequences for felt security, sense of safety, and day-to-day life. The majority (of young people) were in no doubt that using drugs and caring for children did not mix and had come to believe that drugs came first and were more important than they were. (Kroll and Taylor 2008: 2)

If these are the voices from children living in the midst of their parent's drug habit, it is no less important to hear the voices of drug-using parents themselves as they articulate what they see as being the impact of their drug use on their children. In research with recovered addicts who were parents (McIntosh and McKeganey 2002) and with current addict parents (Barnard 2007), the adults have spoken at length about the many ways they felt their drug use had compromised the lives of their children. Parents spoke with regret at how they had sometimes failed to protect their children from harm during the period of their drug use. One of the recovered drug users interviewed by McIntosh and McKeganey, for example, commented:

> My eldest son had bruises on the side of his face and I think that it was my partner that hit him but I was too out of my face to notice. I just hold onto things like that, what could have happened and in fact what has happened.

Other parents talked about the mood swings that had characterized the period when they had been using illegal drugs and of how this had impacted upon their children:

> When I was on drugs if I was to go two days without it I'd take it out on my kids. I would turn around and say "it's your fault I've no got drugs". If they moaned for the least wee thing I'd jump down their throat. I'd not hit them but I knew in my own mind I shouldn't have been doing that. It wasn't their fault I was on drugs so why should I let them suffer?

I couldn't look after Sarah when I was strung out. I had to have drugs in me. I'd be shouting and bawling at her and a couple of times I even sort of hit her. I know I was violent. I wouldn't get her dressed or anything until I had my drugs in me but it was a real struggle you know to get up off the chair. So she was left to her own devices sort of you know, to wander about the house with just underwear on. Her night dress on from the night before.

Some parents talked about how in time they came to recognize that the family home they shared with their children had become a place that no child should grow up within:

I was running about with folk that were injecting and I was injecting myself. I was taking temazepam, valium, acid really just anything at all. Not eating or sleeping my house was a mess, folk coming into my house at all hours having parties, it was really disgusting, the lifestyle I was leading was disgusting, and it was scary as well 'cos I had my wee boy with me and he was seeing everything that was going on around him.

I mean the two of us were doing the same, leaving needles lying about and people were coming and saying "is it alright if I have a hit?" and "aye no bother, batter in, on you go", and that just not right.

Some of the parents spoke about the impact of having repeatedly exposed their children to petty and sometimes serious criminality, and of how this had impacted upon the child's own behaviour:

My eldest boy was treble streetwise cos he was brought up that way. He'd be in the jail and things like that with us (visiting relatives) and I'd take him out stealing with me, get the jail and my mum would need to come down to the police station and get him and things like that.

Those parents who had recovered from their drug problem spoke at length about how focused they had been on the drugs they were using and how this had inevitably resulted in the neglect of their children:

You only care about yourself, you think you care about everybody else but number one comes first and that's yourself, and if you're lucky, if you've got anything left they get it. But you would take it off them to give to you. I mean at the time I wouldn't admit it but now I would.

The more people told me I had a problem the more I would deny I had a problem. And it was one night when I'd sold all the furniture in the house and the children were really starving, and instead of running about trying to get them food I was running about trying to get my drugs. In the end I think the shame caught up with me, and the guilt.

Its like the only thing that was at the front of my mind was drugs, where am I going to get this where am I going to get that. Whereas in actual fact I should have been thinking what am I going to give the bairn for his breakfast, his lunch, his tea, what's he doing, who's he out playing with?

Useful as this kind of qualitative research can be in highlighting aspects of the children's experiences it is limited in terms of assessing how representativeness the described events are in terms of the lives of these young people. To get some idea of the scale and the range of harm that these children may experience it is necessary to turn to some of the quantitative research that has been undertaken.

The Impact of Parental Drug Use on Children: The Results from Quantitative Research

Since the early 1980s there has been a growing body of research looking at the impact of parental drug use on children – most of that research emanates from the United States and most of it relates to the impact of mother's rather than father's drug use. Research has been undertaken on the impact of babies exposed in-utero to their mother's drug use. It has been shown that babies born to cocaine-dependent mothers are at increased risk of being born prematurely, of having a smaller head size and of being at lower birth weight compared to babies born to non-cocaine-dependent mothers. Lewis and colleagues have reported data from a follow-up study of babies exposed in-utero to maternal cocaine use:

Cross sectional analysis revealed more cocaine group offspring exhibited suspicious or abnormal neurological signs at birth and across all testing periods. (Lewis et al. 2004: 306)

Further the authors of this report note that:

Data reported here indicate the presence of a dose response effect of gestational cocaine exposure among preschool age children. Levels of cocaine dose were related to rates of abnormal neurological exams as well as deficits in mental and motor development. (Lewis et al. 2004: 314)

Concern over the impact of maternal drug use on the unborn child is not, however, confined solely to the consumption of illicit drugs. Research has shown that methadone, widely prescribed to dependent drug users, can have a serious adverse effect on the unborn child. According to Jansson and colleagues (2005):

> Administration of methadone to pregnant women is associated with profound effects of fetal neurobehavioral functioning...The effects were pervasive and evidenced in fetal heart rate, motor activity, and their inter-relation....The long term sequale of daily repeated depression of motor activity and heart rate are unknown, but potentially present a distinct mechanism through which methadone may exert and effect on development beyond the neurotoxic effects of the substance itself. (Jansson et al. 2005: 614–616)

Further the authors of this report conclude that:

> The strategy (of methadone maintenance) has persisted despite evidence that methadone generates effects on the neonate that are as deleterious, if not more so, than heroin on neonatal abstinence syndrome. (Jansson et al. 2005: 616)

Alongside the research into the impact of prenatal exposure to various drugs, studies have also been undertaken into the longer-term impact on children of being raised within a drug-dependent household. Research has shown that children with drug-dependent parents are at increased risk of abuse and neglect (Cohen and Brook 1987, Famularo et al. 1989, Tracy 1994, Chaffin et al. 1996). According to the National Center on Addiction and Substance Abuse at Columbia University:

> Parental substance abuse is one of the main problems facing families who are reported for child maltreatment. Parents with substance abuse problems are approximately three times likelier to report abuse towards their children and four times likelier to report neglect than parents without substance abuse problems. (The Nation Center on Addiction and Substance Abuse 2005: 2)

> Children of drug abusing parents, particularly drug abusing mothers, are more likely to be disobedient, aggressive, withdrawn, and detached. These children also tend to have fewer friends lower confidence in their ability to make friends and a greater likelihood of being avoided by their peers. (The Nation Center on Addiction and Substance Abuse 2005: 12)

Dawe and colleagues have summarized the body of research looking at the longer-term impact of parental drug use on children in the following way:

> The outcome for children raised in families in which either or both parents use illicit substances is generally poor. Such children are at high risk of child abuse and neglect, and early conduct and behavioral problems, school failure and adolescent substance abuse. Many of the families are headed by single parents, experience social isolation, financial difficulty and high levels of (maternal) depression and anxiety. Parenting practices are often characterised by inconsistent emotional neglect and an authoritarian style. (Dawe et al. 2003: 299)

Research has identified that children raised within drug-dependent households are at increased risk of using illegal drugs themselves (McKeganey et al. 2004) and of forming associations with other peers with a range of behavioural problems:

> The children of drug dependent fathers showed an augmented level of affiliation with deviant peers beyond that found in comparison children at each time point assessed. (Moss et al. 2003: 123)

Other researchers have looked at the health needs of children with drug-dependent parents and found that these children often fail to receive appropriate health care. Cornelius and colleagues, for example, surveyed the health needs of nearly 400 boys within families where one or both parents had a substance abuse problem. The researchers concluded that:

> The data from this study provide evidence that paternal substance use disorder is associated with poor dental condition, poor oral hygiene, a greater need for dental treatment and inadequate levels of dental treatment utilisation among their offspring. (Cornelius et al. 2004: 982)

Shulman and colleagues (2000) reported on the results of an outreach medical service provided to the children of substance abusing parents within the United States. During the first 3 years of the service 100 children were assessed by the research team:

> 50% scored in the borderline range of intellectual functioning, 19% scored in the range of mental retardation. Approximately 68% of the children demonstrated a variety of speech and or language impairments. Emotional

or behavioral disorders were diagnosed in 16% of the children. Eighty three percent of the children had medical or nutritional disorders or both. Common physical examination findings included microephaly, hyptertonia dysmorphism, and obesity. (Shulman et al. 2000: 1931)

Follow-up information on the assessed children identified that 59% were receiving a variety of interventions as recommended, 18% were not eligible for the advised interventions, 6% of children were not receiving the recommended intervention and 17 children were receiving services of an unknown kind. Of 27 children who were referred for additional medical consultations only 48% were completed (Shulman et al. 2000: 1931).

Perhaps the most obvious way in which parental drug use can have an impact on young children is in the level of neglect they are likely to experience. Street and colleague reported the results of a 5-year follow-up study of 71 infants born to drug-dependent mothers matched with 142 babies borne to non-drug-dependent mothers. The results of this study provide considerable cause for concern:

> Half of the children born to self-declared drug using mothers who received prenatal input were subjected to child protection by age 5 years. This represents a three-fold increase over controls from similar socio economic circumstances. The risk is almost certainly higher for those drug-using women who do not seek help during pregnancy. One could question whether drug addiction and adequate parenting are mutually incompatible. A key marker of good enough parenting is the ability to put the child's needs above ones own needs. Addiction entails a need to satiate ones own needs above all else. Perhaps we should not be surprised at these dismal findings. (Street et al. 2007: 206)

We know from the work of John Bowlby and others that the attachment a newborn baby feels towards a parent (principally the mother) is crucial for the child's subsequent healthy psychological development (Bowlby, 1999). Attachment is developed in the many hours that a parent will spend with their child, responding to his or her needs and sounds, establishing eye contact with the child, and engaging in reciprocal verbal and non-verbal communication. The addicted parent, experiencing the daily cycle of acute drug use and drug withdrawal, may simply not be able to bond in these subtle ways with their child. The difficulties of bonding may be even greater where the newborn is crying inconsolably as a result of the distressing effects of drug withdrawal.

At the present time we know relatively little about the long-term impact of early exposure to parental drug dependency. Research carried out at the University of Edinburgh with the survivors of parental drug and alcohol problems raises the possibility that the adverse effects that arise as a result of the young persons exposure to their parent's drug and alcohol use may well persist over many years. Many of the individuals interviewed in this study had struggled to develop long-lasting and stable relationships with other people (Bancroft et al. 2004):

> Building an independent life was no easy trajectory for most of these young people, and their accounts suggest no sense of a gradual transition to adulthood. Many had experienced a foreshortened childhood through the taking on of caring responsibilities and learning to look after themselves. Role reversal between parent and child itself was sometimes described as making the transition to independent living difficult as concern was still felt for the parent left behind. (Bancroft et al. 2004: 36)

This research raises the possibility that young people exposed to their parent's substance misuse may be in need of help and support not only for the first few years of life but well into their adulthood. The implications of that for services, including the cost of those services, is substantial given the numbers of young people we now know are living within drug-dependent households.

How Effective are Services at Repairing the Damage to Children from Parental Drug Dependence?

Whilst there is a need for services to support young people growing up in the midst of their parent's drug dependency, it is important to establish how effective those services are likely to be in meeting the needs of young people. Within the United States, where there is more extensive experience of family support services, Catalano and colleagues evaluated an intensive family support intervention (Catalano et al. 1999, 2002, Haggerty et al. 2008). The "Focus on Families" project involved 53 hours of small group training with parents, 5 hours of family retreat and 32 twice-weekly 90-minute meetings. Children were involved in 12 sessions and case managers supported families for 9 months with one home visit and two telephone calls per week. Parents were paid $3 per assignment to enhance the level of their involvement within the programme. Parents and young people were assessed at 6th and 12th month.

By any standard the "Focus on Families" intervention would be regarded as an intensive intervention. At the 12-month evaluation point whilst there had been a reduction in parent's drug use, an increase in household routines and a decrease in domestic conflict, there had been only very slight impact on the children. Indeed the older children were more resentful at the impact of the intervention within their family – perhaps having already accommodated to the relative lack of household routines and structure within their family home.

Another intensive intervention with vulnerable families was the "Parents Under Pressure" programme evaluated by Dawe and colleagues. This intervention was targeted on vulnerable families and involved parents taking part in ten training modules aimed at reducing the potential for child abuse and neglect amongst the methadone-maintained parents. The importance of this intervention can be gauged from the finding in other research that 41% of mothers and 25% of fathers with a substance abuse disorder scored in the clinical range on the Child Abuse Potential Inventory (Chaffin et al. 1996, Ammerman et al. 1999). The evaluation of the Parents Under Pressure programme identified improvements in a number of areas of family functioning, leading the research team to judge that the intervention might ameliorate some of the risks faced by children within substance misusing families. However, Dawe and colleagues point out that:

> Despite the statistical and clinical significance of the intervention, 36% of Parents Under Pressure group showed continued high risk status over the course of the study. (Dawe et al. 2003: 388)

Similarly, Suchman and colleagues reviewed a range of interventions aimed at increasing parenting capacity and concluded that:

> Taken together finding from these well designed clinical trials of parent training programs indicate that whereas they may have some short term efficacy for increasing parents behaviour management strategies aimed at reducing children's conflict producing behaviours, they do not lead to long term improvements in the quality of parental child relationships or children's psychological adjustment. (Suchman and Luthar 2000: 180)

In the light of these studies we may need to draw the uncomfortable conclusion that once children have been significantly exposed to the reality of their parent's drug use, and harmed as a result of that exposure, we simply do not have the services in place, or indeed the available knowledge and skill, to substantially repair the damage resulting from that exposure. If it is accepted that services are likely to have only a modest impact on repairing the damage of children's early exposure to parental drug dependency, the question then inevitably arises as to whether it might be more appropriate to remove children from the source of that harm at an earlier point rather than assume that services will be able to repair the damage associated with early exposure to parental drug misuse.

Unfortunately here again there has been very little research on the impact of removing children from their drug-dependent parents with which to guide professional decision-making. One reason for this might be because the policy option of removing children from their birth family is deeply controversial. One study that has been undertaken on this issue was carried out by Ornoy and colleagues in Israel and involved comparing the outcomes of three groups of children: those who remained with their heroin-dependent mothers, those who had been born to heroin-dependent mothers and then placed for adoption with non-drug-dependent families, and those born into non-drug-dependent families in similar socio-economic circumstances. According to Ornoy and colleagues, when the children in the three groups were assessed it was found that:

> Children born to parents with heroin dependency raised at home and those of low SES exhibited intellectual impairment both on verbal and performance skills. They also had impaired reading and arithmetic skills. Children born to mothers with heroin dependency but who were adopted at a young age had normal intellectual and learning abilities, except for some reduced function on the performance Wechsler Intelligence Scale for Children–Revised. We found a high rate of ADHD among all children born to parents with heroin dependency, including those adopted, as well as in children with low parental SES. The highest rate of ADHD was in children born to mothers with heroin dependency raised at home, being twice that observed in the other groups. Mothers of these groups of children also had a high rate of ADHD. (Ornoy et al. 2001)

On the basis of this small study, placing children of heroin-dependent mothers within non-drug-using families might improve some of the outcomes for children. Ornoy's findings though are enormously challenging in questioning the commonly held assumption that children will be invariable better off to the extent that they remain with their biological parents. Other recent research is also leading us to question that orthodoxy. Connolly and colleagues have compared the educational attainment of "looked after children" (i.e., children living under local authority care) and children remaining in the care of their parents. The authors of this study found that the looked after children did particularly well in terms of the level of their educational attainment indicating that the local-authority-provided educational programmes were able to repair some of the deficits often experienced by children within vulnerable families:

> Young people reported to have high levels of involvement in the pilots appeared to have made appreciably more progress than those with less involvement in reading and writing, an effect which is statically significant. It is reasonable to conclude that since there was a particular emphasis on literacy across the pilots, this additional support was effective in achieving improvement in reading and writing... About 40% of the young people participating in the pilots advanced by one 5–14 national Assessment level, much better than the average progress reported for all looked after children and similar to advances made by non-looked after children nationally. Again this finding was statistically significant. (Connolly et al. 2008)

There is little doubt that children can be harmed as a result of being brought up within chaotic, drug-dependent households and that the harm children may experience can influence their lives over many years. A question remains however, as to whether it is the majority of children who are being harmed as a result of their exposure to their parent's serious drug problem or only a minority of children. This is an important question that bears upon the capacity of services to help these children. If the proportion of children adversely affected by their parent's drug dependency is small then we may well be able to provide the necessary support to these families and limit the damage arising from that exposure. If, however, either the majority or indeed even a large minority of children are harmed as a result of that exposure then the sheer scale of the problem may already be beyond our capacity to cope. Regrettably there have been very few studies that are able to assist in determining which of these scenarios is likely to apply. Nevertheless if it is the case that parental drug dependency is having a substantial and widespread effect on undermining parenting capacity then we ought by now to be seeing the indications of this in some of the child support services that are already available for children.

In England over the 12-month period to March 2009 there were 37,900 children who became the subject of a child protection plan as a result of concerns for their welfare. That figure represents an increase from 33,300 in 2007 to 34,000 in 2008. Forty-five per cent of those children were the subject of child protection plans as a result of neglect with that percentage increasing from 43% in 2005 to 44% in 2007 (National Statistics 2009). Neglect was also the most common reason for placing a child on the protection register in Scotland (45%) and Wales (47%). Although it is not possible to say with certainty that parental drug dependency was the factor behind the level of neglect identified in these figures it is likely that this is playing an increasing role in leading to children being referred to social work services. In Scotland, for example, the Children's Reporter Administration highlighted the growing impact of parental drug dependence in its annual report for the year 2003/04:

> This report provides details of a further rise in the number of referrals on grounds of a lack of parental care (up 12% since 2002/03) as well as reporting a 28% increase in referrals where the child was the victim of an offence. The influence of alcohol and drugs is becoming an ever more prominent feature in the lives of children experiencing difficulties: both in their own lives and in the lives of the adults responsible for them. The disrupted pattern of family life, the neglect that is so often a consequence of parental drug use, the dependency and poverty of aspiration in so many families suggest strongly that we are dealing with children on the wrong side of the opportunity gap. (Scottish Children's Reporter Administration Annual Report 2003/04)

The Response of Services

To date the response of services has been to focus attention on the children who are thought to be at the greatest risk. The trouble with this strategy is that it pushes the bar of tolerable harm too high and leaves many children unsupported. Within this scenario, for example, whilst we may respond to the child who is being regularly exposed to his or her parent's drug use we may be more inclined to hold off from intervening in a family where the child is being intermittently exposed to their parents drug use. In effect then services are operating a kind of triage judgement that concentrates services on the children at greatest risk and by implication failing to help those children who are judged to be less vulnerable but who may still be at significant risk of some harm.

Whilst it may be possible to build a protective network of services around the most vulnerable families the very provision of that support can fundamentally change the child's experience of his or her family life. Children within supported families may be taken to school and collected from school each day, they may be regularly fed by services going into the family home in the morning, evenings and weekends. The children may be supported in their homework by paid or volunteer staff. In addition to the support that the children are receiving their parents may be participating within family support programmes and the families may be monitored on a regular basis by social work staff. In the face of that intensive and costly involvement of services two things are very evident. First, we should not be in any doubt that the experience of a child within such a family approximates in any way to a normal childhood. Second, we need to recognize that whilst it may be possible to provide intensive support to some families, for some of the time, it will not be possible to support anything like the number of families that require such a high level of support for anything like the length of time that support may be needed.

In conclusion we need to recognize that whilst in our policy statements and in our professional aspirations we may talk about the importance of meeting the needs of children within drug-dependent households, the reality is that we do not have anything like the level of resources to support the number of children that we now know are living within those circumstances. As a result despite our fine words and fine policies the majority of children living within drug-dependent households still have to cope (or not) on the basis of their own resources. There is though an alternative to how we are responding to the problem of parental drug dependence.

A Radical Alternative for Meeting the Needs of Children in Drug-Dependent Families

The first element of a radically different approach to meeting the needs of children in drug-dependent families is to recognize the incompatibility between parental drug dependence and child welfare. Second is to recognize that it is the needs of children, not their parents, which are paramount. The challenge for services working in accordance with those two principles is to work to take the drugs out of the families or to take the children out of the families. Allowing children to continue to be exposed to the reality of their parent's drug dependency is to violate both of those principles.

But how long should services leave children to live in the midst of their parent's drug dependency? This is a difficult issue which is made all the more problematic as a result of the fact that the parent's recovery from their drug problems can take many years to come about whilst the damage to children arising from that exposure misuse may occur within a matter of months. If we are going to adhere to the principle that it is the rights of the child that are paramount (rather than those of the parent) then we have to recognize that the critical time frame here has to be that of the child rather than that of the slowly recovering drug-dependent parent. We have to ensure that parents have access to high-quality drug-dependency treatment that can enable them to overcome their drug dependency. What we cannot do is to afford the parents the luxury of a long period of time over which their recovery may or may not actually occur before intervening decisively to protect the children involved. To do that would be to leave the children for too long within circumstances where they are being harmed.

We need to place a clear time frame on parents capacity to resolve their drug problem; conveying to parents in the clearest of terms that they have a fixed time frame, say 18 months, over which to cease their drug use or face the reality of services planning for the permanent relocation of their children within non-drug-dependent households. That suggestion sounds harsh for many people and the preferred response may be for services to work with addict parents, encouraging them to reduce their drug use and gradually take on their rightful parenting responsibilities. The trouble with the latter approach is that whilst it may seem more respectful of the needs of the adult it may leave the child exposed to the harms of their parent's drug dependency for many years.

Within the United States the Adoption and Safe Families Act has written into Federal law that where a child has been fostered for more than 15 of the last 22 months parents will be given a specific time period to resolve their problems or face having their child placed permanently for adoption. The Adoption and Safe Families Act arose out of the recognition that where children were being continuously moved within the child-care system, they were in danger of being further harmed as a result of the lack of consistency in their care. Within the United Kingdom we do not have legislation approximating to the Adoption and Safe Families Act and as a result there is no time frame attached to parents' efforts at resolving their drug use, no official limit placed on the length of time that services will work with parents, and no limit on the number of times that a child may be temporarily fostered as a result of their parent's drug use. The outcome may well be a system of support to vulnerable families that sounds preferable but which leaves most children unsupported. The benefits of the Adoption and Safe Families legislation is that it clarifies for everybody involved (parents, children and services) that where children are being harmed as a result of their parent's drug use that the parents themselves have to resolve that behaviour or lose their children. A further benefit of the Adoption and Safe Families Act is also the clear obligation that it places upon services to work with drug-dependent parents to enable them to overcome their dependency and to take up their parental responsibilities.

The Problem of Scale

Behind all of the plans to help children exposed to their parent's drug dependency is the issue of numbers. If the current estimates of there being in excess of 300,000 children in the United Kingdom with one or both parents with a serious drug problem is accurate then we are facing a massive challenge in terms of the sheer scale of the problem. Moreover if the number of children living within the circumstances of their parent's chaotic drug habit is itself hampering the capacity of services to respond to the needs of these children then there is a need somehow to reduce the numbers of children being born to drug-dependent parents. If the issue of removing children from drug-dependent households is regarded as controversial, no less so is the option of trying to reduce the numbers of children born to drug-dependent parents in the first place. Within the United States there are projects where addict women are paid cash in return for agreeing to be sterilized. It is difficult to see that such a move would ever be socially acceptable within the United Kingdom. However, what may be acceptable is to offer female drug users payment in return for their use of long-term contraception. For many people this will be a suggestion that is itself socially unacceptable. If we reject that suggestion out of hand we need to be able to offer an alternative means of providing the level of support to the number of children that we believe are now being exposed to their parent's chaotic drug habit. Paying female addicts to use long-term contraception is unquestionably controversial and at some fundamental level offends our own sense of the right of the individual to choose when to have a family and for that choice to be unfettered by the state. However if it is the state, rather than the adult addict, that has to meet the needs of the children within these families, then perhaps there is no alternative to seeking some means of reducing the numbers of children being born to drug-dependent parents.

Finally, if children are being left within the circumstances where they continue to be exposed to their parent's drug dependency, then we need a better way of knowing what kind of risks the children are being exposed to on a day-to-day basis. At the moment our best way of finding this out is for social work staff to interview children on a periodic basis. However, this is by no means guaranteed to reveal the reality of what the children involved are indeed being exposed to. As an alternative we may need to consider whether it is appropriate to install within the family homes where drug users are looking after dependent children some means, whereby the children can report their concerns or through which social work staff can obtain a sense of what is happening within the family home without relying upon either the child or the parent disclosing what is happening. To suggest that closed circuit television should be placed within the family home of addict parents would be to offend many people on the basis that such a move would compromise the adult's rights to privacy. But which is the more important right here that of the child to be free from harm or that of the adult to a private life? If we judge that the adult's privacy is more important than the rights of the child then we should not criticize social work staff for failing on occasion to identify the risks to children. If we say that the rights of the child are paramount then we should also recognize that some level of invasion of the adult's privacy might be necessary to fully protect the children involved.

Conclusion

There is a deep fear on the part of services and policy makers at requiring drug-dependent parents to choose between their children and their drugs. The fear in part has to do with the possibility that many parents may choose to continue to use illegal drugs over their children and in the process deliver a massive child care problem to the state. That fear is almost certainly impeding our ability to help the children within these families. On the basis of the available statistics, the majority of these families are already breaking down with the result that many of these children are already being cared for by other adults. At the moment we have very little idea as to where the majority of these children are living or who is looking after them. The proposal for services to be much clearer about the harms drug-dependent parents are causing children, and of the importance of forcing parent's to choose between their children and their drug use, may be to formalize a process that is already occurring. Shifting policy in this direction however would amount to nothing less than a revolution in how we are tackling parental drug dependence. If we fail in this regard then irrespective of all of our fine sounding words and well-intentioned policy statement children will continue to pay the price of their parent's drug addiction. In due course, those young people will have children of their own and, in all probability many of their children will suffer the same neglect and abuse and another generation of children will be harmed in the process.

KEY DISCUSSION QUESTIONS

1. Is parental drug dependency compatible with providing a safe and nurturing environment for children to grow up within?

2. Do social work services currently have the capacity to support the number of children that we now estimate are growing up within the circumstances of their parents chaotic drug use?

3. In meeting the needs of the children of chaotic drug-dependent parents whose time frame should apply that of the child who may be harmed within a matter of months or that of the parent who may take many years to recovery from their drug dependency?

4. Should we be more prepared to remove children in circumstances of parental drug dependency?

5. Where does the greater harm lie? In intervening within a family where no intervention was required or in failing to intervene within a family where there was a need for such intervention?

6. Is it ethical socially acceptable to try to reduce the number of children born to drug-dependent parents, or is this an intervention too far?

7. Is placing cctv equipment within the homes of addict parents an invasion of the adults privacy or an important means of finding out what is happening to the children involved?

Chapter 7

Drug Legalization: Solution or Social Problem?

Introduction

Drug law reform is sweeping across the countries of central and southern America. The Argentine Supreme Court has ruled that it is unconstitutional to prosecute individuals for possessing drugs for their personal use. The court argued that adults should be free to make lifestyle decisions without the intervention of the state (Jenkins 2009). Mexico is similarly considering the benefits of decriminalizing drug possession as it faces the reality of drug gangs that are more heavily armed than the national military and 5,376 drug-related murders in a single year (BBC News 9 December 2008). It has been reported that Brazil and Ecuador are also proposing to follow the Latin American route to drug decriminalization and in due course perhaps full legalization (Jenkins 2009). In 2001, Portugal decriminalized the possession of small amounts of illegal drugs for personal use. Within the context of these developments questions are being increasingly asked whether drug legalization or some form of decriminalization should now be pursued more broadly. Writing in the *Observer* newspaper the respected philosopher John Gray has argued strongly in favour of legalization:

> In rich societies like Britain, the US and continental Europe, the drug war has inflicted multiple harms. Since the inevitable result is to raise the price of a serious drug habit beyond what many can afford, penalising use drives otherwise law-abiding people into the criminal economy. As well as criminalising users prohibition exposes them to major health risks. Illegal drugs can't easily be tested for quality and toxicity and overdosing are constant risks. Where the drugs are injected there is the danger of hepatitis and HIV being transmitted. Again criminalising some drugs while allowing a free market in others distracts attention from those that are legal and harmful as alcohol. Whilst it is certainly possible that legalisation could see more people take drugs a drug users life would be much safer and healthier than at present. (Gray 2009)

These views echo those of the influential broadsheet journalist Simon Jenkins:

> The policy of deploying the full might of the state against the production, supply and consumption of illegal drugs has not worked. Pretty much anyone in the developed world who wants to take illicit substances can buy them. Those purchases fund a multi-billion dollar global industry that has enriched mighty criminal cartels, for whom law enforcement agencies are mostly just a nuisance, rarely a threat. Meanwhile, the terrible harm that drug dependency does to individuals and societies has not been reduced. Demand and supply flourish. (Jenkins 2009)

For these commentators, and many others, the failure of prohibitionist drug policies to reduce levels of drug use is often cited as the strongest argument in favour of legalization. But how persuasive are the arguments for liberalizing the drug laws in this way and what might be the downside of drug legalization or decriminalization?

The Arguments For Legalization

Key to the arguments for legalization is the claim that drug prohibition has failed to effectively deal with the drugs issue. The evidence for that failure is largely presented in terms of the claim that illegal drugs are widely available within most countries; that between 60% and 70% of crime may be connected to the drugs trade; that prohibition artificially pushes up the price of illegal drugs so as to make those drugs literally worth more than their weight in gold; that prohibition drives drug users underground exposing them to a variety of health risks; that the drugs are produced, stored and transported in uncontrolled and unhygienic conditions and as a result often pose a serious health risk to users; and that prohibition creates a tier of super rich criminals who are prepared to trade in illegal drugs. Legalization or decriminalization, it is often said, is an answer to most, if not all, of these problems.

But is the case for the failure of prohibitionist drug policies well made or poorly made? Within the United Kingdom there are estimated to be approaching 400,000 problematic drug users. Large as that figure may sound it still only represents around 1.0% of the UK population. Similarly, on the basis of the 2008/09 British Crime Survey it has been estimated that there are around 980,000 people aged from 16 to 59 who have used cocaine in the last year, around 586,000 who have used ecstasy in the last year, and around 203,000 who have used hallucinogens in the last year. There are also estimated to be around 2.5 million who have used cannabis in the last year. Whilst again these are large numbers, the estimate of the number of people in the United Kingdom using cocaine in the last year only amounts to 3% of the adult population, the figure for ecstasy is 1.8%, and the figure for cannabis 7.9%. These percentages are all a long way from the percentage of the population consuming the tobacco or alcohol. Smith and Foxcroft (2009) have reported that in 2006, 71% of men and 56% of women in the United Kingdom drank alcohol at least one day in the last week (Smith and Foxcroft 2009). According to the Office for National Statistics (2009) 21% of the adult population in the United Kingdom are smokers. Compared to the percentages of the population using these legal drugs the level of use of the illegal drugs is tiny. Far from standing as evidence of the failure of restrictive drug laws the low level of illegal drug use in society may then be the clearest indication of the success of those laws in confining illegal drug use to such a small proportion of the adult population.

There is little doubt that one of the by-products of making certain drugs illegal is to increase the price of those substances when they are then sold on the black market. As a result of that price inflation the sale of illegal drugs unquestionably makes a relatively small number of people exceedingly wealthy. Moreover those who sit at the top of drug dealing networks are also likely to be hugely influential in their own communities and beyond, ruling though a combination of fear and financial muscle. The fact of their wealth, however, hardly seems reason enough to legalize the drugs trade. What would seem more appropriate is to ensure that drug enforcement agencies are rapidly able to identify and target those individuals and freeze their financial assets pending a clear examination as to the source of their fantastic wealth.

Within the United Kingdom, the Transform Drug Policy Foundation which supports drug legalization has published the results of a cost-effectiveness review of drug prohibition and drug regulation which, they argue, makes a powerful financial case for legalization (Transform 2009). The Transform report looked at the possible impact of legalization under four different scenarios: one where the level of heroin and cocaine use following legalization reduced by 50%, one where it remained at the present level, one where it increased by 50%, and a worst-case scenario where it increased by 100%. According to Transform, £13.9B of the estimated total cost of drugs to the United Kingdom (£16.7B) is made up of the criminal justice costs and the cost of drug-related criminality. In the event that heroin and cocaine were legalized these criminal justice costs would reduce massively such that even in the face of a possible 100% increase in the level of heroin and cocaine use there would still be an overall £4.6B cost saving to the United Kingdom. On the face of it this is a powerful case for drugs legalization.

However, the statistics within the Transform report bare closer inspection. Firstly, the proposed worst-case scenario following legalization of a 100% increase in the percentage of the population using heroin and cocaine is highly questionable. A 100% increase in the size of the problematic drug-using population in the United Kingdom would see a rise of just under 1% to just under 2% of the UK population, that is an increase from around 400,000 to 800,000. On the basis of the latest British Crime Survey figures a 100% rise in the level of cocaine use in the last year would see an increase in prevalence from 3% to 6%. On this basis the so-called "worst-case scenario" proposed by Transform actually looks rather modest, particularly given Transform acknowledgement that:

> With the existence of such limited empirical evidence it is difficult to estimate whether prevalence would increase if prohibition were replaced by legal regulatory model, if so by how much, and what the corresponding costs in terms of problem use would be. (Transform 2009: 34)

In the absence of clear evidence as to the likely scale of any increased use of heroin and cocaine, it is important to ensure that modelling a "worst-case" scenario is indeed just that, that is, modelling the worst possible outcome following drug legalization. In this respect it may be more appropriate to calculate the cost to society following legalization of an increase in the prevalence of problematic drug use not from 1% to 2% but from 1% to 10% or 15%.

The response from the advocates of drug legalization to a hypothesized increase of that order in drug use prevalence is simply to say that such an increase would never occur because most people who wish to use illegal drugs are already able to do so. However, the number of people who are willing or inclined to use drugs when those substances are illegal is not necessarily the same as the percentage of people who would be prepared to consume those drugs in the event that they became legal. The scenario that one would need to consider under the so-called "worst possible outcome" model would be one where a major shift in social attitudes towards drug consumption followed on from legalization possibly resulting in a much greater willingness to at least experiment with various forms of drug consumption. It is important to add in a realistic time frame in considering the possible impact of drug legalization and whilst the Transform modelling is limited to the 12 months following legalization a more realistic time frame would be around 10 years. But still the question remains as to whether over that time frame there would be even a remote possibility that the level of heroin use in society could rise above 10%?

Although not an obvious parallel it is interesting to consider the level of opium use in China in the late 1800s and early 1990s following at the time of the Opium Wars:

> By the end of the 1930s, it was estimated that 10 percent of the Chinese nation (about 40 million people) were opium addicts.... Opium poppy growing at the time was still so common as to be found in the suburbs of Canton. Domestic production and importation continued unabated until 1949 when after four years of bitter civil war, the Kuomintang army was defeated by the Communists. Within months of assuming control, in February 1950, the Communist government State Administrative Council banned poppy growing, the production, importation and sale of opium and all narcotics. Only a required quantity of licit medicinal opium was produced under rigorous control. ... Opium stocks were publicly burned, divants were destroyed, dealers were either killed or sent for "political reeducation" in labour camps. Poppy fields were burnt and ploughed. Pipes were publicly destroyed. Opium taking was listed officially as unhealthy anti-social anti-socialist and a capitalist activity. Addicts were not condemned for their vice

but offered medical help and rehabilitation centres were set up. Those who were antagonistic towards treatment were sent to labour camps whilst those who re-addicted were paraded before the public as criminals and imprisoned. Between 1949 and 1953 the addict population dramatically shrank. By 1960 China was virtually free of drug addiction. (Booth 1998: 168/169)

Plainly, one cannot say on the basis of the Chinese experience that the legalization of heroin would result in a similar level of consumption and dependency. What the Chinese experience does reveal is the fact that the 1% figure for current heroin use should not be regarded as an impermeable barrier. Legalization carries with it the very real possibility that over time the prevalence of heroin use within society could increase well beyond its current level.

The argument that is typically directed against the possibility of such an increase in the use of heroin, under a legalized regime, is to emphasize that the government would seek to regulate the heroin market in such a way as to ensure that use of the drug would be remained very limited. That proposal though, somewhat flies in the face of the assertion that restrictive government drug policies have already largely failed to reduce the availability of illegal drugs on the streets. Certainly if one looks at tobacco, where there is a large counterfeit market, the difficulties governments face in regulating a legal product are all too evident. Equally, the existing legal restrictions banning the sale of alcohol to minors is plainly not stopping young people from accessing alcohol.

One way in which it is often proposed to limit the availability of drugs under a regulated market is to assert that medical practitioners would have the responsibility for making drugs such as heroin or cocaine available to those who wished to use them. There is though a deep irony in that proposal given that it was liberal prescribing practices on the part of medical practitioners in the 1950s and 1960s which fuelled the growing heroin problem within the United Kingdom (Spear 2002).

One of the other arguments presented in favour of drug legalization is that this policy would undermine the economic base of the criminal gangs that profit from the drugs market. Whilst legalization would undoubtedly have an impact on the activities of criminal gangs it is difficult to believe that those gangs would simply cease their criminal activities and move into the sphere of legal drug production. What is more likely is that the gangs would continue their involvement in the drugs trade by targeting those individuals who might be excluded from a government-regulated drug market (e.g. young people), or switch the area of their criminal involvement to some other area of illegal activity. Under a regulated drug market then there may well be a need for continuing and possibly even greater criminal justice input to ensure that the market for legal drugs supply was not undermined by the activities of the illegal gangs providing easier and cheaper access to the drugs.

Another of the presumed benefits of a legally regulated drug market is the proposal that this would allow the government to derive substantial tax benefits from drug sales. This hypothesized benefit from legalization might, however, reduce dramatically in practice. In the event that national government were able to impose a tax on the sale of the currently illegal drugs it would be possible for the illegal drug suppliers to offer their product at a reduced price, and in the process undermine legitimate drug sales. National governments could easily find themselves in a price war with the illegal drug producers and suppliers creating, a downward pressure on price that could substantially reduce the tax revenue. Aside from the price war, there is also the question of whether it is right in a moral sense for national governments to derive an income (taxation) from selling what are in effect amongst the most dependency inducing products available.

In terms of the possible costs that could increase under a legalized drug regime, one of the key areas could be the need to substantially expand the provision of drug treatment services. The assumption on the part of those favouring legalization is that any increase in those drug treatment costs would be offset by the cost saving of a reduced enforcement budget. However, the degree to which enforcement spending could be reduced under a legalized drug regime are far from certain, and one could face a situation where drug treatment costs were rising whilst enforcement costs were falling at a slower than anticipated rate resulting in fewer savings than had been expected from legalization.

A further downside of legalizing the currently illegal drugs, and taking a role in regulating the subsequent drug market, is the adverse impact such a move could have on drug prevention efforts. At the present time the message on illegal drugs from government is very clearly focussed on discouraging use, and reducing the harms associated with that use. In a situation where the government was simultaneously seeking to discourage drug use on the part of young people, whilst actively engaged in the business of drug supply, it is hard to see how those prevention efforts would not be undermined.

Heroin Prescribing

Under a regulated drug market substances such as heroin and cocaine could be provided by medical practitioners working within specially designated clinics. This form of provision is already being piloted in the United Kingdom as part of the Random Opiate Injecting Trials being led by the National Addiction Centre in London (Strang et al 2010). These trials entail providing heroin for injection to individuals with a long history of heroin dependency and who have failed to respond to alternative addiction treatments (including substitute prescribing). The early positive results from this trial have been outlined to the national media and have led some politicians to call for the wider use of heroin prescribing (Laurance 2009, Oakeshott 2009, Travis 2009).

The research team involved in this study have stressed that medically prescribed heroin may be an effective treatment for only a tiny proportion of those who have become dependent upon the drug rather than a possible pathway through which a much wider range of individuals could gain access to heroin. One reason why medically prescribed heroin may be deemed appropriate for only a small proportion of the overall heroin-using population (those who have a long-standing dependency on the drug) is because of the anxiety which many doctors would feel at the risk of turning an individual's occasional heroin use into a pattern of long-term chronic use as a result of having made the drug more widely available. Equally, limiting heroin to only a small percentage of individuals who have developed a long-standing dependency may also have the danger of being seen to reward addiction and treatment failure – the message from government being that if you are not dependent on the drug you buy your own heroin, but once you become dependent and failed to respond to other treatments the government will provide the drug to you for free.

Heroin-prescribing schemes have been positively evaluated in a number of international studies in Switzerland (Perneger et al. 1998, Uchtenhagen et al. 1999, Rehm et al. 2005, Nordt and Stholer 2006), Germany (Haasen et al. 2007), the Netherlands (Bammer et al. 2003, Van Den Brink et al. 2003). These studies have found that heroin prescribing is associated with a reduction in individual's drug use, in their risk behaviour, in their likelihood of experiencing an overdose and in their involvement in criminal activities. There are some indications from the Swiss research that heroin prescribing may have resulted in a reduction in the incidence of new cases of heroin use within the country.

Part of the difficulty in interpreting the results from these studies is the problem of identifying the extent to which the positive outcomes are the result of the heroin prescribing or other aspects of the clinical regime – for example, the level of psycho-social support dependent drug users being prescribed heroin were receiving. Research in this area has also failed to indicate whether it is possible to shorten the length of time that drug users remain dependent through the route of heroin prescribing. Heroin prescribing is expensive at around £15,000 per drug user per year compared to around £2,800 per user per year for methadone prescribing. The Royal College of General Practitioners have stated that in their view "there would be no added value from general practitioners prescribing heroin to their patients" (Home Affairs Committee, 2002, Vol iii, Ev 244). By contrast, the National Treatment Agency has stated that prescribing injectable heroin 'may be beneficial for a minority of heroin misusers'.

Within the United Kingdom, the National Treatment Agency has set out a number of key principles which they say should underlie any programme of heroin prescribing including that the programme "must be supported by locally commissioned and provided mechanisms for supervised consumption" and that it should be delivered by specialist doctors (NTA 2003). As Luty has pointed out, however, "mainstream drug treatment services would find it very difficult to create an injectable service in line with current guidelines even if they wished to – which most do not" (Luty 2005).

It is not hard to see why many doctors would be wary of prescribing heroin to addicts for fear that they may be beginning a process from which they would find it extremely difficult to extricate themselves at the point at which they begin to feel that continued prescribing was no longer in their patient's interests. There are probably many doctors who would question whether prescribing heroin to a dependent heroin user actually amounts to treatment in the normal sense of the word even if it resulted in lower levels of drug-use-related risk behaviour. If it was found to be the case that heroin prescribing resulted in sustained long-term benefits for individuals, and ultimately led to significant numbers of drug users ceasing their use of heroin after a period of prescribed use, then it may well be that over time the pressure for wider heroin prescribing would grow and this option would become much more widely available.

In a situation where medical practitioners were prescribing heroin it is easy to see how the pressure might increase for them in due course to also take on prescribing of other drugs, for example cocaine, LSD, ecstasy. Prescribing heroin then could rapidly become the thin end of a wedge of much wider range of drug prescribing that in the end could fundamentally change the role of the doctor. One wonders, for example, whom the addict would turn to in the event that they decided to discontinue their drug use given that their doctor may have become their major drug supplier.

Clearly then there are a range of risks associated with major drug law reform but how have those countries that have changed their drug laws actually fared?

The International Dimension

The country that has come the closest to decriminalizing all forms of illegal drug use is Portugal, which, in 2001, introduced a new law ending the use of penal sanctions for the possession of small amounts of illegal drugs for personal use. This change in the law also involved setting up a system of what are called "drug dissuasion commissions" which the individual would appear before as a way of trying to discourage further drug use. Where it is deemed appropriate these commissions can levy a fine, they can ban the individual from going to certain venues, and they can suspend the individual's right to practice (e.g., where the individual is a doctor). The commissions comprising three people including a social worker, a medical practitioner, and a legal advisor have a responsibility to review each individual case within 72 hours of the individual being referred to the panel. Importantly Portugal has retained the use of legal sanctions, including prison, for those people who are found to be dealing drugs or involved in drug production.

Despite the widespread attention that Portugal has received as a result of its drug law reforms, the evidence on the impact of those changes is far from extensive. Hughes and Stevens (2009) have looked at the data on whether overall levels of drug use in Portugal have changed in the wake of the new laws, and have also interviewed a range of key informants within Portugal on what they judge the effect of the changed drug laws to be. On the basis of the limited quantitative information available, Hughes and Stevens report that:

> ... while cannabis use among young people may have increased, heroin use
> has decreased. The Portuguese authorities have recorded a reduction in the

number of heroin users who are entering treatment for the first time. It seems that initiation into heroin use is falling whilst cannabis use may be rising towards the levels experienced in some other European countries. (Hughes and Stevens 2009: 3)

According to Hughes and Stevens, Portugal has witnessed a dramatic reduction in drug-related deaths falling 59% from 1999 to 2003, and a reduction in drug-related diseases with a 17% reduction in the number of new HIV cases from 1999 to 2003. With regard to drug-related crime it has been noted that the number of crimes "linked strongly to drugs" actually rose by 9% from 1999 to 2003 (Tavares et al. 2005). On the basis of the interviews with key informants there would appear to be considerable good will within Portugal towards the changes in drug laws. However, Hughes and Stevens caution against the idea that the Portugal offers a template for other countries to follow by way of drug law reform:

> The Portuguese experience cannot provide a definitive guide to the effects of decriminalisation of drugs but only indications of the results of decriminalisation in the specific Portuguese context. It is not possible to tell the extent to which changes were caused by decriminalisation or the wider drug strategy. (Hughes and Stevens 2009: 9)

In contrast to the liberalization of the drug laws in Portugal, Sweden decided to toughen its drug laws in the late 1960s as a way of avoiding what was seen to be a rising tide of drug use within a number of European countries. Antonio Maria Costa, head of the United Nations Office of Drugs and Crime, has commented positively on what Sweden has achieved as a result of adopting a zero tolerance drug policy:

> Drug use in Europe has been expanding over the past three decades. More people experiment with drugs and more people become regular users, with all the problems this entails for already strained national health systems. There are thus suggestions, at the European level, that drug polices have failed to contain a widespread problem. Sweden is a notable exception. Drug use levels among students are lower than in the early 1970s. Lifetime prevalence and regular drug use amongst students and among the general population are considerably lower than in the rest of Europe. In addition, bucking the general trend in Europe drug abuse has actually declined in Sweden over the last five years. (Costa 2006: 5)

The goal of Swedish drug policy from the late 1960s has not simply been to contain its drug problem but rather to create a society free from the use and trade in illegal drugs. In the early to mid-1960s Sweden was pursuing rather liberal drug policies, including allowing drug users to determine the quantities of opiates and amphetamines prescribed to them by their doctor. The Swedish heroin-prescribing initiative came to be judged as a failure by the late 1960s and was eventually closed down. In the 2-year period from 1965 to 1967 there were 3,300,000 dosages of amphetamines and 600,000 dosages of opiates provided to around 150 drug users registered with the programme. It was known at the time that many of those who were attending the clinic were distributing their medication to other drug users who were not attending the clinic (UNODC 2007). There were indications over the 2-year period of the project that the number of individuals arrested by the police with signs of drug injecting was increasing – rising from 20% in 1965 to 33% in 1967. The worry at that time was not simply that the project was failing to reduce the level of drug injecting in Stockholm, but that it may actually have begun to fuel an increase in injecting (Bejerot 1975). The project was formally closed by the Swedish government in 1967 following the fatal overdose of a young woman who had been participating within the prescribing clinic.

From the late 1960s drugs policy in Sweden dramatically changed. One of the most influential figures in bringing forward a change in Swedish drug policy was Nils Bejerot who had undertaken research within Swedish prisons, and who repeatedly urged the Swedish government to adopt a zero tolerance approach towards illegal drug use. According to Bejerot it was only by adopting a tough stance in relation to illegal drugs that Sweden had any chance of avoiding what he saw as the impending "addiction epidemic". In 1969 the Swedish government approved a ten-point plan for tackling the problem of illegal drugs which included a substantial increase in government spending on the drugs issue, the agreement to use wire-tapping to gather intelligence on the operation of the drugs trade, increasing the legal penalties for drug offences, improving the link between services and increasing the provision of abstinence-based drug treatment services. The Swedish drug policy was strengthened further in 1978 with the expressed statement that

> The struggle against drug abuse may not be limited only to reducing its existence but must aim at eliminating drug abuse. Drug abuse can never be accepted as a part of our culture. (ONDCP 2007: 105)

And further that:

> The basis for the struggle must be that society cannot accept any other use of narcotic drugs than what is medically motivated. All other use is abuse and must be forcefully be opposed. (ONDCP 2007: 105)

In addition to strengthening enforcement and treatment, the Swedish government also committed itself to facilitating a massive cultural shift away from the previous growing tolerance around illegal drugs. The necessity as seen at the time was to make everybody at every level in Swedish society responsible for changing the perception of illegal drugs:

> everybody who comes in contact with the problem must be engaged, the authorities can never relieve individuals from personal responsibility and participation. Efforts by parents, family, and friends are especially important. Also schools and non-governmental organisations are important instruments in the struggle against drugs. (ONDCP 2007: 19)

Further changes in Swedish drug polices came in the late 1980s and early 1990s with the stipulation that drug use itself, not simply drug dealing, was a criminal offence with police officers empowered to require a blood or urine sample in circumstances where they suspected an individual to have been using illegal drugs. In the period since the 1990s, Swedish drug policy has continued its zero tolerance approach in the commitment to reduce the number of people using illegal drugs, to increase the number of people ceasing their drug use and to reduce the availability of illegal drugs within Sweden.

Do Drug Policies Make a Difference to Drug Consumption?

It has been suggested that drug policies in general have only a limited impact on overall levels of illegal drugs use (Transform 2009). Nevertheless, over the period that restrictive drug policies have been applied in Sweden, the country has bucked the European trend of escalating drug use. The largest study of drug use amongst school students in Europe is the ESPAD survey undertaken in 35 countries and involving more than 100,000 students aged from 15 to 16 (Hibell et al. 2007). Levels of lifetime cannabis use amongst students in this study is 45% for the Czech Republic, 31% for France, 28% for the Netherlands, 33% for

Switzerland, 29% for the United Kingdom and 7% in Sweden. The percentage of pupils who perceived cannabis to be "very easy" or "fairly easy" to obtain ranged from 66% for the Czech Republic, 42% for France, 49% for the Netherlands, 51% for the United Kingdom and 28% for Sweden. Lifetime use of illicit drugs other than cannabis by pupils ranges from 11% for Austria, 11% for France, 16% for the Isle of Man, 9% for the United Kingdom and 4% for Sweden. The consistent picture across these data is that of lower levels of illegal drug use amongst young people in Sweden than amongst the other European countries studied. Indeed most of the other countries included within the ESPAD research would simply marvel at the possibility of restricting illegal drug use amongst their own young people to that found in Sweden.

The United Nations Office on Drugs and Crime produces an annual review of drug statistics from across the world for the 15–64 age range. In the 2009 World Drugs Report the annual prevalence for opiates misuse across 34 European countries ranges from a high of 1.68 for Scotland down to one of the lowest recorded levels of 0.17 for Sweden. The figures for cocaine abuse ranges from a high of 2.0 for Monaco down to 0.5 for Sweden; the figure for cannabis use ranges from a high of 10.0 for Monaco down to one of the lowest for Sweden at 2.1. The annual prevalence for ecstasy across 34 European countries ranges from a high of 1% for Estonia down to a low of 0.2 for Sweden. The consistent picture across these drug prevalence data is of Sweden having a smaller drug problem than almost all of the European countries listed. These data do not prove that the low level of drug abuse in Sweden is attributable to the restrictive drug policies within that country, but they do show that there is nothing inevitable about the high level of illegal drug use that is found in many other European countries.

Conclusions

For a country to enjoy a level of illegal drug use akin to that in Sweden it may well be necessary to adopt a similar range of drug policies. This may well mean a shift from perceiving the main aim of drug policies to be about reducing or minimizing the harm associated with illegal drugs to substantially reducing drug use itself; recognizing that illegal drug use poses a major threat to society rather than seeking to accommodate to that problem. It may be necessary to adopt tougher enforcement policies, abstinence-focussed treatment and widespread prevention.

It may only be possible to reduce the levels of illegal drug use in any society by succeeding in changing the perception of illegal drug use as someone else's problem to perceiving it as a problem for society as a whole such that parents, employers, schools, politicians, the media and young people are all engaged in tackling the creeping social acceptance of illegal drugs and working towards reducing the overall level of illegal drugs use.

Whatever the financial gain associated with the policy of legalization or decriminalization (and these may well have been exaggerated) there is an acknowledged risk that such a shift in a country's drugs laws could result in a significant rise in the overall level of drug use. By contrast, the zero tolerance approach towards illegal drugs holds out the possibility of reducing the overall level of drug consumption without the risk of a marked increase in drug usage. In these terms then Sweden may offer a better template for other countries to tackle their own drug problems than Portugal.

KEY DISCUSSION QUESTIONS

1. To what extent is it desirable or achievable for a country to aim to rid itself of illegal drugs?
2. Are there benefits in a country aiming to become drug free even if it is accepted that this is an unachievable goal?
3. One of the consequences of a country adopting restrictive drug laws is that a significant sector of its population will acquire a criminal record at a young age – is there a way in which this can be avoided without going down the road of legalization?
4. If a country were to legalize all drugs what would stand as the best evidence that such a policy had worked and what would stand as evidence of the policy having failed?
5. How reversible is the policy of drug legalization?
6. Under a fully legalized regime how widespread could drug use become and what might be the most effective barrier guarding against the proliferation of such drug use within a legalized regime?

Chapter 8

The Politics of Drugs Research: A Journey into the Cold

Introduction

There is a hidden controversy in the world of drugs policy that is rarely acknowledged and hardly ever discussed. It is a controversy that became a global news story in the winter of 2009 when the British Home Secretary dismissed his chief drugs advisor Professor David Nutt. That controversy concerns the relationship between the science and the politics of drugs research and it is a controversy that runs very deep.

For a variety of reasons researchers rarely write about their experience of undertaking studies that brings them into conflict with government officials and others in authority. The impression that researchers feel more comfortable conveying is one where they apply for research grants, undertake their studies and report their findings. The simplicity of that image conveys an impression of research as a largely trouble-free process of incremental illumination and scientific advance. It is an image that in relation to drugs, research can be as far from the reality as it is possible to get. This chapter draws on aspects of my own research to illustrate some of the difficulties and challenges that one can face in undertaking research that questions the orthodoxy of establishment opinion. As I will show in this chapter, those difficulties can surface at any point in the research process, from seeking funding, to undertaking research, to presenting findings, and to stimulating public debate. Each of these moments in the research process can generate flash points of conflict between researchers and those in authority. However, as the health service researcher Professor David Hunter has noted:

> We need research and analysis of the type that both challenges and seeks to understand the nature of policy and its impact – that is, strong policy research that is prepared to speak truth to power and occasionally to rock the boat. Otherwise we will continue to accumulate knowledge and stockpile research findings that simply tell us what we already know and goodness knows we have enough of these already. But if that is all we do as researchers, then we are seriously failing in our moral duty to speak truth to power. (Hunter 2008: 43)

As this chapter will show, the reality of "speaking truth to power" can be discomforting and costly both professionally and personally. However, unless researchers are prepared to openly describe the difficulties they experience in speaking truth to power, the scientific contribution to public policy debate will be less than it should be and those in authority will be less well served by science than they need to be.

One of the few researchers to have been prepared to describe the challenges of undertaking research on a politically sensitive topic is Allyson Pollock who, along with a number of colleagues, has undertaken research on the impact of the private finance initiative on the UK National Health Service (see Pollock 2004: 221). That research brought Pollock into direct conflict with both political figures and senior civil servants. As Pollock has described it the pressure on her research unit "was destabilising and time-consuming. Much of our work had to be put on hold while the unit fought for survival. This, no doubt, was the object of the attack" (Pollock 2006: 220). From reading her experience, it appears that when a government feels that one of its main policies is being attacked it can all too easily find itself discrediting the science.

This reveals something about the experience of undertaking research on a sensitive topic and the reality of presenting challenging and critical findings to those in authority. In the remainder of this chapter I will describe those occasions when my own research has brought me into conflict with authority and the exile that one can find oneself in when one pushes unwelcome findings on to the professional, political and public arena.

Methadone – the Quick Road to Controversy

One of the first controversial reports I produced involved looking at drug users' views of prescribed methadone. For some of the drug users I interviewed, methadone was spoken of as a life saver; a prescribed drug that had enabled them to develop a level of stability in their lives that had been largely absent in the midst of their dependence on illegal drugs. For others however, methadone was described as a drug that had compounded their addiction and made their lives infinitely worse. The report I produced on the basis of those interviews was titled "Methadone: Life Saver or Life Sentence?" to reflect those contrasting views. I presented the paper at an academic conference in Scotland and included the analysis in a book I was writing on the recovery from dependent drug use (McIntosh and McKeganey 2002).

Following the academic conference a number of the newspapers in Scotland covered the story of the drug users' critical views of methadone. Within days of the articles appearing I was asked to attend one of the main drug treatment agencies in Glasgow to explain the report I had written. I arrived at the agency on a Saturday morning and was shown into a meeting room where the staff were assembled. Once through the polite introductions, the questions came thick and fast: Why had I used the term "addict" to refer to the drug users I had interviewed? Why had I used the term "life sentence" to refer to methadone? Why had I published the report before it had been peer reviewed? Why had I sought the media coverage of my research and why couldn't I see how much damage I was doing to the people I was researching? I asked one of the staff members what term they would prefer me to use when writing about my respondents. "We use the term drug user" was the immediate reply, "addict or drug abuser serves to stigmatize our clients and makes their lives that much more difficult". The term "drug user", I said, "makes it sound as if the people you are treating are in control of their drug use when in reality they are utterly dependent on the drugs they are using". As the meeting progressed the gap between my sense of what I had written and the views of the assembled staff became steadily greater and the session ended with very little sense of a common understanding. If that had been my first taste of the conflict that drugs research can lead one into I knew that it was not going to be the last.

What Do Drug Users Want from Treatment: Abstinence or Harm Reduction?

The next point where I became forcefully aware of the controversy that drugs research can generate arose in the context of an evaluation of drug treatment services in Scotland. As part of the research my colleagues and I had asked drug users what changes in their drug use they were seeking to achieve as a result of having made contact with a drug treatment agency. At the point, months earlier, when my research team had been designing the questionnaire we would use in this research, the question about drug users' aspirations from treatment did not strike me as particularly controversial. In due course, however, the answer to that question turned out to be one of the most controversial areas of my research.

By far the largest proportion of the thousand plus drug users we interviewed said that they had only one goal in mind – which was to become drug free (McKeganey et al. 2004). In contrast, only a tiny proportion of those surveyed said that they were looking for harm reduction support along the lines of advice as to how to use their drugs with lower risk, or identifying forms of safer drug use. The fact that most of the drug users interviewed expressed a wish to become drug free indicated that in their aspirations at least, they were at odds with the predominant direction of drug treatment services in Scotland which to this day are heavily weighted towards harm reduction.

As I began to discuss the research results with various colleagues, I constantly found myself having to defend the study we were undertaking and the line of analysis. Academics, drug treatment specialists and civil servants all variously advised me that the analysis could stir controversy and sow the seeds of discontent undermining a fledgling consensus in the world of addictions treatment. To me that sounded an inadequate reason not to explore what drug users themselves wanted to get out of treatment and for that reason I continued to pursue the line of enquiry. I presented an early version of the analysis of drug users' aspirations to a cross party group of politicians at the Scottish Parliament. Halfway through my presentation the chair interrupted me to say that he had "heard enough already about abstinence". A few months later I prepared a paper reporting the results of this analysis for one of the leading addiction journals. In due course the editor wrote to me to say that the paper had been rejected. According to the referees, the analysis of what drug users wanted to get out of their treatment was largely predictable. The paper was subsequently published in a different academic journal and was the subject of an international discussion involving a range of academics and drug policy commentators (McKeganey et al. 2004).

Once published it was soon clear to me that the paper had touched a raw nerve. The Scottish Drugs Forum which represents the views of drug users and the voluntary sector, and which is a strong supporter of the harm reduction approach to drug treatment, described the research as "unhelpful and manipulative" (BBC 2004). A presentation of the results of the paper at a meeting of addiction psychiatrists drew strong criticism; the analysis, it was claimed, pointed to nothing more revealing than the "obvious finding" that people who contact drug treatment services say they want to become drug free. I sensed, however, that the negativism towards the paper ran a good deal deeper than the claim that its findings were obvious.

As a result of the press coverage that followed the academic publication, politicians in both Scotland and England had picked up on the results of the analysis. It was clear that within the political sphere questions were beginning to be asked about whether drug treatment services were indeed sufficiently focused on enabling drug users to become drug free or whether they were too focused on maintaining drug users in a state of continuing dependence. At a medical conference, where I presented the results of the analysis, a number of doctors expressed their annoyance at the fact that politicians were beginning to express critical comments about the goals of drug treatment. The view of those doctors was that politicians had no right to interfere in this area and that those who were stirring their interest were causing considerable harm to the field.

In a follow-up analysis to the paper on drug users' aspirations I looked at how many drug users actually managed to become drug free after nearly 3 years after they had started their addictions treatment. In the case of those receiving methadone the proportion was around 3% whilst for those receiving residential rehabilitation approaching 30% were drug free (McKeganey et al. 2004). Once the academic paper setting out these results was published, the Scottish media began reporting the findings. Many of the articles were stinging in their criticisms of drug treatment services. *The Sunday Times* ran the headline "Methadone Programme Fails 97% of Heroin Addicts" (Womersley 2006). *The Scotsman* newspaper ran a major article reporting that Methadone was 96.6% Ineffective (Macmahon 2006). Within that article Annabel Goldie, leader of the Scottish Conservatives, was quoted as saying:

> Methadone, which is meant to be a bridge, is no such thing as these findings sharply and disturbingly reveal. The way forward, if we are serious about reducing drug addiction in Scotland and helping to keep more people off drugs, is to expand rehabilitation facilities. (Macmahon 2006)

In the same article a spokesperson from the Scottish Government provided their comment on the research:

> "there is no one size fits all approach for those seeking to come off drugs" and the Executive are committed to expanding the range of available treatment options. (Macmahon 2006)

An earlier article in *The Scotsman* newspaper had produced a similar comment from the government indicating their growing irritation with the results of the research:

> It is high time we ended the unhelpful obsession in trying to prove whether abstinence or harm reduction strategies are best. The most effective treatment will always depend on the circumstances of the individual addict there is no "one size fits all" solution. (Gordon 2006)

Surprisingly at this time I was invited to meet with Scotland's First Minister whose office had issued its own statement on the results of my research:

> The First Minister respects the work of Neil McKeganey. He is in no doubt that these issues are among the most pressing in Scotland and he is as frustrated as the public about people being in long-term programmes rather than becoming drug free. (Barnes 2006: 1)

In due course the First Minister announced that he was going to expand the residential rehabilitation sector in Scotland and initiate an independent review of Scotland's methadone programme.

Called to Account

The low point in my relationship with civil servants came in the context of an evaluation into a Scottish-based drugs counselling project. The early results from the evaluation were far from promising; the project was struggling to contact its target group and suffering from a lack of managerial clarity. An interim report outlining these problems was circulated to the health board funding the project and to the government department funding the research. A planned meeting of the grant holders on the study provided an opportunity to review the progress of the research and consider the difficulties that had already been identified in how the project was working.

Two weeks before the planned grant holder meeting I was telephoned by the civil servant overseeing the research and asked if it would be all right for her to attend the grant holder meeting. This was not an unusual request and it was easy to extend her an invitation. A few days later I received a further telephone call from same the civil servant asking if it would be acceptable for her to attend the meeting with her line manager. Again it was easy to agree to this request. The following day I received another call from the civil official asking if it would be possible for a senior civil servant to chair the meeting and for one of their secretarial staff to take the minutes. Although this was beginning to sound rather heavy handed it was hard to decline the request.

A few days before the meeting was scheduled to take place a colleague sent me a copy of his invitation to the meeting. The emailed invitation had been circulated to a wide range of people inside and outside of the government and including the manager of the project we were evaluating. Along with an invitation to the meeting, the email contained a request from the civil servant to be supplied with any critical comments on my own work and promising to brief any complainant about my response once the meeting had concluded.

I was shocked by the content of the email. I felt as if my position was being undermined. By circulating the email to the manager of the project we were evaluating I was concerned that the research has been jeopardized. If in due course we produced a final report that was critical of the management style within the project, in my view the project manager could simply cite this email as proof that the Scottish government itself had lost faith in the research team undertaking the evaluation.

In the grant holder meeting, I was asked to provide an account of the progress of the research so far. In my opening presentation, I asked the chair for clarification as to whether the meeting was confidential to those who were in attendance or whether it was an open meeting. The chair was clearly puzzled by my question. On an overhead projector I put up an image of the email inviting me to the meeting, which made no mention of the request from the civil servant for critical comments on my own work. I then showed an image of the email that had been sent to me by my colleague which contained the request for critical comments on my own work along with the promise to brief any complainants once the meeting had concluded. The first email, I explained, made it appear that the meeting was limited to those in attendance, whilst the second effectively opened the meeting to anyone who provided adverse comment on my work. I ended my opening presentation by asking why the civil servant manager of the research study had chosen to send an email that had effectively undermined the very research she was supposed to be managing.

The meeting ended with the civil servant who had sent the original email asking that I send to her every email that I had written and received in connection with the research project in both hard copy and the electronic file.

Over the next few weeks I received numerous further emails and official letters from the civil servant, most of which were copied to colleagues within the Scottish Government. For a number of weeks I tried to deal with this correspondence without involving other colleagues. I slept fitfully and often woke in the middle of the night rehearsing the response that I would then draft the following day. Each morning at work when I checked my mail I consciously looked for the all too familiar envelope from the government. If there were such a letter I would set it aside and open it days later. This was the only way that I felt able to control the situation. Further emails came from the civil servant with the last one stating that I would "be hearing from her colleagues" in due course. At that point I sent a one-line message back to the civil servant, copied to all of those who had been included in the circulation list of her last email to me, stating simply "there is such a thing as harassment". From that point on I did not receive another email, phone call or letter from the civil servant in question.

I realized at that point that I needed to alert senior managers at the University of Glasgow about what was happening. The response from within the University was that the research contract needed to be terminated on the basis that it was unacceptable for any academic to be working under the level of pressure I was experiencing from the government. The university duly wrote to the Scottish Government terminating the contract and explaining that the University would be happy to refund that portion of the grant that had already been spent on the research to date. The Scottish Government did not request any such repayment.

At the same time that these events were unfolding I received a letter from another civil servant within a different part of the civil service informing me that research I had undertaken for a committee looking into Scotland's prostitution laws was going to be audited. The letter explained that I would be required to provide civil servants with copies of all my interviews with prostitute women, all field notes that I had written, and any other material I had put together in the course of the research. In nearly 20 years of research for the government I had never received such a letter and I could not help but feel that it was connected to the difficulties I was experiencing with civil servants on the other project. I pulled all of the information together and set about the laborious task of removing any personal identifiable information from all of the tapes and all of the field notes that I had written. There was simply no way that I was going to hand over data to the government that would have allowed civil servants to identify women engaged in prostitution. In due course I forwarded the material to the civil servant who had requested the information and wrote a letter of resignation from the Scottish Government committee on which I had been asked to sit reviewing the prostitution laws in Scotland. Weeks later I received a letter from the Scottish Government informing me that my work had passed the audit. The results of this research were later published in McKeganey (2006).

Forecasting the UK Drug Problem

This research was undertaken as part of the UK Foresight "Brain Science and Addiction Project". The project involved an evidence-based assessment of what the UK drug problem might look like in 25 years time. As part of that project my colleagues and I reviewed the growth of the UK drug problem over the last 50 years and considered the possibility that the prevalence curve might continue upwards approaching 1,000,000 problematic drug misusers by 2025. Such an increase would represent a growth in the scale of problematic drug misuse from just less than 1% of the adult population to approaching 3%. In an accompanying narrative my colleagues and I began to explore the possible impact of such a growth in the addict population. Our thinking on this issue was shaped by the view that many of the existing services responding to the drugs problem were already being stretched to breaking point and beyond. For example, it has been estimated that there may be in excess of 300,000 children with drug-dependent parents in the United Kingdom – if only half of those children are being adversely affected by their parent's drug use then that number is already beyond the capacity of social work services to support the families involved. The idea of a twofold or threefold increase in the number of children with addict parents was a shocking prospect with which social work services would be simply unable to cope. Similarly, it has been estimated that at present around 40% of injecting drug users are already Hepatitis C positive – a threefold increase in the numbers of drug injectors who were Hepatitis

C positive would have an impact on the health service that was beyond anything we had seen to date. It has been estimated that between 60% and 70% of crime is connected to drugs misuse – a threefold increase in drug-related criminality would be beyond the capacity of our enforcement agencies to cope without a massive increase in the enforcement budget. Since drugs misuse is already having an enormous impact on the prison system a threefold increase in the numbers of drug-using prisoners would challenge the prison system's capacity beyond breaking point and prisons themselves would simply become holding stations for our addict population.

The review also looked at the possible impact on the economy of a threefold increase in drug user numbers. At the present time the illegal drugs trade generates funding that is being laundered through the legitimate economy. In the event of a threefold increase in the amounts of illegal money flowing into the legal economy there would be a danger that the legitimate economy itself would be undermined by drug money. There would be companies, we reasoned, whose employers had no idea at all that they were working for a business whose origins could be traced back to the drugs trade. In due course it would simply be impossible to distinguish between the legal business world and the illegal business world, at which point the drugs trade would have succeeded in attaining financial respectability. Finally, the report looked at the possibility that upper echelons of the drugs trade would try to secure political influence as a way of protecting their enormous financial resources. In time the very democratic institutions that we largely take for granted within the United Kingdom could come under the influence of the drugs trade possibly through the route of donations to political parties.

As the report setting out these possible impacts was being written I began to ponder how the civil servants would respond to the arguments, and whether they would hold to their promise to publish the state of science reviews. The UK Foresight Programme is avowedly about developing challenging views of the future, but I felt that the report we were about to submit was even more challenging than civil servants would have been expecting. Is it possible, I pondered, that the government could actually publish a report, which suggested that the democratic institutions of government could in due course come to be corrupted by the drugs trade?

As the project moved towards its conclusions the issue of publication began to loom large. I had been asked to submit an executive summary of the review for inclusion within a press pack that would be circulated to those invited to a media briefing. With the executive summary submitted I flew to Malta for a family holiday. Almost immediately on landing in Malta my mobile rang – an official from the Foresight team told me that there was a problem with our executive summary and that it might not be included along with the other reviews in the material soon to be released to the press. Over the next few days and on the basis of editorial comments from London I re-wrote parts of the executive summary and faxed these to the Foresight office and took part in lengthy telephone conversations with officials. With the publishing deadline days away, and no decision having been taken on whether to include our report, I began to feel that our work was unlikely ever to see the light of day.

A list of further editorial changes was faxed from London and I realized at that point something that had eluded me in the discussions with officials. The officials with whom I had been discussing changes had kept reassuring me that we were only ever talking about changes to the executive summary. I realized though that all of the changes I had agreed to make to the executive summary would also have to be made to the full report. There was simply no way that it would have been sensible to change the executive summary in key ways and leave the full report intact. I explained this to the officials and said that if they wanted any further changes that they had to make those themselves and publish the review under their name. To the credit of the Foresight Team and the UK Government Chief Scientist, who argued in favour of publication, the decision was taken to include the sociology review in the published material. The officials insisted though that our report include a unique disclaimer on the front cover of the review to the effect that:

> Government notes this independent review of the science, which includes scenarios of possible levels of future problem use. The scenarios range from a decrease in problem users to an increase. The data does not reflect recent Government data. The Government highlights that the latest surveys show that the proportions of 16–24 year olds reporting that they have ever taken any drug has fallen by 13% in comparison to 1998 and the proportion reporting that they have ever taken class A drugs has fallen by 24% in comparison to 1998. This data suggests a recent decrease in levels of use of certain illicit drugs. It should be noted that this paper only looks in detail at the implications of worst-case scenarios. (McKeganey et al. 2005)

An Unwelcome Voice

At the end of 2009 with a new drug strategy in place in Scotland, the Minister with responsibility for drugs matters announced that he was disbanding the main drug advisory committee that had sat for many years and advised successive drugs ministers. The new committee, the minister announced, would facilitate the delivery of the new road to recovery drug strategy and "ask the difficult questions" that would assist in the implementation of the strategy. When I looked at the membership of the committee I was surprised that out of the 17 available places five had been allocated to methadone-prescribing doctors, there was nobody on the committee representing the views of children, nobody from education and nobody from the residential rehabilitation sector. There was only a single policeman on the committee, a single recently retired academic and two places for recovered addicts who could attend meetings on an alternate basis. In an article in *The Scotsman* newspaper I wrote that the composition of this committee was imbalanced, that whatever difficult questions it went on to ask it was unlikely to look first at how to reduce the numbers of addicts in Scotland on methadone and I suggested that just as the Advisory Council on the Misuse of Drugs in England held its meeting in public so might the new Scottish drugs advisory committee (McKeganey 2009).

The minister penned his own article in the following week's newspaper rejecting what he described as my "cynical, snide and misinformed commentary" and insisting that they would not be following my advice (Ewing 2009). The minister's language clearly showed how irritated he had been that I had criticized his new commission. Whatever one feels about the legitimacy or otherwise of the views I had expressed, the message that I took from this was "do not criticize the government and if you criticize the government then you had better expect a vigorous response". No premium then was to be put on critical public debate on how the government was tackling Scotland's drugs problem.

But Does Any of this Matter?

In setting out an autobiographical account of the kind of conflicts that I have been involved in over a 20-year period one question will immediately come to the fore – does any of this matter? Is what

I have written evidence of a cussed academic who fails to listen to wise counsel from others or evidence of a deeper problem to do with how those in authority respond to difficult and challenging research. A more timorous researcher would in all probability not have found himself or herself embroiled within these kinds of disputes, nor perhaps would one who was reliant on the government for their continued employment. But I believe that academic tenure affords a degree of protection when it comes to criticizing government policy and addressing the difficult question of how far one pushes those in authority to confront challenging research findings. As David Hunter has observed, there is a moral dimension to that process:

> Should researchers whose work seriously challenges the prevailing orthodoxy remain neutral of passive bystanders, or become unwitting accomplices in bad faith? Or should they become vocal advocates for what their findings reveal. As researchers we could simply take the view that our job is done once the research is done, and with luck, in the public domain for all to see. It is then for others to use it in seeking to influence policy and practice. But this would be to reject (the) belief that policy analysts, including many researchers, have a moral duty to speak truth to power and in a way that guarantees a hearing. (Hunter 2009: 46)

In my own case many of the difficulties that I have experienced have arisen because of my refusal to simply do the research and "move on". In repeatedly presenting my research findings on drug users' aspirations for abstinence, on the limited achievements of Scotland's national methadone programme, on the failures to meet the needs of children with addict parents I have exasperated many political figures, civil servants and drug treatment professionals. To many of them it will have seemed that I pursued these issues either because of a love of the media or a love of conflict. I know that there have been occasions when my colleagues and I have tended for research contracts from the government only to be told that we did not even make the short list of bidders. There have been other occasions when my colleagues and I have been impeded in our research by methadone-prescribing clinicians who have refused us access to "their patients". Speaking truth to power can be difficult and costly, but the alternative of framing one's research findings in a way that avoids offending those in authority would seem to undermine the very reason to do the research in the first place.

Are You In the Tent or Outside of the Tent?

One of the choices that confront researchers working in the public policy arena is that of deciding where they are going to stand on the "in
the tent outside of the tent" divide. For some of those working in the
public policy arena there is a view that you stand a greater chance of
influencing policy if you are able to secure a position inside the policy tent. For others however, the compromises that may be required
to secure a position inside the tent can seem too great and as a result
they remain on the outside commenting on the public policy decisions
of those inside the tent. Whatever the personal preferences of those
involved, I believe that the very distinction of either being "in the tent
or outside of the tent" harms the public policy process and stifles the
debate on how we may tackle some of our most intractable social
problems.

The clearest example of this occurred recently in the publication in
Scotland of the drug death figures for 2008. The report from the General
Registrar Office in Scotland announced that there had been 576 drug-
related deaths in 2008 – an increase of 26% on the previous year and
the highest recorded total at that point. One might have thought that
the figure would have generated a vigorous public debate on the failure
to reduce the overall level of drug-related mortality in Scotland. In fact
the opposite was the case. *The Herald* newspaper ran a story under the
headline "Drug related death rates rise by 34% in Scotland" (Campsie
2009). The article included a statement from a Scottish government
spokesperson:

> As a legacy of long-term drug misuse over recent decades, drug-related
> deaths may continue to rise over the next few years, especially among older
> men. It's a long-term problem with no single solution. That is why we must
> continue to take action to tackle this issue now and for the long-term.
> (Campsie 2009)

Within the article there was not a single comment from the hundreds of doctors treating addicts in Scotland, nor from any of the
academics studying drug addiction, nor from any of the drug treatment agencies. Within *The Scotsman* newspaper there was a greater
range of voices quoted, but the views expressed were equally uncritical
(Thompson 2009 – 13 August). The Scottish Drugs Forum, a national
drug information charity commented that:

It is difficult to tell exactly why older drug-users are increasingly featuring among the drug death statistics. However, many will have been using drugs – primarily heroin – for a long time. As a result, their physical health will have deteriorated and many will have become increasingly socially isolated over the years. This could make them more vulnerable to accidental or deliberate overdose.

A spokesperson for the Turning Point drugs treatment charity commented that:

> Turning Point Scotland is working to ensure we provide a programme of interventions particularly designed for people who do not engage with support services and are therefore more exposed to the serious health risks, including the risk of overdose by the prolonged and persistent drug use.

The report from the registrar general had included the finding that methadone had been found to be connected to approaching one-third of the addict deaths (General Register Office 2009). Again one might have thought that this statistic would have led to a discussion as to the possible downside of Scotland's methadone programme. The reality was very different. One of the key figures in the Scottish addictions medicine establishment cautioned against the view that Scotland might need to look in detail at its methadone programme. Dr Roy Robertson, chairman of the National Drug Related Death Forum, was quoted as saying:

> Every country that has drug-use problems debates this constantly and incessantly, about the relative value of methadone against the risks. We know that methadone, by and large, is a successful treatment. (Thompson 2009)

Within this article the only voices critical of government drug policy were from the parliamentary opposition parties. Cathy Jamieson, former Justice Minister in the previous Labour administration, was quoted as saying:

> The rise in the number of drug-related deaths is extremely worrying, and we need action from ministers to reverse the trend." She said: "The SNP promised a 20 per cent increase in funding for drugs treatment in their manifesto, but, like so many other promises, they have failed to deliver it. Ministers have also cut budgets to local agencies supporting drug addicts.

Annabel Goldie, Leader of the Scottish Conservatives, was quoted as saying that the Scottish drug-related deaths figures reflected "a wasted decade".

It is impossible to know why there was such reticence to criticize government policy in the face of such dramatic statistics. Part of that reluctance may have had to do with the fear that organizations might lose their funding if they were seen to criticize government policy. For other there may have been a feeling that their position "inside the tent" would have suffered had they made any critical comment. Whatever the reason, the greater loss is in the contraction of the public debate on such an important topic. In the absence of critical commentary an impression is created that the current government must be doing all that it can to reduce drug-related deaths and that only the politically motivated could possibly suggest otherwise.

If we are to reinvigorate the process of public debate we need to recognize that dissent is not something to be guarded against, resisted, punished and stifled but to be encouraged and nurtured. That will mean re-discovering a sense of the value of independent research on the part of those in authority and re-discovering a sense of courage on the part of those undertaking research. It will mean setting aside the "in the tent outside of the tent" divide that favours consensual comment and accepting rather than shackling the critical voice of science as it contributes to that debate.

Conclusions

In this chapter I have described some of the difficulties I have experienced in my research not because I think these events are commonplace but because they reveal something about the challenges one can face in undertaking research on a politically sensitive and controversial subject. The phrase "evidence based policy" trips so easily off the tongue as to make one think that there is always a seat available for researchers at the policy-making table, and that in presenting their evidence researchers will always find a receptive audience from those in authority. The reality, as I have sought to illustrate, can be very different. Researchers sometimes have to work very hard to ensure that their voice is heard and that the evidence they have gathered does indeed get a hearing.

In the wake of the dismissal of the government chief drugs advisor David Nutt, there has been a renewed commitment on the part of government and the science community to try to specify the terms of a relationship that can protect the right of scientists to comment critically on areas of public policy whilst, at the same time, continuing to provide scientific expertise to government. The Sense About Science charity has been actively involved, with government, in trying to agree a core set of principles for the provision of scientific advice to government (Sense about Science 2009). Those principles cover the importance of academic freedom, the importance of ensuring that scientists providing advice to government are able to undertake their work independently of politicians' interests, and that ministers will give proper consideration to advice from scientists – rather than simply reject that advice out of hand where it conflicts with a political priority. It is too early to say whether these principles will enable a healthier relationship to develop between the two spheres of politics and science. On the basis of my own experience it is important to recognize that challenges to the independence of science do not arise solely from those with political power. Indeed whenever scientists are reporting unwelcome findings to those in authority similar issues can arise that can challenge the very heart of the scientific endeavour. The question then becomes whether it is possible for those in authority to relinquish the control they exert over the various aspects of the research process deciding what gets funded, how findings are reported and how the policy debate moves forward?

KEY DISCUSSION QUESTIONS

1. To what extent should drugs research be kept separate from government?
2. Is it possible to truly overcome the divide between being "in the tent and outside of the tent" in the area of public policy?
3. Are there any benefits in the policy divide between being "in the tent and outside of the tent" that what we should seek to nurture?
4. Where should the limits be drawn in the contribution of researchers to public policy debate?
5. Are there occasion when researchers use their authority as scientists to express what are largely personal views and if so how can one ensure that a clear distinction is able to be drawn between the two domains of personal views and scientific views?
6. What are the characteristics of a healthy relationship between science and politics?

Chapter 9

Conclusion:
So What's Morality
Got to Do with It?

Introduction

In this final chapter I would like to look at the moral dimension of our
views and responses to illegal drugs. For the last 20 years our drug policies have been guided by the principle of pragmatism. That principle,
applied to the drugs issue, has rarely been defined but consists largely
in the view that one should accept the inevitability of illegal drug use
and seek to minimize the various harms associated with that use. The
principle of pragmatism, closely associated with the philosophy of harm
reduction, places one about as far from the principle of moral judgement as it is possible to get. Whereas the notion of moral judgement
might characterize drug use as something that ought not to be occurring, a behaviour that offends some deeper moral code, the principle
of pragmatism eschews any such judgement and concentrates solely on
how the harms associated with that behaviour might be reduced.

Stated in this way it is easy to see why those who support the philosophy and practice of harm reduction favour the principle of pragmatism.

In the case of needle and syringe exchange services, for example, the moral questions about whether it is right or wrong to provide individuals with the means to use illegal drugs, or about the rightness or wrongness of the drug using behaviour itself, are set aside in favour of a pragmatic appraisal of the public health benefits associated with reducing drug users' risks of sharing non-sterile injecting equipment.

Much of the current thinking and writing to do with illegal drugs has been heavily influenced by the principle of pragmatism. The principle of pragmatism has been so influential within the drugs sphere that it has become almost a term of abuse to suggest that someone's view of illegal drug use is rooted in a moral view of the world. The principle of pragmatism has also been heavily influential in drug policy terms. Within the UK drug strategy, for example, there is not a single mention of a moral dimension in terms of how we are tackling our drugs problem.

The absence of a moral dimension, and the reluctance to talk about drug misuse in moral terms, is puzzling when one thinks of the enormous harms that arise from the use of illegal drugs. Given the level of harm to individuals, to families and to communities it is odd that we should have become so hesitant about expressing a moral view of the world of illegal drug use. One of the reasons why the principle of pragmatism has become so influential within the drugs sphere has to do with the dominance of the medical or public health model. From within the public health/medical perspective the key questions that one confronts in relation to illegal drugs are to do with reducing the adverse effects of the drug use that is occurring, whether that be in terms of treating individuals drug dependency or reducing their drug-related risk behaviour. There is simply no place it seems within that discourse to exercise any moral judgement on the drugs issue.

The absence of moral judgement within this public health/medical model in relation to illegal drug use contrasts markedly with the role of moral judgements within the educational domain in relation to sex education. It is now widely accepted that young people should be encouraged to see sexual behaviour not simply as a matter of biology or of the satisfaction of their own individual wishes and desires but in terms of the social and inter-personal impact of their behaviour. Educating young people about sex is seen in these terms as having to do with placing sex within the context of healthy, loving and mutually respectful relationships. Within the domain of sex education far from shying away from moral judgements we have placed those judgements at the very centre of our notion of a healthy sexual relationship. In the case of illegal drugs by contrast, we have largely unburdened ourselves of the responsibility for a moral view, preferring instead to adhere to the principle of pragmatism which covers illegal drug use in a cloak of moral agnosticism.

But why might one seek a moral dimension in the drugs debate and what purpose could it serve. There is merit in answering those questions in relation to a concrete example by focussing on a young person who is considering starting to smoke cannabis. As the parent or guardian of that young person you might explain the various potential harms that he or she might experience as a result of such drug use. However, since the statistical probability of the individual experiencing those harms is fairly remote it is difficult to believe that the simply presenting the evidence of potential harm would be sufficient to reduce the likelihood of the individual using illegal drugs. Equally, one might convey to the young person something of the social harms that they could experience if, for example, they were arrested in possession of cannabis. Those harms could include the young person acquiring a criminal record. Again though the statistical probability of being arrested in possession of cannabis is, as we saw, extremely remote. As a parent one might seek to use ones authority over the young person to reduce the likelihood of the drug use occurring; explaining, for example, that illegal drug use is a breach of the rules of the household in which the young person is living. In addition to each of these things one might also convey the view that illegal drug use is simply wrong because it offends a moral code.

But what is the moral code that drug use offends? Within some societies there is a view that the human body is not the possession of each individual. Instead there is a view that the human body is really the possession of an almighty spirit such that it is the responsibility of the individual to look after the body in any way they can, for example eschewing drug and alcohol use. Such a moral code, however, is likely to apply to only a small number of people with deeply held religious views. Religious morality is though only one possible moral code that might apply in this context. Another moral code has to do with the relative value placed on meeting the needs of the individual as opposed to meeting the needs of the group or the wider society.

Drug use at its heart is about pursuing individual needs and desires whether for pleasure, respite of psychological pain, or individual curiosity. In a context in which one perceives oneself, and one's own needs and desires, as the key determinant of one's actions, it is easy to see how the use of illegal drugs may be seen as a matter purely for the individual to determine. The issue of whether drugs offend a moral code is largely irrelevant from within such a view. If however, one adopts a view that places the needs of others, one's family or the wider society over the inclination to pursue ones own needs, then drug use may come to be seen in an entirely different light as something to be avoided rather than encouraged.

There are probably two reasons why the moral agnosticism in relation to illegal drugs has occurred. First, there is the liberal view of drug use that can be traced back to at least the 1960s in which using drugs such as cannabis, LSD was seen in largely positive terms as a way of enabling individuals to think creatively and break some of what were seen as the shackles of conventional behaviour. Secondly, there is the evident loss across our secular and pluralistic society of anything approximating a commonly agreed moral code. As a result of these two developments drug use itself has been placed within a kind of moral vacuum.

But does it matter that drug use has been placed within that moral vacuum? It is almost certainly the case that the most powerful determinant of whether an individual chooses to use illegal drugs is not the legal penalties associated with such use, or the mental health harms that may flow from such use, but the reactions of other people. We are as humans enormously attuned to the reactions of others and forever seeking their approval. If we are to effectively tackle our drug problem we may well require all of the possible means available to influence the choices individuals make in relation to illegal drugs including those that have a moral dimension.

To develop a moral view of illegal drugs use will require a fundamental change in our drug polices from focussing on reducing the harm associated with such use to focussing first and foremost on reducing the level of drug use itself. We may need to recognize that the inclination to use illegal drugs, seen in terms of the pursuit of personal pleasure, causes too much social harm to continue to be seen as a matter of purely individual choice. Illegal drug use may be an individual freedom too far – a freedom that fractures rather than binds society and for that reason alone needs to be socially devalued.

What in practical terms might it mean to adopt a more moral stance on illegal drug use? The first thing to say here is that this would not require one to regard those using illegal drugs as immoral in themselves, rather it would be to view the drug use itself in moral terms. Instead of being couched in morally neutral terms, drug use would be viewed as a behaviour, which is self-focussed and which disregards the views and needs of others. It would be to see drug use as a behaviour that is about putting one's own needs and desires above those of the wider society, one's family, friends and community. It would in a sense be to stigmatize drug use.

Recently there has been much debate around stigma as it relates to drug use with a number of the drug legalization groups arguing in favour of challenging the stigma typically associated with illegal drugs and illegal drug users. The Release drugs charity, for example, sponsored an advertising campaign in London in which London busses carried a large advert announcing that Nice People Take Drugs (O'Hara 2009, Release 2009). That campaign was designed expressly to challenge the stigma associated with drug use and drug users. Following a number of complaints to London Transport, the Nice People Take Drugs advert was removed from the busses because it was felt that the message within the advert came too close to encouraging people to use illegal drugs.

Whilst there has been an influential and valuable campaign challenging the stigma associated with mental illness, attempts to challenge the stigma associated with drug use may be entirely misplaced. If we are to work to reduce the level of drug use in society, far from normalizing drug use and presenting the drug using lifestyle as an entirely acceptable "life style" choice perhaps what we need instead is to retain a view of drug use as a stigmatized activity.

Stigma can be used as a social device designed to reduce what are seen to be socially harmful behaviours. In the case of drink driving campaigns, for example, stigma has been used as a marketing strategy to encourage the view that those who drink and drive are socially irresponsible. Within such campaigns driving under the influence of alcohol is seen not as a form of socially valued risk taking, but as a selfish, socially irresponsible behaviour that threatens the lives of "innocent others".

In the case of illegal drugs there may well be a degree to which stigma has been an important social barrier reducing the wider adoption of a pattern of illegal drug use. Different drugs are associated with different levels of stigma and different levels of use. In the case of cannabis, the most widely used illegal drug, there is very little stigma associated with its use. From politicians to pop stars, individuals can report their use of cannabis with little or no adverse impact on their career. When it comes to Class A drug use the level of stigma goes up, the level of reported use goes down, and the consequences of use become more dramatic. Cocaine is more stigmatized than cannabis but less stigmatized than heroin. In quantitative terms the level of its use sits between the two and revelations of its use can have seriously adverse consequences on one's career – depending of course on the nature of the career in question. In the case of heroin by contrast, we have a drug more stigmatized than any other and whose use, even by rock and pop stars, can be seen as indicative of personal destitution and weakness. One of the positive outcomes of stigmatizing heroin in this way may well have been that its use remains relatively rare.

For many people the suggestion that there may be some merit in retaining a clear sense of the stigma associated with drug use, and retaining a moral view of drug use itself, will be seen as offensive and provocative in the extreme. The response to that suggestion may well be to point out that the last thing drug users need or want is to be stigmatized or viewed as immoral as a result of their drug use. Curiously those who are of that view are drawing a parallel between the drugs an individual is using and the individual's own identity and are, in that sense, reducing the individual to the drugs he or she is using which is potentially stigmatizing in itself. In contrast by maintaining a distinction between the drugs the individual is using and the person himself it ought to be possible to retain a view of drug use as appropriately stigmatized without at the same time stigmatizing the individual. Retaining moral judgements about drug use and accepting the stigma directed towards drug use if not drug users may be an important part of an effective approach aimed at tackling the use of illegal drugs in society.

KEY DISCUSSION QUESTIONS

1. What do we lose from a full appreciation of the harms of illegal drugs by adopting a position of moral neutrality about such drug use?
2. How appropriate is the principle of pragmatism directed towards the use and sale of illegal drugs?
3. What are the benefits if any of adopting a moral approach to illegal drugs?
4. Does the approach of moral neutrality towards the use of illegal drugs serve to normalize illegal drug use?
5. Can one draw a distinction between the issue of morality as applied to drug use and the issue of morality as applied to drug users?
6. Are there positive benefits associated with retaining the stigma associated with illegal drug use?

Bibliography

Abuldrahim, D., Gordon, D., and Best, D. (2006) *Findings of a Survey of Needle Exchanges in England*. London: National Treatment Agency.

Advisory Council on the Misuse of Drugs (ACMD) (1988) *AIDS and Drug Misuse*, Part 1. London: HMSO.

Advisory Council on the Misuse of Drugs (ACMD) (1993) *AIDS and Drug Misuse*, Update Report. London: HMSO.

Advisory Council for the Misuse of Drugs (ACMD) (2003) *Hidden Harm: Responding to the Children of Problem Drug Users*. London: HMSO.

Advisory Council on the Misuse of Drugs (ACMD) (2005) *Further Considera-tion of the Classification of Cannabis under the Misuse of Drugs Act 1971*. London: Home Office.

Advisory Council on the Misuse of Drugs (ACMD) (2008) *Cannabis: Classifi-cation and Public Health*. London: Home Office.

Advisory Council on the Misuse of Drugs (ACMD) (2010) *Consideration of the Cathinones*. London: HMSO.

Allardyce, J., and MacLeod, M. (2002) On the Trail of the First Minister. *Scotsman Newspaper*, 13 October.

Ammerman, R., Kolko, D., Kirisci, L., Blackson, T., and Dawes, M. (1999) Child abuse potential in parents with histories of substance use disorder. *Child Abuse & Neglect* 23 (12), December: 1225–1238.

Andreasson, S., and Allebeck, P. (1990) Cannabis and mortality among young men: A longitudinal study of Swedish conscripts. *Scandinavian Journal of Social Medicine* 18: 9–15.

Arsenault, L., Gannon, M., and Murray, R. (2007) Causal association between cannabis and psychosis: Examination of the evidence focus. *American Psychiatric Association* 5, Spring: 270–278.

Ashton, M. (2008) *The New Abstentionists*. London: Drugscope.

Audit Commission (2002) *Changing Habits: The Commissioning and Manage-ment of Drug Services*. London: Audit Commission for Local Authorities and the National Health Service for England and Wales.

Audit Commission (2004) *Drug Misuse: Reducing the Local Impact*. London: Criminal Justice National Report Audit Commission for Local Authorities and the National Health Service for England and Wales.

Audit Scotland (2009) Drug and Alcohol Services in Scotland, available at http://www.auditscotland.gov.uk/docs/health/2009/nr_090326_drugs_alcohol.pdf.

Bammer, G., van den Brink, W., Gschwend, P., Hendriks, V., and Rehm, J. (2003) What can the Swiss and Dutch trials tell us about the potential risks associated with heroin prescribing? *Drug Alcohol Review* 22: 363–371.

Bancroft, A., Wilson, S., Cunningham-Burley, S., Backett-Millburn, K., and Masters, H. (2004) *Resilience and Transition Among Young People: Surviving Parental Drug and Alcohol Misuse*. York: Joseph Rowntree Foundation.

Barnard, M. (2007) *Drugs and the Family*. London: Jessica Kingsley Press.

Barnes, E. (2006) Methadone Fails 97% of Drug Addicts. *Scotland on Sunday Times*, 29 October 2006.

BBC (2004) Abstinence Call in Drug Study, http://news.bbc.co.uk/2/hi/uk_news/scotland/3741256.stm.

BBC (2005) Goldie lambasts methadone system, http://news.bbc.co.uk/2/hi/uk_news/scotland/4432912.stm. Accessed 15 July 2010.

BBC (2007) Family bid to aid young addicts, http://news.bbc.co.uk/1/hi/scotland/glasgow_and_west/6279481.stm. Accessed 15 July 2010.

BBC (October 2007) Drug "rewards" given to addicts, http://news.bbc.co.uk/1/hi/uk/7049934.stm. Accessed 15 July 2010.

BBC (2009) Straw moots heroin prescription 20 September 2009, http://news.bbc.co.uk/1/hi/uk/8265641.stm. Accessed 15 July 2010.

BBC (March 2010) Government adviser Eric Carlin quits over mephedrone, http://news.bbc.co.uk/1/hi/uk/8600911.stm. Accessed 15 July 2010.

BBC (March 2010) Mephedrone may be banned, chief drug adviser indicates, http://news.bbc.co.uk/2/hi/uk_news/8601315.stm. Accessed 15 July 2010.

BBC News (2008) Mexico Drug Gangs Killing Surge December 9, http://news.bbc.co.uk/2/hi/7772771.stm. Accessed 15 July 2010.

Bejerot, N. (1975) Drug abuse and drug policy. *Acta Psychiatrica Scandinavica Supplement* 256: 3–277.

Berridge, V. (1999) *Opium and the People. Opiate Use and Drug Control Policy in Nineteenth and Early Twentieth Century England*. London: Free Association Books.

Berridge, V., and Mars, S. (2004) History of addictions, *Journal of Epidemiology and Community Health* 58: 747–750.

Berridge, V., and Strong, P. (1993) *AIDS and Contemporary History*. Cambridge: Cambridge University Press.

Black, C., MacLardie, J., Mailho, J., Murray, L., Sewel, K. (2009) *Scottish Schools Adolescent Lifestyle and Substance Abuse Survey (SALSUS) Smoking Drinking and Drug Use Among 13–15 Year Olds in Scotland*. NHS Scotland.

Blakey, D. (2008) *Disrupting the Supply of Illicit Drugs into Prisons*. A Report for the Director General of National Offender Management Service.

Bloor, M., Gannon, M., Hay, G., Jackson, G., Leyland, A., and McKeganey, N. (2008) Contribution of problem drug users' deaths to excess mortality in Scotland: Secondary analysis of a cohort study. *British Medical Journal* 337: a478, doi: 10.1136/bmj.a478.

Bloor, M., McIntosh, J., McKeganey, N., and Robertson, M. (2008) "Topping Up" methadone: An analysis of patterns of heroin use among a treatment sample of Scottish drug users. *Public Health*, doi: 10.1016/j.puhe.2008.01.007.

Bloor, M., Neale, J., and McKeganey, N. P. (2006) Persisting local variations in the prevalence of hepatitis C virus among Scottish problem drug users: results from an anonymous screening study. *Drugs: Education, Prevention and Policy* 13, 189–191.

Blunkett, D. (2001) Blunkett calls for cannabis debate http://news.bbc.co.uk/1/hi/uk_politics/1429178.stm.

Booth, M. (1998) *Opium: A History*. New York: St Martin's Press.

Boreham, R., Fuller, E., Hills, A., and Pudney, S. (2006) *The Arrestee Survey Annual Report Oct 2003 – Sept 2004*. England and Wales: Home Office.

Bowlby, J. (1999) *Attachment*. Attachment and Loss Vol. I (2nd ed.). New York: Basic Books.

Boyd, D. (2008) UKDPC Non Consensus on Recovery. *Addiction Today*, June 06.

Bruneau, J., Lamothe, F., and Franco, E. (1997) High rates of HIV infection among injecting drug users participating in needle exchange programs in Montreal: Results of a cohort study. *American Journal of Epidemiology* 143: 994–1002.

Bullock, T. (2003) Changing levels of drug use before during and after imprisonment. In M. Ramsay (ed.), *Prisoners Drug Use and Treatment: Seven Studies*. London: Home Office Research Study 267.

Burrows, D. (2005) Towards a regulated market for illicit drugs: Effectis of the harm reduction model of controlled drug availability. *International Journal of Drug Policy* 16: 8–9.

Campsie, A. (2009) Drug – Related Death Rates Rise By 34% in Scotland Drug. *Herald Newspaper*, Tuesday, 1 September 2009.

Canadian Centre on Substance Abuse (1996) *Harm Reduction: Concepts and Practice: A Policy Discussion Paper*. Canadian Centre on Substance Abuse (CCSA) National Working Group on Policy.

Carrell, S. (2010) Disgraced Former Glasgow Council Leader Stephen Purcell Admits Cocaine Use and Fear of Blackmail Plot, *Guardian*, 29 March 2010, 15.02 BST.

Casey, J., Hay, G., Godfrey, C., and Parrot, S. (2009) *Assessing the Scale and Impact of Illicit Drugs Market in Scotland*. Edinburgh: Scottish Government Social Research.

Catalano, R. F., Gainey, R. R., Fleming, C. B., Haggerty, K. P., and Johnson, N. O. (1999) An experimental intervention with families of substance abusers: One-year follow-up of the focus on families project. *Addiction* 94 (2): 241–254.

Catalano, R. F., Haggerty, K. P., Fleming, C. B., Brewer, D. D., and Gainey, R. R. (2002) Children of substance abusing parents: Current findings from the focus on families project. In R. J. McMahon and R. D. V. Peters (eds), *The Effects of Parental Dysfunction on Children* (pp. 179–204). New York: Kluwer Academic Press/Plenum Publishers.

Centre for Social Justice (2007) *Breakthrough Britain Volume 4 Addictions Towards Recovery.*

Chaffin, M., Kelleher, K., and Hollenberg, J. (1996) Onset of physical abuse and neglect: Psychiatry substance abuse and social risk factors from prospective community data. *Child Abuse and Neglect* 20: 191–203.

Cohen, P., and Brook, J. (1987) Family factors related to the persistence of psychopathology in childhood and adolescents. *Psychiatry* 50: 332–345.

Comiskey, C., Kelly, P., Leckley, L., O'Dull, B., Stapelton, R., and White, D. (2009) *The ROSIE Study: Drug Treatment Outcomes in Ireland.* A Report for the National Advisory Committee on Drugs.

Connell, K. (2007) *Methaphetamine and the Changing Face of Child Welfare.* Practice Principle for Child Welfare Workers.

Connelly, G., Forrest, J., Furnivall, J., Siebelt, L., Smith, I., and Seagrave, L. (2009) *The Educational Attainment of Looked after Children – Local Authority Pilot Projects: Final Research Summary Research Findings No.41/20 Scottish Government 2008.*

Cornelius, J., Clark. D., Weyant, R., Bretz, W., Corby, P., Mezzich, A., Kirisci, L. (2004) Dental abnormalities in children of fathers with substance use disorders. *Addictive Behaviours* 29 (5) July: 979–982.

Costa, A. M. (2006) *World Drugs Report 2006.* United Nations Office of Drugs and Crime.

Daily Mail (2009) Heroin for addicts on the NHS is the way to cut crime, say the Liberal Democrats, 21 September.

Darke, S., Ross, J., Mills, K., Williamson, A., Haarvard, A., and Teeson, M. (2007a) Patterns of sustained heroin abstinence amongst long terms dependent heroin users: 36 months findings from the Australian Treatment Outcome Study (ATOS). *Addictive Behaviours* 32 (9): 1897–1906.

Darke, S., Ross, J., and Teeson, M. (2007b) The Australian Treatment Outcome Study (ATOS): what have we learn about treatment for heroin dependence? *Drug and Alcohol Review* 26 (1), January: 49–54(6).

Davies, T., Dominy, N., Peters, A., and Bath, G. (1995) HIV in injecting drug users in Edinburgh prevalence and correlates. *Journal of Acquired Immune Deficiency Syndrome and Human Retrovirology* 18 (4): 399–405.

Dawe, S., Harnett, P., Rendalls, V., and Staiger, P. (2003) Improving family functioning and child outcome in methadone maintained families: The parents under pressure programme. *Drug and Alcohol Review* 22 (3): 299–307.

Department of Health (2010) *Updated Guidance for Prison Based Opioid Maintenance Prescribing.* London.

Des Jarlais, D. C., Friedman, S. R., Novick, D. M., Sotheran, J. L., Thomas, P., Yancovitz, S. R., Mildvan, D., Weber, J., Kreek, M., Maslansky, R., Bartelme, S. et al. (1987) HIV-1 infection among intravenous drug users in Manhattan, New York City, From 1977 through 1987. *JAMA* 1989, 261 (7): 1008–1012.

Des Jarlais, D. C., Friedman, S. R., Sotheran, J. L., Wenston, J., Marmor, M., Yancovitz, S. R., Frank, B., Beatrice, S., Mildvan, D. (1994) Continuity and change within an HIV epidemic. Injecting drug users in New York City, 1984 through 1992. *JAMA: The Journal of the American Medical Association* 271 (2): 121–127.

Des Jarlais, D. C., Marmor, M., Paone, D., Titus, S., Shi, Q., Perlis, T., Jose, B., and Friedman, S. R., (1996) HIV incidence among injecting drug users in New York City syringe-exchange programmes. *Lancet* 348 (9033): 987–991.

Dijkgraaf, M., van der Zanden, B., de Borgie, C., Blanken, P., Van Ree, J., Van den Brink, W. (2005) Cost utility analysis of co-prescribed heroin compared with methadone maintenance treatment in heroin addicts in two randomised trials. *British Medical Journal* 330: 1297.

Dinsmore, D. (2010) I'm sorry...I let everybody down. *Scottish Sun*, 29 March.

Ditton, J., and Speirits, K. (1981) *The Rapid Increase of Heroin Addiction in Glasgow during 1981*. Background Paper No 2. Department of Sociology, Glasgow: University of Glasgow.

Donoghoe, M. C., Stimson, G. V., Dolan, K., and Alldritt, L. (1989) Changes in HIV Risk Behaviour in Clients of Syringe-exchange Schemes in England and Scotland. *AIDS* 3 (5) May: 267–272.

Drugscope (2009) *Drug Treatment at the Crossroads – What's It for, Where It's at and How to Make It Even Better*. Drugscope Publications.

Effective Interventions Unit (2004) *Residential Detoxification and Rehabilitation Services for Drug Users: A Review*. Scottish Executive.

Erwin, J. (2005) Doing Time with Porridge, *Guardian*, Wednesday 5 October.

European Monitoring Center for Drugs and Drug Addiction (EMCDDA) (2008) *The State of the Drug Problem in Europe*. Lisbon.

European Monitoring Center for Drugs and Drug Addiction (EMCDDA) (2009) *The State of the Drug Problem in Europe*. Lisbon.

European Monitoring Centre for Drugs and Drug Addiction (EMCDDA) (2009) *Statistical Bulletin*. Lisbon.

Ewing, F. (2007) *Inaugural Speech Glasgow Addictions Service Second Christmas Conference*. Glasgow: Glasgow Addictions Service.

Ewing, F. (2009) Drugs commission has a vital role to play on Road to Recovery. *Scotsman*, 12 December.

Famularo, R., Kingcherff, R., Bunshaft, D., Spivak, G., and Fenton, T. (1989) Parental compliance to court ordered treatment intervening in cases of child maltreatment. *Child Abuse and Neglect* 13: 507–514.

Farrell, M. (2008) *NTA Response to Conservative Statement on Methadone*, Press Statement from National Treatment Agency, 23 December.

Fergusson, D., Jorwood, L., and Beautrais, A. (2003) Cannabis and educational achievement. *Addiction* 98: 1681–1692.

Fiks, K., Johnson, H., and Rosen, T. (1885) Methadone maintained mothers 3 year follow up of parental functioning. *International Journal of the Addiction* 20: 651–660.

Fitzgerald, J. (2005) Policing as public health menace in the policy struggles over public injecting. *International Journal of Drug Policy* 16: 203–206.

Fitzgerald, J. (2009) Mapping the experience of drug dealing risk environments an ethnographic case study. *International Journal of Drug Policy* 20: 261–269.

Ford, R. (2006) Inmates Win Cold Turkey Payouts. *Times*, 14 November.

Frei, A. (2001) Economic evaluation of the Swiss project on medically prescribed heroin substitution treatment. *Psychiatrische Praxis* 28: S41–4.

Frischer, M., Bloor, M., Finlay, A., Goldberg, D., Green, S., Haw, S., McKeganey, N., and Platt, S. (1991) A new method for estimating the prevalence of injecting drug use in an urban population: Results from a Scottish city. *International Journal of Epidemiology* 20 (4): 997–1000.

Frisher, M., Crome, I., Martino, O., and Croft, P. (2009) Assessing the impact of cannabis use on trends in diagnosed schizophrenia in the United Kingdom from 1996 to 2005. *Schizophrenia Research* 113 (2–3): 123–128.

Gardham, D. (2009) Jack Straw calls for heroin on prescription. *Sunday Telegraph*, 20.

Gardner, E. L. (2003) Addictive potential of cannabinoids: The underlying neurobiology. *CPL Chemistry and Physics* 121: 267–297.

General Register Office (GRO) (2009) *Drug Related Deaths in Scotland 2008.* Scottish Government.

General Register Office for Scotland (2008) *Drug-Related Deaths in Scotland in 2007.* Scottish Government.

General Register Office for Scotland (2009) *Drug-Related Deaths in Scotland in 2008.* Scottish Government.

Goldie, A. (2005) *Goldie Lambasts Methadone Programme.* http://news.bbc.co.uk/1/hi/scotland/4432912.stm.

Gordon, D., Burn, D., Campbell, A., and Baker, O. (2008) *The 2007 User Satisfaction Survey of Tier 2 and 3 Services Users in England.* London: National Treatment Agency for Substance Misuse.

Gordon, L., Tinsley, L., Godfrey, C., and Parrott, S. (2006) The economic and social costs of Class A drug use in England and Wales, 2003/04. In Singleton, N., Murray, R. and Tinsley, L. (eds), *Measuring Different Aspects of Problem Drug Use: Methodological Developments. Home Office Online Report 16/06.* London: Home Office.

Gordon, T. (2006) Residential rehab call by McConnell. *The Herald*, 3 November.

Gossop, M., Griffiths, P., and Strang, J. (1988) Chasing the dragon: Characteristics of heroin chasers. *British Journal of Addiction* 83: 1159–1162.

Gossop, M., Darke, S., Griffiths, P., Hando, J., Powis, B., Hall, W., and Strang, J. (1995) The Severity of Dependence Scale (SDS): Psychometric properties of the SDS in English and Australian samples of heroin, cocaine and amphetamine users. *Addiction* 90: 607–614.

Gossop, M., Marsden, J., and Stewart, D. (2001) *NTORS after 5 Years. Changes in Substance Use, Health and Criminal Behaviour Five Years after Intake.* London: Crown Office.

Gossop, M., Marsden, J., Stewart, D., and Rolfe, A. (2000) Reductions in acquisitive crime and drug use after treatment of addiction problems: 1-year follow-up outcomes. *Drug and Alcohol Dependence* 58: 165–172.

Gossop, M., Marsden, J., Stewart, D., and Treacy, S. (2001) Outcomes after methadone maintenance and methadone reduction treatments: Two year follow-up results. *Drug & Alcohol Dependence* 62: 255–264.

Gossop, M., Trakada, K., Stewart, D., and Witton, J. (2005) Reductions in criminal convictions after addiction treatment: 5-year follow-up. *Drug and Alcohol Dependence* 79: 295–302.

Gray, J. (2009) The case for legalising all drugs is unanswerable. *Observer*, 13 September.

Gyngell, K. (2009) Spectacular results or spectacular spin behind Jack Straw's call for heroin prescribing. *Centre for Policy Studies*, 25 September.

Gyngell, K. (2009) *The Phoney War on Drugs*. Centre for Policy Studies Report.

Haasen, C., Verthein, U., Degkwitz, P., Berger, J., Krausz, M., and Naber, D. (2007) Heroin assisted treatment for opioid dependence: A randomised, controlled trial. *British Journal of Psychiatry* 191: 55–62.

Haggerty, K., Skinner, M., Flemming, C., Gainey, R., and Catalano, R. (2008) Long-term effects of the focus on families project on substance use disorders among children of parents in methadone treatment. *Addiction* 103 (12): 2008–2016.

Hartgers, C., van Ameijden, E. J., van den Hoek, J. A., and Coutinho, R. A. (1992) Needle sharing and participation in the Amsterdam Syringe Exchange program among HIV-seronegative injecting drug users. *Public Health Reports* 107 (6): 675–681.

Hartnoll, R., Mitcheson, M. C., Battersby, A., Brown, G., Ellis, M., and Flemming, P. (1980) Evaluation of heroin maintenance in controlled trial. *Archives of General Psychiatry* 37: 877–884.

Hathaway, A. (2001) Shortcomings of harm reduction: Toward a morally invested drug reform strategy. *International Journal of Drug Policy* 12 (2): 125–137.

Haw, S. (1985) *Drug Problems in Greater Glasgow*. London: Standing Conference on Drug Abuse.

Hay, G., Gannon, M. (2006) Capture-recapture estimates of the local and national prevalence of problem drug use in Scotland. *International Journal of Drug Policy* 17: 203–210.

Hay, G., Gannon, M., McKeganey, N., Hutchinson, S., and Goldberg, D. (2005) *Estimating the National and Local Prevalence of Problem Drug Misuse in Scotland*, ISD Scotland, Scottish Executive Report (available at http://www.drugmisuse.isdscotland.org/publications/abstracts/prevalence3.htm).

Hay, G., Gannon, M., Casey, J., and McKeganey, N. (2009) Estimating the National and Local Prevalence of Problem Drug Misuse in Scotland. *Executive Report*, University of Glasgow. Information and Statistics Division Scottish Government.

Hay, G., Gannon, M., MacDougall, J., Millar, T., Williams, K., Eastwood, C., and McKeganey, N. (2008) *National and Regional Estimates of the Prevalence of Opiate Use and/or Crack Cocaine Use 2006/07: A Summary of Key Findings*. Home Office Research Report 9.

Hayes, P. (2007) *Foreword to National Treatment Agency Annual Report 2007/08*. NTA: London.

Health Protection Agency (2004) *Shooting Up Infections Among Injecting Drug Users in the United Kingdom in 2003*.

Health Protection Agency (2005) *Shooting Up Infections Among Injecting Drug Users in the United Kingdom in 2004*.

Health Protection Agency (2006) *Shooting Up Infections Among Injecting Drug Users in the United Kingdom in 2005*.

Health Protection Agency (2007) *Shooting Up Infections Among Injecting Drug Users in the United Kingdom 2006*.

Health Protection Agency (2009) *Shooting Up Infections Among Injecting Drug Users in the United Kingdom 2008.*

Health Protection Agency (2010) *Shooting Up Infections Among Injecting Drug Users in the United Kingdom 2009.*

Heather, N., Wodak, A., Nadelmann, E. and O'Hare, P. (eds) (1993) *Psychoactive Drugs and Harm Reduction: From Faith to Science.* London: Whurr Publishers.

Hedrich, D. (2004) *European Report on Drug Consumption Rooms.* European Monitoring Centre for Drugs and Drug Addiction Office for Official Publications of the European Communities.

Heimer, R., Bray, S., Burris, S., Khoshnood, K., and Blankensip, M. (2002) Structural Interventions to Improve Opiate Maintenance *International Journal of Drug Policy* 13 (2): 103–111.

Herning, R., Better, W., Tate, K., and Cadet, J. (2001) Mariiuana users are at increased risk for stroke. *Annals of the New York Academy of Sciences* 939: 413–415.

Hibell, B., Guttorrmsson, U., Ahistrom, S., Balakireva, O. et al. (2007) *The 2007 ESPAD Report.* Lisbon: European Monitoring Centre for Drugs and Drug Addiction.

Hickman, M., Higgins, V., Hope, V., Bellis, M., Tilling, K., Walker, A., and Henry, J. (2004) Injecting drug use in Brighton, Liverpool, and London: Best estimates of prevalence and coverage of public health indicators. *Journal of Epidemiology and Community Health* 58: 766–771 doi:10.1136/jech.2003.015164.

Hoare, J. (2009) *Drug Misuse Declared: Findings from the 2008/09 British Crime Survey.* Home Office Statitical Bulletin 12/09. London: Home Office.

Home Office (1998) *Tackling Drugs to Build a Better Britain.* London: HMSO.

Home Office (2002) *Updated Drug Strategy Directorate.*

Home Office (2008) *Drugs: Protecting Families and Communities.* The 2008 Drug Strategy.

Home Office (2007) *Crime in England and Wales 2006/07*, ed. Nicholas, S., Kershaw, C., Walker, A. Home Office Statitical Bulletin. London: Home Office.

Home Office (2009) *Extending Our Reach: A Comprehensive Approach to Tackling Serious Organised Crime.*

Hough, A. (2010) Mephedrone: government adviser Dr Polly Taylor quits as drugs row escalates. *Telegraph*, 29 March.

Huber, G. L., Griffith, D. L., and Langsjoen, P. M. (1988) The effects of marihuana on the respiratory and cardiovascular systems. In G. Chesher, P. Consroe, and R. Musty (eds), *Marijuana: An International Research Report.* National Campaign against Drug Abuse Monograph Number 7, Canberra: Australian Government Publishing Service.

Hughes, C., and Stevens, A. (2009) *The Effects of Decrimalisation of Drug Use in Portugal.* Oxford: The Beckley Foundation Drug Policy Programme.

Hunt, N., Ashton, M., Lenton, S., Mitcheson, L., Nelles, B., and Stimson, G. (2003) *A Review of the Evidence-Base for Harm Reduction Approaches to Drug Use.* London: Forward Thinking on Drugs.

Hunt, N. (2004) Public health or human rights: What comes first? *International Journal of Drug Policy* 15: 231–237.

Hunt, N. (2005) Public health or human rights? Author's rejoinder to responses. *International Journal of Drug Policy* 16 (1), January 5–7.

Hunter, D. J. (2008) Speaking truth to power: On the discomfort of researching the contemporary policy process. In L. McKee, E. Ferlie, and P. Hyde, (eds), *Organising and Reorganising: Power and Change in Health Care Organisations*. Basingstoke: Palgrave Macmillan.

ISD (2009) *Drug Misuse Statistics Scotland 2009*. Scottish Government.

International Harm Reduction Association (IHRA) (2009) *What is Harm Reduction?* Available at http://www.ihra.net/files/2010/05/31/IHRA_HRStatement.pdf.

International Narcotics Control Board (INCB) (2009) Report. *INCB United Nations*. Available at http://www.incb.org/incb/en/annual-report-2009.html.

James, E. (2005) Doing time with Porridge. *Guardian*, 5 October.

Jansson, L. DiPietro, J., and Elko, A. (2005) Fetal response to maternal methadone administration. *American Journal of Obstetrics and Gynecology* 193 (3): 611–617.

Jenkins, S. (2009a) Prohibition's failed. Time for a new drugs policy. *The Observer*, Sunday 6 September.

Jenkins, S. (2009b) The War on Drugs is Immoral Idiocy. We Need the Courage of Argentina *Guardian*, 3 September.

Joseph Rowntree Foundation (2006) *The Report of the Independent Working Group on Drug Consumption Rooms JRF.*

Kerr, T., Tyndall, M., Li, K., Montaner, J., and Wood, E. (2005) Safer injection facility use and syringe sharing in injection drug users. *Lancet* 366: 316–318.

Kerr, T., Stoltz, J., Tyndall, M., Li, K., Zhang, R., Montaner, J., and Wood, E. (2006) Impact of a medically supervised safer injection facility on community drug use patterns: A before and after study. *British Medical Journal* 332: 220–222.

Kerr, T., Tyndall, M., Lai, C., Montaner, J., and Wood, E. (2006) Drug related overdoses within a medically supervised safer injection facility. *International Journal of Drug Policy* 17 (5): 436–441.

Kerr, T., Tyndall, M., Li, K., Montaner, J. and Wood, E. (2005) Safer injection facility use and syringe sharing in injection drug users. *The Lancet* 366. (9482): 316–318.

Kerr, T., Tyndall, M. W., Zhang, R., and Lai, C. (2007) Circumstances of first injection among illicit drug users accessing a medically supervised safer injection facility. *American Journal of Public Health* 97 (7): 1228–1230.

Kroll, B., and Taylor, A. (2008) Interventions for children and families where there is parental drug miuse, *Executive Summary*. Department of Health Drug Misuse Research Initiative.

Kushlick, D., and Rolles, S. (2004) Human rights versus political capital. *International Journal of Drug Policy* 15: 245.

Lakhani, N. (2009) UK drug rehabilitation service is 'collapsing'. *Independent*, Sunday 1 February.

Laurance, J. (2009) Clamour grows for heroin on the NHS. *Independent*, Monday 14 September.

Leshner, A. (1997) Addiction is a brain disease, and it matters. *Science* 278: 45–47.

Levine, Harry G. (2001) The secret of world-wide drug prohibition: The varieties and uses of drug prohibition. *Hereinstead*, October, On-line: http://www.hereinstead.com/sys-tmpl/worldwide/.

Lewis, M., Misra, S., Johnson, H., and Rosen, T. (2004) Neurological and developmental outcomes of prenatally cocaine exposed offspring from 12 to 36 months. *American Journal of Drug and Alcohol Abuse* 30 (2): 299–320.

Liriano, S., and Ramsay, M. (2003) Prison drug use before prison and the links with crime. In M. Ramsay (ed.) *Prisoners Drug Use and Treatment: Seven Studies*. London: Home Office Research Study 267.

Luty, J. (2005) New guidelines for prescribing injectable heroin in opiate addiction. *Psychiatric Bulletin* 29: 123–125.

Lynskey, M., Coffey, C., Degenhardt, L., Carlin, J., and Patton, G. (2003) Longitudinal study of the effects of adolescent cannabis use on high school completion. *Addiction* 98: 685–692.

MacDonald, M., Law, M., Kaldon, J., Hales, J., and Dore, G. (2003) Effectiveness of needle and syringe programmes for preventing HIV transmission. *International Journal of Drug Policy* 14 (5/6): 353–357.

MacDougall, D. (2002) Prisons Offering Drugs to Inmates. *Scotsman*, 30 March.

Macmahon, P. (2006) Methadone '96.6% ineffective'. *Scotsman*, 30 October.

Maher, L., and Dixon, D. (1999) Policing and public health law enforcement and harm minimization in a street level drug market. *British Journal of Criminology* 39 (4): 488–512.

Maria Costa, A. (2006) *Foreword to the World Drugs Report 2006*. United Nations Office of Drugs and Crime.

Marsden, J., Eastwood, B., Bradbury, C., Dale-Pererra, A., Farrell, M., Hammond, P., Knight, J., Ranhawa, K., and Wright, C. (2009) Effectiveness of community treatments for heroin and crack cocaine addiction in England: A prospective, in-treatment cohort study. *Lancet* 374: 1262–1270.

Mcauley, A., Lindsay, G., Woods, M., and Louttitt, D. (2009) Responsible management and use of personal take home naloxone Supply: A pilot project. *Drugs Education Prevention and Policy* 17: 388–399.

McElrath, K. (2002) *Prevalence of Problem Heroin Use in Northern Ireland*. Belfast: Queens University.

McIntosh, M., and McKeganey, N. (2002) *Beating the Dragon: The Recovery from Dependent Drug Use*. Harlow: Pearson.

McIntosh, J., Bloor, M., and Robertson, M. (2008) The health benefits of reductions in individuals use of illegal drugs. *Journal of Substance Use* 13: 247–254.

McIntosh, J., and Saville, E. (2006) The challenges associated with drug treatment in prison. *Probation Journal* 53: 230–246.

McKeganey, N. (2006) Street prostitution in Scotland: The views of working women. *Drugs: Education, Prevention and Policy* 13 (2) April: 151–166.

McKeganey, N., Connelly, C., Knepil, J., Norrie, J., and Reid, L. (2000) *Interviewing and Drug Testing of Arrestees in Scotland*. Crime and Criminal Justice Research Findings 48. Central Research Unit Scottish Executive.

McKeganey, N., Casey, J., Mcgallagly, J., Hay, G. (2009) Heroin seizures and heroin use in Scotland. *Journal of Substance Use* 14 (3–4): 240–249.

McKeganey, N., and Barnard, M. (1992) *AIDS Drugs and Sexual Risk Lives in the Balance*. Buckingham: Open University Press.

McKeganey, N., Barnard, M., and McIntosh, J. (2002) Paying the price for their parents Addiction: Meeting the needs of the children of drug dependent parents. *Drugs Education Prevention and Policy* 9 (3): 233–246.

McKeganey, N., Bloor, M., Robertson, M., Neale, J., and MacDougal, J. (2006) Abstinence and drug abuse treatment: Results from the drug outcome in Scotland study. *Drugs Education Prevention and Policy* 13 (6): 537–550.

McKeganey, N., Casey, J., McGallagly, J., and Hay, G. (2009) Heroin seizures and heroin use in Scotland. *Journal of Substance Use* 14 (3–4): 240–249.

McKeganey, N., Morris, Z., Neale, J., and Robertson, M. (2004) What are drug users looking for when the contact drug services Abstinence or harm reduction. *Drugs Education Prevention and Policy* 11 (5): 423–435.

McKeganey, N., Neale, J., Lloyd, C., and Hay, G. (2002) State of Science Review: Sociology. Foresight brain science. *Addiction and Drugs Project*. Available at http://www.foresight.gov.uk/Brain%20Science/Sociology.pdf.

McKeganey, N., Neale, J., and Robertson, M. (2005) Physical and sexual abuse among drug users contacting drug treatment services in Scotland. *Drugs: Education Prevention and Policy* 12 (3): 223–232.

McKeganey, N. P. (2008) Should heroin be prescribed to heroin misusers? *British Medical Journal* 336: 71 (12 January), doi:10.1136/bmj.39422.503241.AD.

McKeganey, N. (2009) Drugs Advisory Body May Be Too Linked to Government to Work. *Scotsman*, 8 December.

McKeganey, N. P., Bloor, M., Robertson, M., Neale, J., and MacDougall, J. (2006) Abstinence and drug abuse treatment: Results from the drug outcome research in Scotland study. *Drugs: Education, Prevention & Policy* 13 (6): 537–550.

McKeganey, N. P., and Norrie, J. (1999) Pre-teen drug users in Scotland. *Addiction Research* 7: 493–507.

McKeganey, Neil (2006) The lure and the loss of harm reduction in UK drug policy and practice. *Addiction Research and Theory* 14 (6): 557–588.

McKeganey, N., McIntosh, J., MacDonald, F., Gannon, M., Gilvarry, E., McArdle, P., and McCarthy, S. (2004) Preteen children and illegal drugs. *Drugs Education Prevention and Policy* 11 (4): 313–327.

McLellan, T., Skipper, G., Campbell, M., and Du-Pont, R. (2008) Five year outcomes in a cohort study of physicians treated for substance use disorders in the United States. *British Medical Journal* 337: a2038.

McSmith, A., and Castle, S. (2006) Britain 'Deserves Its Drugs Problem', Says UN. *Independent Newspaper*, Tuesday 27 June.

McVeigh, J., Beynon, C., and Bellis, M. (2003) New challenges for agency based syringe exchange schemes analysis of 11 years of data (1991–2001) in Merseyside and Cheshire, United Kingdom. *International Journal of Drug Policy* 14: 399–405.

Mehra, R., Moore, B., Tetrault, J., and Fiellin, D. (2006) The association between Marijuana smoking and lung cancer a systematic review. *Archives of Internal Medicine* 166: 1559–1367.

Measham, F., Moore, K., Newcombe, R., and Welch, Z. (2010) Tweaking, bombing, dabbing, and stockpiling: the emergence of mephedrone and the perversity of prohibition. *Drugs Alcohol Today* 10 (1): 14–21.

Metrebian, N., Carnwath, Z., Mott, J., Carnwath, T., Stimson, G., and Sell, L. (2006) Patients receiving a prescription for diamorphine (heroin) in the United Kingdom. *Drug Alcohol Review* 25: 115–121.

Ministry of Justice (2008) *Arrests for Recorded Crime: Notifiable Offences and the Operation of Certain Police Powers under PACE.* England and Wales 2006/07 National Statistics.

Milloy, M. J., Kerr, T., Mathias, R., Zhang, R., Montaner, J., Tyndall, M., Wood, E. (2008) *The American Journal of Drug and Alcohol Abuse Addiction and Urban Health Research Initiative Non Fatal Overdose among a cohort of active injection drug users recruited from a safe injection facility.*

Ministry of Justice (2009) *Sentencing Statistics Quarterly Brief for October to December 2008.* England and Wales.

Moore, T. H., Zammit, S., Lingford-Hughes, A., Barnes, T., Jones, P., Burke, M., and Lewis, G. (2007) Cannabis use and risk of psychotic or affective mental health outcomes: A systematic review. *Lancet* 370: 319–328.

Moskalewicz, J., Barrett, D., Bujalski, M., Dąbrowska, K., Klingemann, H., Struzik, M. (2007) Harm reduction coming of age: A summary of the '18th International Conference on the Reduction of Drug Related Harm' – Warsaw, Poland: 13–17 May 2007. *International Journal of Drug Policy* 18 (6): 503–508.

Moss, H., Lynch, K., and Hardie, T. (2003) Affiliation with deviant peers among children of substance dependent fathers from pre-adolescence into adolescence: Associations with problem behaviors. *Drug and Alcohol Dependence* 71 (2), 20 August: 117–125.

Mugford, S. K. (1993) Harm reduction: Does it lead where its proponents imagine? In Heather, N., Wodak, A., Nadelmann, E. A., O'Hare, P. (eds), *Psychoactive Drugs and Harm Reduction: From Faith to Science.* London: Whurr Publishers.

Nadelmann, E. A. (1993) Progressive legalizers, progressive prohibitionists and the reduction of drug related harm. In Heather, N., Wodak, A., Nadelmann, E. and O'Hare, P. (eds), *Psychoactive Drugs and Harm Reduction From Faith to Science.* London: Whurr Publishers.

National Institute for Health and Clinical Excellence (NICE) (2007a) *Methadone and Buprenorphine for the Management of Opioid Dependence.* London (UK): National Institute for Health and Clinical Excellence, January 37p. (Technology appraisal guidance no. 114).

National Institute for Health and Clinical Excellence (NICE) (2007b) *Psychosocial interventions and opioid detoxification.* London (UK): National Institute for Health and Clinical Excellence.

National Institute for Health and Clinical Excellence (NICE) (2008) *Methadone and buprenorphine for managing opioid dependence.* London (UK): National Institute for Health and Clinical Excellence.

National Institute for Health and Clinical Excellence (NICE) (2009) *Needle and syringe programmes: Providing people who inject drugs with injecting equipment.* London (UK): National Institute for Health and Clinical Excellence.

National Statistics (2009) *Referrals, Assessment and Children and Young People Who are the Subject of a Child Protection Plan*, England – Year ending 31 March 2009.

National Treatment Agency (NTA) (2003) Injectable heroin (and injectable methadone): Potential Roles int Drug Treatment. *Executive Summary* (www.nta-nhs.uk.).

National Treatment Agency (NTA) (2007) *NTA Responds to BBC Story on Treatment Efficacy.* Available at http://www.drugscope.org.uk/newsand events/newsarchivepages/November2007/NTA-responds-BBC-claims.

National Treatment Agency (NTA) (2008) *Annual Report 2007/8.* Published by National Treatment Agency.

National Treatment Agency (NTA) (2009) *Largest Assessment of Treatment Programmes in England for Heroin and Crack Cocaine Addicts Shows Drug Treatment Works.* 01 October 2009.

National Treatment Agency for Substance Misuse (2009) Getting to Grips with Substance Misuse Among Young People the Data for 2007/08.

Newman, R. (2005) Comment on 'What are drug users looking for when they contact drug services: Abstinence or harm reduction?' by Neil McKeganey, Zoë Morris, Joanne Neal, & Michele Robertson. *Drugs: Education, Prevention, and Policy* 12 (4) 265–266.

Newsbusters (2009) CNN Praises UK Government Giving Drugs to Junkies, accessed at http://newsbusters.org/blogs/carolyn-plocher/2009/10/14/cnn-praises-uk-government-giving-drugs-junkies.

Nordt, C., and Stohler, R. (2006) Incidence of heroin use in Zurich, Switzerland: A treatment case register analysis. *Lancet* 367: 1830–1834.

Nutt, D. (2009) Equasy: An Overlooked Addiction with Implications for the Current Debate on Drug Harms. *Journal of Psychopharmacology* January 23 (1): 3–5.

Nutt, D., King, L., Saulsbury, W., Blakemore, C. (2007) Development of a rational scale to assess the harms of drugs of potential misuse, *Lancet* 369: 1047–1053.

O'Brien, S., Hammond, H., and McKinnon, M. (2003) *Report of the Caleb Ness Inquiry.* Edinburgh: Edinburgh and the Lothians Child Protection Committee.

Oakeshott, I. (2009) Jack Straw Call for Heroin Precribing on the NHS. *Times*, 19 September.

Office for National Statistics (ONS) (2009) Deaths related to drug poisoning in England and Wales. Available at http://www.drugfree.org.au/fileadmin/Media/Global/DGDTHS0809.pdf.

O'Hara, M. (2009) Nice People Take Drugs Ads Pulled from London Buses. *Guardian*, 9 June.

ONDCP (2009) *World Drugs Report.* ONDCP: Vienna.

Ornoy, A. (2003) The impact of intrauterine exposure versus postnatal environment in neurodevelopmental toxicity: Long-term neurobehavioral studies in children at risk for developmental disorders. Proceedings of EUROTOX 2002, The XL European Congress of Toxicology. *Toxicology Letters* 140–141.

Ornoy, A., Segal, J., Bar-Hamburger, R., and Greenbaum, C. (2001) Developmental outcome of school-age children born to mothers with heroin dependency: Importance of environmental factors. *Developmental Medicine & Child Neurology* 43 (10): 668–675.

Parker, H. (2007) Between the lines new drug strategies must reflect changing consumption patterns. *The Guardian*, Wednesday 18 April 2007.

Parker, H. (2008) *The ACCE (alcohol, cannabis, cocaine, ecstasy) Profile Challenge: Responding to Changing Alcohol and Drug Misuse Trends.* National Drug Treatment Conference 2008.

Parker, H. (2009) Between the Lines: New Drug Strategies Must Reflect Changing Consumption Patterns. *The Guardian*, Wednesday 18 April 2007.

Parker, H., Aldridge, J., Measham, F. (1998) *Illegal Leisure: The Normalisation of Adolescent Recreational Drug Use Among English Youth.* London: Routledge.

Parker, H., Bakx, K., and Newcombe, R. (1988) *Living with Heroin: The Impact of a Drugs Epidemic on an English Community.* Oxford: Open University Press.

Pearson, G. (1987) *The New Heroin Users.* Oxford: Oxford Blackwell.

Percy, A. (2005) 16th International Conference on the reduction of drug related harm, Belfast, Northern Ireland, 20–24th March 2005. *International Journal of Drug Policy* 16 (2005) 199–202.

Perneger, T., Giner, F., del Rio, M., and Mino, A. (1998) Randomized trial of heroin maintenance programme for addicts who fail in conventional drug treatments. *British Medical Journal* 317: 13–18.

Phillips, R. (2009) Drugs treatment: Drug treatment at the crossroads What it's for, where it's at and how to make it even better? *Drugscope Report London: Drugscope.*

Pollock, A. (2004) *NHS PLC.* London: Verso Books.

Primarolo, D. (2008) *Speech by Rt Hon Dawn Primarolo MP Minister of State for Public Health.* National Conference on Injecting Drug Use.

Pudney, S., Badillo, C., Bryan, M., Burton, J., Conti, G., and Iacovou, M. (2006) Estimating the Size of the illicit drugs market. In Singleton, N., Murray, R., and Tinsley, L. (eds), *Measuring Different Aspects of Problem Drug Use: Methodological Developments* (2nd edition). Home Office Online Report 16/06.

Rawlins, M. (2002) *Letter to Home Secretary David Blunkett on the Reclassification of Cannabis.* Published under The Reclassification of Cannabis within the Misuse of Drugs Act 1971. Advisory Council on the Misuse of Drugs.

Rawlins, M. (2005) *Michael Rawlins letter to Home Secretary within ACMD Report Further consideration of the classification of cannabis under the Misuse of Drugs Act 1971.* Advisory Council on the Misuse of Drugs.

Rawlins, M. (2008) *Letter to Home Secretary Jacqui Smith on the Reclassification of Cannabis and published in Cannabis Classification and Public Health Advisory Council on the Misuse of Drugs.*

Rehm, J., and Fischer, B. (2008) Should heroin be prescribed to heroin misusers? Yes, *British Medical Journal* 336: 70 (12 January), doi:10.1136/bmj.39421.593692.94.

Rehm, J., Frick, U., Hartwig, C., Gutzwiller, F., Gschwend, P., and Uchtenhagen, A. (2005) Mortality in heroin-assisted treatment in Switzerland 1994–2000. *Drug Alcohol Depend* 79: 137–143.

Rehm, J., Gschwend, P., Steffen, T., Gutzwiller, F., Dobler-Mikola, A., Uchtenhagen, A. (2001) Feasibility, safety, and efficacy of injectable heroin prescription for refractory opioid addicts: a follow-up study. *Lancet* 358: 1417–1420.

Reinarman, C. (2004) Public health and human rights: The virtues of ambiguity. *International Journal of Drug Policy* 15: 239–241.

Release (2009) http://www.release.org.uk/nice-people-take-drugs. Available at http://www.release.org.uk/nice-people-take-drugs.

Rey, J., and Tennant, T. (2002) Cannabis and mental health: More evidence establishes clear link between use of cannabis and psychiatric illness. *British Medical Journal* 325 (7374): 1183–1184.

Robbe, H. (1994) *Influence on Marijuana on Driving*. Institute for Human Psychopharmacology, Maastricht: University of Limburg.

Roberts, M. (2004) Comment on 'What are drug users looking for when they contact drug services: Abstinence or harm reduction?' by Neil McKeganey, Zoë Morris, Joanne Neal, & Michele Robertson. *Drugs: Education, Prevention, and Policy* 12 (4): 261–263.

Robertson, J. R., Bucknall, A. B. V., Welsby, P. D., Roberts, J. J. K., Inglis, J. M., and Peutherer, J. F. (1986) Epidemic of AIDS related virus (HTLV–III/LAV) infection among intravenous drug abusers. *British Medical Journal* 292: 527–529 (22 February), doi:10.1136/bmj.292.6519.527.

Rowan, G., Chatham, L., Jie, G., Simpson, D. (2000) Services provided during methadone treatment: A gender comparison. *Journal of Substance Abuse Treatment* 19: 7–14.

Royal College of General Practitioners (2002) *Royal College of GPs against Increasing Heroin Prescribing*. Available at http://cms.rcgp.org.uk/staging/news_and_events/news_room/archived_news_releases/archive_back_to_1998/press_releases_2002/royal_college_of_gps_against_i.aspx.

Salmon, A. M., van Beek, I., Amin, J., Kador, J., and Maher, L. (2010) Impact of a supervised injecting facility on ambulance attendances at opioid-related overdoses in Sydney, Australia. *Addiction* 105 (4): 676–683.

Scottish Advisory Committee on Drug Misuse (2008) *Essential Care: A Report on the Approach Required to Maximise Opportunity for Recovery from Problem Substance Use in Scotland*. Edinburgh: Scottish Government.

Scottish Children's Reporter Administration (2003–04) *Annual Report 2003–04*. Available at http://www.scra.gov.uk/cms_resources/Annual%20Report%202003%2D2004%2Epdf.

Scottish Executive (2005) How many people re receiving methadone hydrochloride mixture for opiate dependence in Scotland and what are the prescribing cots per person. *Scottish Executive ISD*, Edinburgh: The Scottish Government.

Scottish Executive (2006) Hidden harm Next Steps Supporting Children – Working with Parents. *Scottish Executive,* Edinburgh: The Scottish Government.

Scottish Executive (2007) *Statistical Bulletin Criminal Justice Series CrJ/2007/,* 1 January.

Scottish Government (2003) *Getting Our Priorities Right: Good Practice Guidance for Working With Families Affected by Substance Misuse.* Edinburgh: The Scottish Government.

Scottish Government (2008) *The Road to Recovery: A new Approach to tackling Scotland's drug Problem.* Edinburgh: The Scottish Government.

Scottish Government (2009a) *Scottish Crime Survey.* Edinburgh: The Scottish Government.

Scottish Government (2009b) *Statistical Bulletin Crime and Justice Series Recorded Crime in Scotland 2008/09.* Edinburgh: Scottish Government.

Scottish Government (2005) *HM Inspectorate of Prisons HMP & YOI Cornton Vale Inspection* 2–3 February.

Scottish Government (2007) *Review of Methadone in Drug Treatment: Prescribing Information and Practice.*

Scottish Prison Service (2008) *Scottish Prison Survey.* Available at http://www.sps.gov.uk/MultimediaGallery/8bb1f9db-4681-440d-ba30-5f07ed8d09a7.pdf.

Seaman, S. R., Brettle, R. P., and Gore, S. M. (1998) Mortality from overdose among injecting drug users recently released from prison: Database linkage study. *BMJ* 7 February 316 (7129): 426–428.

Sense about Science (2009) *Principles for the Treatment of Independent Scientific Advice.* http://www.senseaboutscience.org.uk/index.php/site/project/421/.

Serious Organised Crime Agency (2008) *Annual Report 2008.*

Shulman, L., Shapiro, S., and Hirschfield, S. (2000) Outreach developmental services for children of patients in treatment for substance abuse. *American Journal of Public Health* 90 (12): 1930–1933.

Simpson, D. D., and Flynn, P. M. (2008) Drug Abuse Treatment Outcome Studies (DATOS): A national evaluation of treatment effectiveness. In Fisher, G. and Roget, N. (eds), *Encyclopedia of Substance Abuse Prevention, Treatment, and Recovery* (pp. 303–307). Thousand Oaks, CA: Sage Publishing.

Simpson, D. (2003) Special section 5 year follow up Treatment outcomes studies from DATOS. *Journal of Substance Abuse Treatment* 25 (3): 23–186.

Simson, G. (1990) AIDS and HIV the Challenge for British Drug Services. *British Journal of Addiction* 85: 329–339.

Singleton, N., Pendry, E., Colin Taylor, C., Farrell, M., and Marsden, J. (2003) *Drug – Related mortality among newly released offenders findings.* Home Office Report 187.

Singleton, N., Murray, R., and Tinsley, L. (2006) *Measuring Different Aspects of Problem Drug Use: Methodological Developments.* Home Office – UK...Home Office Online Reports 16/06.

Smith, K., and Dodd, L. (2009) *Seizures of Drugs in England and Wales 2007/08.* Home Office Statistical Bulletin 08/09.

Smith, L. A., Foxcroft, D. R. (2009) *Drinking in the UK: An Exploration of Trends*. York, UK: Joseph Rowntree Foundation.

Spear, H. B. (2002) *Heroin Addiction Care and Control: The British System 1916–1974*. London: Drugscope.

Stimson, G. (1990) AIDS and HIV Challenge for British drug policy. *British Journal of Addiction* 85: 329–339.

Stimson, G. (2007) Harm reduction coming of age: A local movement with global impact. *International Journal of Drug Policy* 18: 67–69.

Stimson, G. V., Alldritt, L., Dolan, K., Donoghoe, M., and Lart, R. A. (1988) *Injecting Equipment Exchange Schemes: Final Report*, The Pilot Syringe-Exchange Project in England and Scotland: a summary of the evaluation. London: Goldsmiths' College. *Addiction* 84 (11): 1283–1284. Syringe Exchange Schemes: A Report and Some Commentaries.

Stimson, G., and Metrebian, N. (2003) *Prescribing Heroin: What is the Evidence?* York: Joseph Rowntree Foundation.

Stimson, G. V. (1995) AIDS and injecting drug use in the United Kingdom, 1988–1993: The policy response and the prevention of the epidemic. *Social Science and Medicine* 41 (5): 699–716.

Stoermer, R., Drewe, J., Dursteler-Mac Farland, K., Hock, C., Mueller-Spahn, F., and Ladewig, D. (2003) Safety of injectable opioid maintenance treatment for heroin dependence. *Biological Psychiatry* 54: 854–861.

Strang, J. (1993): Drug use and harm reduction: Responding to the challenge. In N. Heather, A. Wodak, E. A. Nadelmann, and P. O'Hare, (eds), *Psychoactive Drugs and Harm Reduction: From Faith to Science*. London: Wburr Publishers Ltd. pp. 3–20.

Strang, J., Darke, S., Hall, W., Farrell, M., and Ali, R. (1996) Heroin overdose: The case for take home naloxone. *British Medical Journal* 312: 1435–1436.

Strang, J., Powis, B., Best, D., and Vingoe, L. (1999) Preventing opiate overdose fatalties with take home naloxone. *Addiction* 94 (2): 199–204.

Strang, J., Manning, V., Mayet, S., Titherington, E., and Offor, L. (2008) Family carers and the prevention of heroin overdose deaths: Unmet training need and overlooked intervention opportunity of resuscitation training and supply of nalonone. *Drugs Education Prevention and Policy* 15 (2): 211–218.

Strang, J., Metrebian, N., Lintzeris, N., Potts, L., Carnwth, T., Mayet, S., Williams, H., Zador, D., Evers, R., Groshkova, T., Charles, V., Martin, A., Forzisi, L. (2010) Supervised injectable heroin or injectable methadone versus optimised oral methadone as treatment for chronic heroin addicts in England after persistent failure in orthodox treatment (RIOTT): A randomised trial. *Lancet* 375: 1885–95.

Street, K., Whittingum, G., Gibson, P., Cairns, P., and Ellis, M. (2007) Is adequate parenting compatble with maternal drug use: A five year follow-up. *Child Care Health and Development* 34 (2): 204–206.

Suchman, N., and Luthar, S. (2000) Maternal addiction child Maladjustment and socio-demographic risk: Implications for parenting behaviour. *Addiction* 95: 1417–1428.

Summerhayes, L. (2006) Why was Michael Left Alone for Six Weeks. *Scotsman*, 22 February.

Syal, R. (2010) Mephedrone Ban Would Do More Harm than Good, Says Ex-Drug Adviser. *Guardian Newspaper*, Thursday 25 March.

Tammi, T., and Hurme, T. (2007) How the harm reduction movement contrasts itself against punitive prohibition. *International Journal of Drug Policy* 18 (2): 84–87.

Tavares, L., Graca, P., Martins, O., Asensio, M. (2005) *External and Independent Evaluation of the National Strategy for the Fight against Drugs and the National Action Plan for the Fight against Drugs and Drug Addiction Horizon 2004*. Lisbon: Portuguese National Insititue of Public Administration.

The Lancet (2007) Rehashing the Evidence on Psychosis and Cannabis *The Lancet* 370 (9584), 28 July 2007–3 August 2007: 292. Available at http://www.thelancet.com/journals/lancet/article/PIIS0140-6736(07)61133-7/fulltext.

The National Center on Addiction and Substance Abuse (2005) *Family Matters Substance Abuse and the American Family*. CASA White Paper Columbia University.

The UK Drug Policy Commission (2008) *Recovery Consensus Group*.

Thompson, T. (2009) *Older Generation Blamed as Drug Deaths Soar. Scotsman Newspaper*, 13 August.

Hand, Timothy and Rishiraj, Amartej Singh (2009) *Seizure of drugs in England and Wales 2008/2009*. Home Office Statistical Bulletin 16/09.

Tracy, E. (1994) Maternal substance abuse: Protecting the child preserving the family. *Social Work* 39: 534–540.

Transform Drug Policy Foundation (2009) A Comparison of the Cost Effectiveness of the Prohibition and Regulation of Drugs. *Transform Drug Policy Foundation* www.tdpf.org.uk.

Travis, A. (2009) Heroin Clinics Would Help Few Addicts, Says Agency Head. *Guardian.co.uk*, Tuesday 15 September.

Uchtenhagen, A., Dobler-Mikola, A., Steffen, T., Gutzwiller, F., Blattler, R., Pfeifer, S. (eds) (1999) *Prescription of Narcotics for Heroin Addicts: Main Results of the Swiss National Cohort Study*. Basel: Karger.

UKDPC (2008) *The UK Drug Policy Commission Recovery Consensus Group*. A vision of recovery July 2008.

UKDPC (2009) *Refocussing Drug Related Law Enforcement to Address harms* Full Review Report.

UKHRA (2001) *Submission to the Home Affairs Drug Strategy Directorate*. UK Harm Reduction Association London.

UNODC (2007) *Sweden's Successful Drug Policy: A Review of the Evidence United Nations Office on Drugs and Crime Vienna*.

United Nations Office of Drugs and Crime (UNODC) (2009) *World Drugs Report*.

United Nations Office on Drugs and Crime (UNODC) (2007) *Sweden's Successful Drug Policy: A Review of the Evidence*. United Nations Office on Drugs and Crime, ONDCP Vienna.

United Nations Office on Drugs and Crime (UNODC) (2009) *World Drugs Report United Nations New York 2009.*

US Department of Health and Human Sciences Substance Abuse and Mental Health Services Administration (2009) Substance Abuse Treatment Advisory. *Emerging Issues in the Use of Methadone* 8 (1): 1–8.

US Department of Justice (2000) *Annual Report Arrestee Drug Abuse Monitoring Programme.*

Van den Brink, W., Hendriks, V., Blanken, P., Koeter, M., van Zwieten, B., and van Ree, J. (2003) Medical prescription of heroin to treatment resistant heroin addicts: Two randomised controlled trials. *British Medical Journal* 327: 310–315.

Van Rees, E. (1999) Drugs as a human right. *International Journal of Drug Policy* 10 (2): 89–96.

Wardle, I. (2009) Drugs Treatment: Drug treatment at the Crossroads: What It's for, Where It's at and How to Make It Even Better? *Drugscope Report. London: Drugscope.*

Willens, T., Biederman, J., and Kiely, K. (1995) Pilot study of behavioural and emotional disturbance in high risk children of parents with opioid dependence. *Child and Adolescent Psychiatry* 34: 779–785.

Williams, M. (2009) Prison Officers Ready to Revolt over Needle Exchange Plans. *Herald*, 30 March.

Winnet, R., and Rayner, G. (2007) Gordon Brown Says Labour Donations 'Illegal'. *Guardian*, 28 November.

Winstock, A. (2010) Results of the 2009/10 Mixmag drug user survey. Oral evidence to the Advisory Council on the Misuse of Drugs.

Wodak, A., and Cooney, A. (2005) Effectiveness of sterile needle and syringe programmes. *International Journal of Drug Policy* 165: s31–s44.

Womersley, T. (2006) Methadone programme fails 97% of heroin addicts. *The Sunday Times*, 29 October 2006.

Wood, E., Tyndall, M. W., Zhang, Rl, Montaner, J. S. G. and Kerr, T. (2007) Rate of detoxification service use and its impact among a cohort of supervised injecting facility users. *Addiction* 102: 916–919.

Wood, F., Bloor, M., and Palmer, S. (2000) Indirect prevalence estimates of a national drug using population: The use of contact-recontact methods in Wales. *Health, Risk & Society* 2 (1), March: 47–58.

Zhu, L., Sharma. M., and Stolina, S. (2000) Delta-90tetrahydrocannabinol inhibits antitumor immunity by a CB2 receptor mediated cytokin dependent pathway. *Journal of Immunology* 165 (1): 373–380.

Author Index

Subject Index

Note: In this index tables are indicated in **bold** type.

Unlinked Anonymous Surveillance
   Programme, 40
upstream disruption, enforcement, 79

visibility, of drug markets, 28
voucher system, drug treatment
   services, 71–2

weak rights/strong rights version, harm
   reduction, 24
wealth, created from drugs, 134–5
What Are Drug Users Looking for
   When They Contact Drug Abuse

Treatment Services – Abstinence or
   Harm Reduction?, 49
women prisoners, drug use, 84
World Drugs Report, 145

young people
   with drug-dependent parents,
      122
   services for, 122–6
youth culture, 9

zero tolerance drug policy, Sweden,
   142–4, 146